ELEMENTARY DEVELOPING AND PRINTING

BY ROBERT HERTZBERG

AMPHOTO
American Photographic Book Publishing Co., Inc.
Garden City, New York

CONTENTS

1

DARKROOM

Answers to the basic questions about darkroom work that you are not at all bashful about asking.

A PLACE FOR DEVELOPING

You are the owner of a high-grade camera and are becoming interested in doing your own developing and enlarging. Especially if you live in an apartment, the first question that probably enters your mind is, "What will I do for a darkroom?"

A quick answer is a second question that might surprise you. "What makes you think you need a darkroom at all?"

Actually, a 100 per cent inky-black space is required only for film development, the initial half of photographic processing, and at that for less than five minutes. This is about as long as it takes to break open a roll of exposed film and to load it into a lighttight tank. All the rest of the developing process — *all* of it — is then done in ordinary room illumination, and the kitchen is as good a spot for the job as any.

Even in small apartments there can be as many as three choices for your temporary dark-darkroom: the kitchen itself, a closet, or the bathroom. Windowless kitchens and bathrooms are common. Since you are most likely to do your processing in the evening, you can blacken such a room merely by turning out the light, closing the door, and putting a towel at the bottom of the door to prevent light leaks from other rooms. If your kitchen does not have a door, you can hang a blanket or a sheet over the opening; however, this soon becomes awkward and inconvenient. For the few minutes of darkness that you need, either put out the lights in adjoining rooms and ask the other members of the family to meditate in the dark, or go into room with a door. Of course, this problem doesn't arise if you live alone.

A normal kitchen is first choice because it has a table and a couple of chairs, and you can sit down and be comfortable in the dark. If it is a galley-type kitchen, with no sitting space, at least it has counters on which you can lay out the film, the tank, and other items.

If your particular kitchen has a window that faces street lights or other apartments, you might have to block it off by means of cardboard cut from cartons, strips of wrapping or drawing paper, or even something as simple as folded newspapers. Use any variety of masking tape to hold the paper in position. Blocking out the window might not be necessary if the shade or blind fits snugly, but it is good insurance against film spoilage.

A linen closet in which you can stand with the door closed behind you is a good second choice place for loading film because a shelf at waist height can be cleared easily to provide a working area. Check the door knob carefully, with someone present outside, to make sure that you can't lock yourself in.

A clothes closet is generally less convenient than a linen closet because bulky garments must be pushed aside or removed to make room for a small table, if there's room for it at all. An alternative is to squat on the floor; with practice, you can have the tank loaded before you become uncomfortable. Again, be sure to check the door for light leakage and certainty of egress.

It is easy to blacken a bathroom window, even for daytime processing, because it is usually much smaller than windows in other rooms and the panes are made of translucent rather than clear glass. You do have to provide a working surface of some sort unless the sink is part of a "vanity" cabinet that has one or two drain boards. A piece of Masonite or stiff cardboard on a plain sink is quite sufficient. If the room doesn't already include

a bath stool, you can readily move in a chair or use the toilet seat
if it's close enough.

At this point you may well be asking, "Why this concern with
the dark? Why not use one of the many 'daylight' tanks I see
advertised in the camera magazines?"

Why? Because all but one of those tanks are misnamed. They
are "daylight processing," not "daylight loading." They must be
loaded in darkness. Processing then proceeds with the lights on.
The one true daylight-loading tank, for 35mm film, is expensive
and of complicated construction, and has a serious catch to its
convenience: When the exposed film in the camera is being
rewound into its cartridge, it must not be rewound completely.
The tapered leader end must stick out of the cartridge just as it
did when the film was put into the camera. This end is needed to
attach to the tank's take-up reel, which is wound up by an
outside knob after the lighttight cover is put on. The trouble is
that it is very difficult with many cameras to tell just when the
leader has come loose from the take-up reel. If you turn the
rewind crank a bit too much, the film end disappears into the
closed magazine. Then you need a darkroom, as with any other
tank.

A PLACE FOR ENLARGING

Enlarging requires a fairly large, flat area for the enlarger and
its accessories and for as many as six open trays measuring
about 12″ × 15″ in size. In an apartment the kitchen is the
obvious and logical place because of its made-to-order facilities:
a sink, with drain boards that are perfect for the trays; a dry
table for the enlarger; electric outlets in several places; a floor
that's easy on the feet; storage space for bottles under the sink or
in closets; stainless steel or glass mixing bowls for preparation of
chemicals; measuring cups; an egg or stove timer; cloth and
paper towels; and so on.

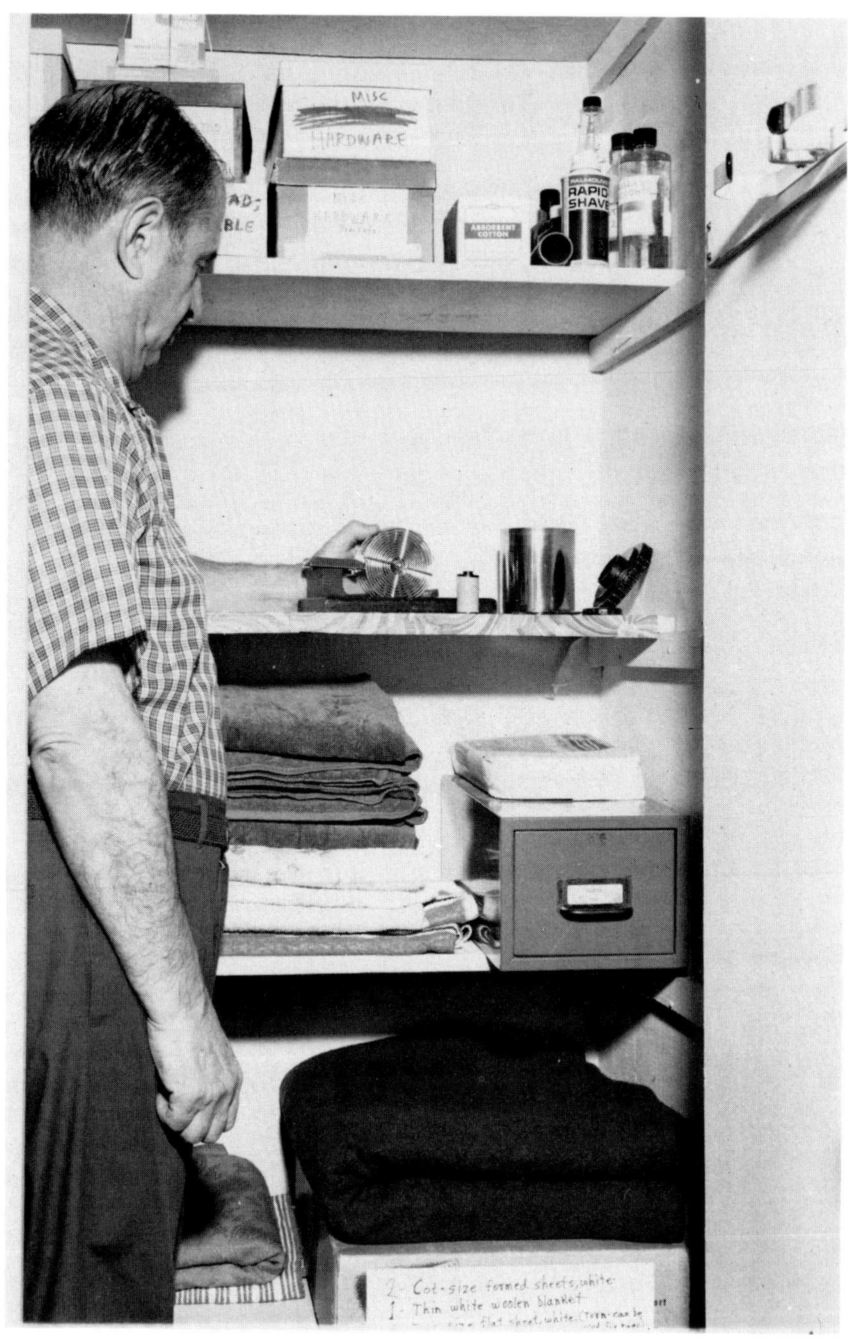

Fig. 1-1. Clear a shelf in a closet and you have an excellent temporary "darkroom" in which you can load exposed film into a developing tank.

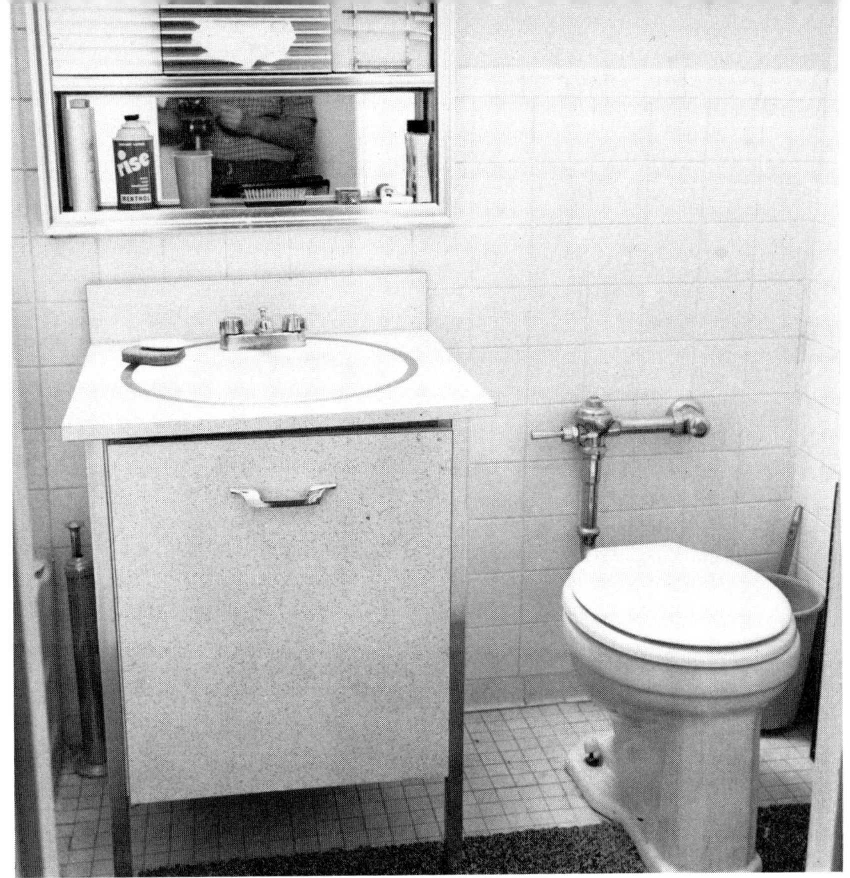

Figs. 1-2a and b. Another good spot is the bathroom. Convert the sink into a work table by adding a top made of hardboard or even stiff cardboard, with short side members to prevent parts of the tank from rolling off in the dark.

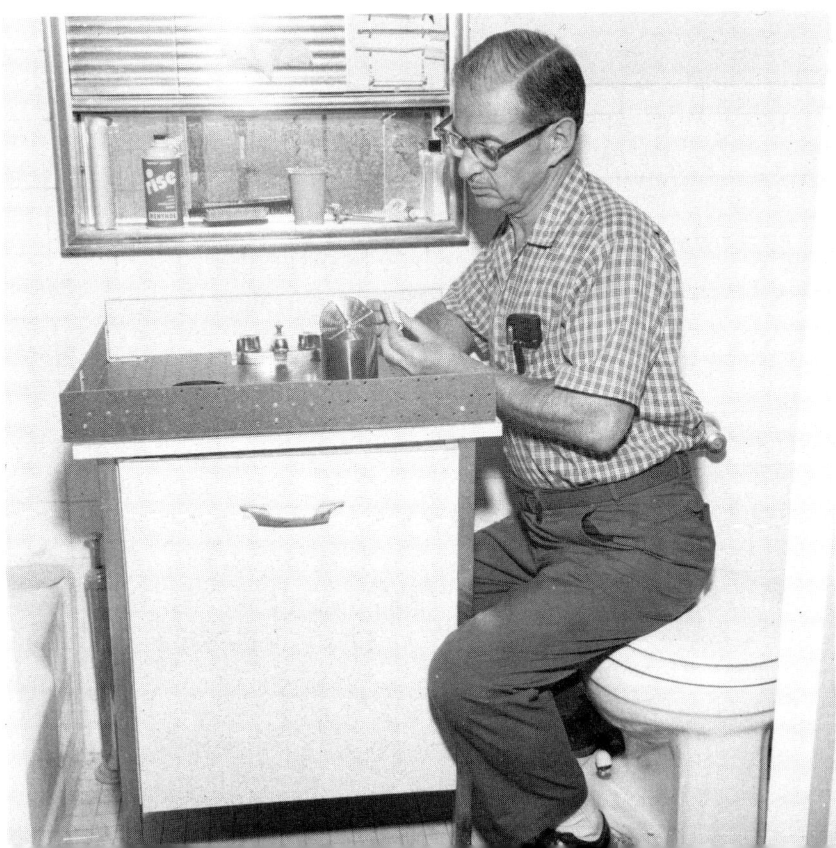

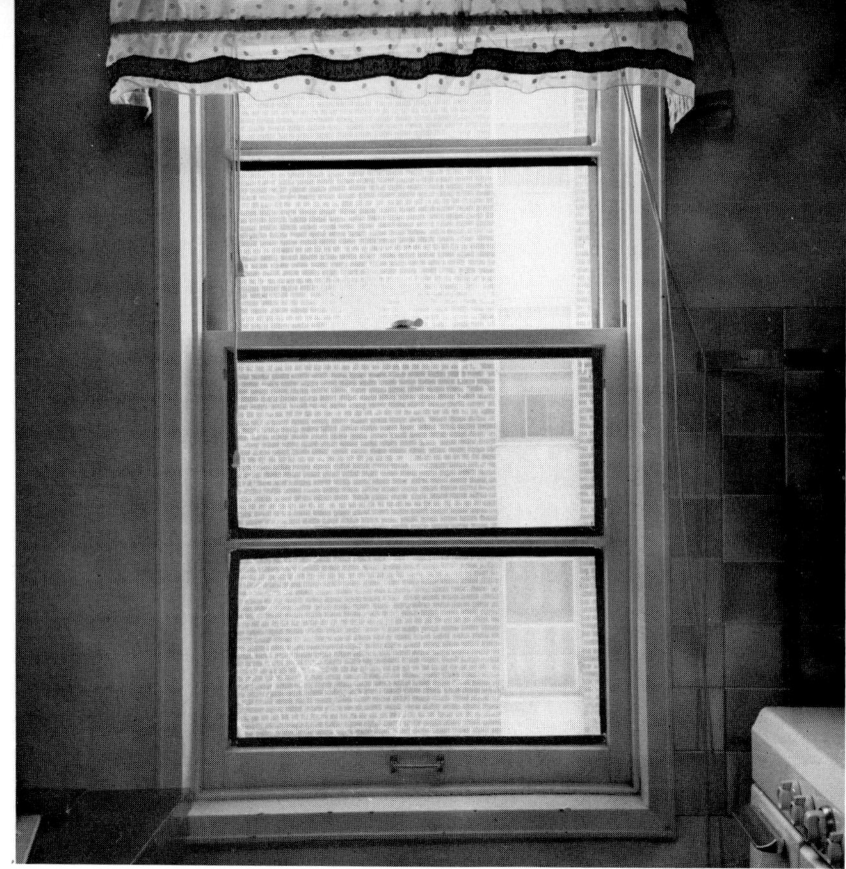

Figs. 1-3a and b. The kitchen is an ideal place for enlarging work, but how do you shut out light? Easily . . . by means of hardboard or cardboard "blinds" cut to fit snugly against the window panes. Keep them in position with pushpins. If the window frames are of aluminum, use short pieces of any sticky tape.

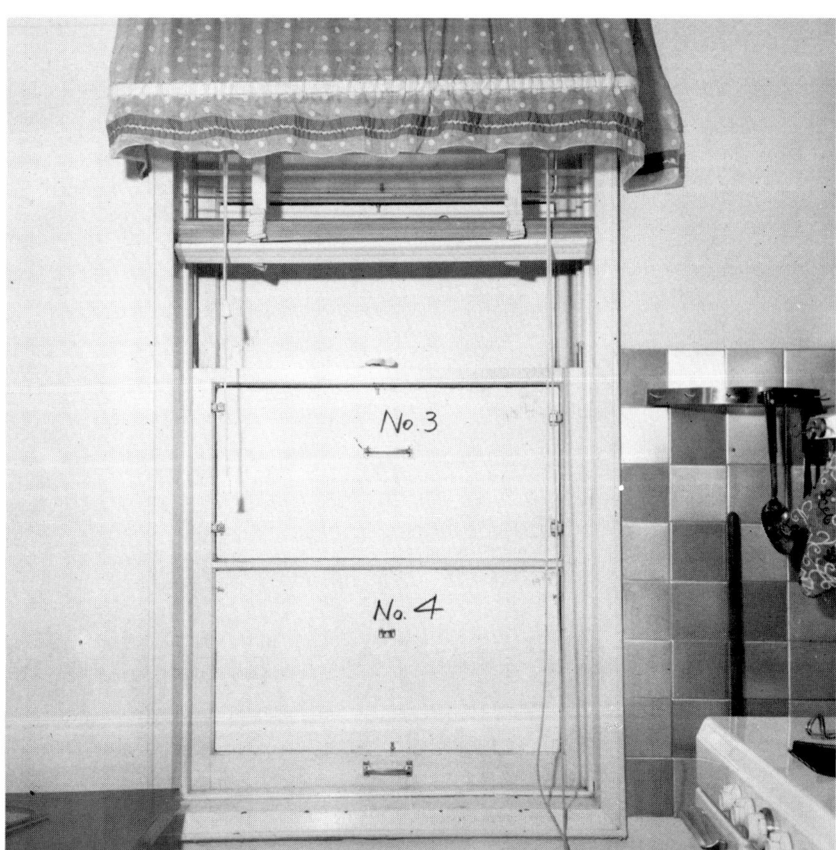

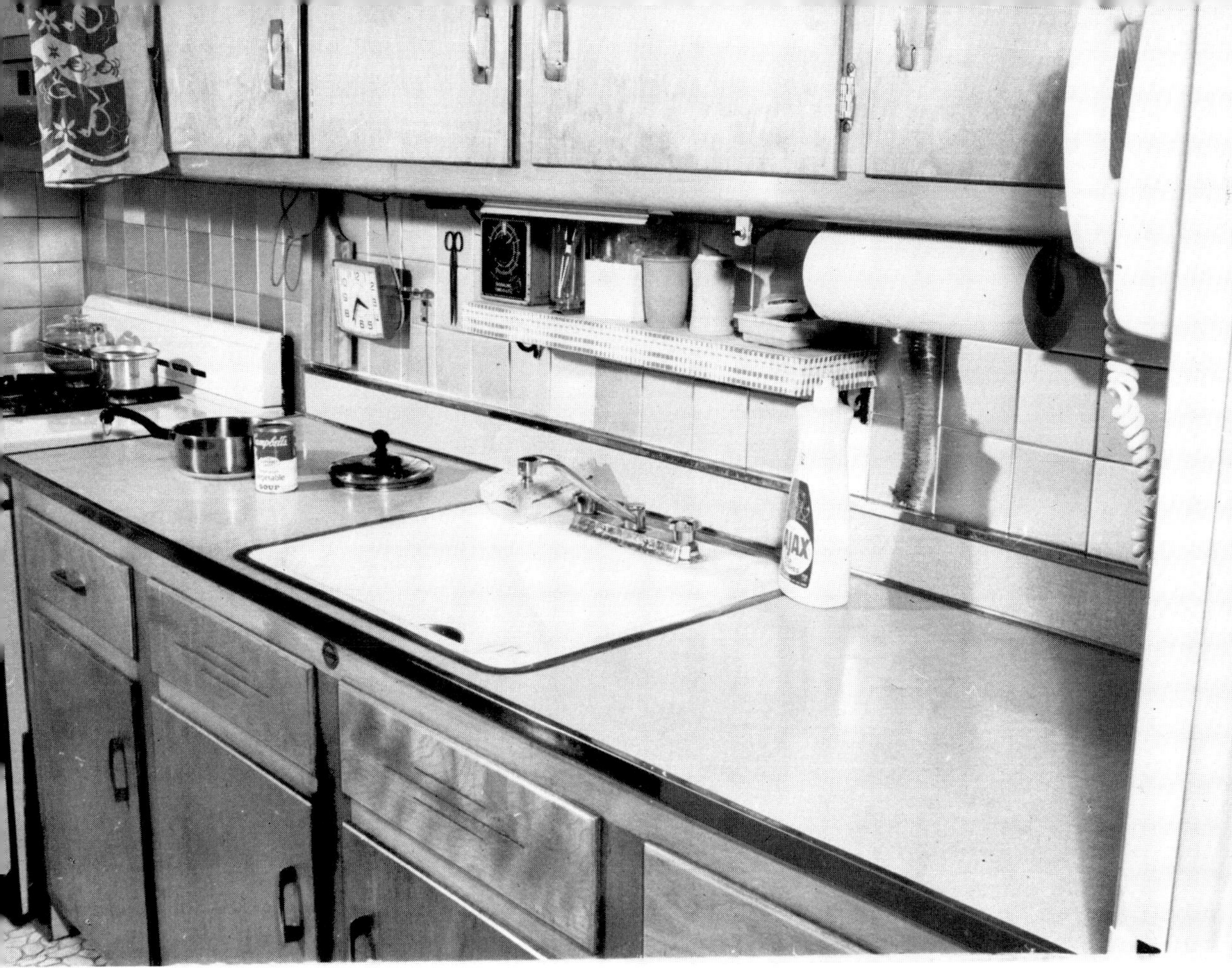

Fig. 1-4. The existing facilities in almost any kitchen are made-to-order for photographic purposes. Here you find water and a sink, counter space for trays and other vessels, electric outlets, a clock, towels, storage space for bottles, and so forth.

Storing the enlarger itself is no problem. With many models made for 35mm and 120 films the head-and-column assembly separates from the baseboard in a couple of minutes, usually without the need for tools, and the two pieces can then be put away in a corner of a clothes closet without interfering with its contents. This disassembly feature is practically forced on equipment manufacturers because of the difficulty and cost of boxing an assembled enlarger for shipment.

The idea of using the bathroom for enlarging might occur to you; if it does, forget it. The room itself is what needs enlarging.

11

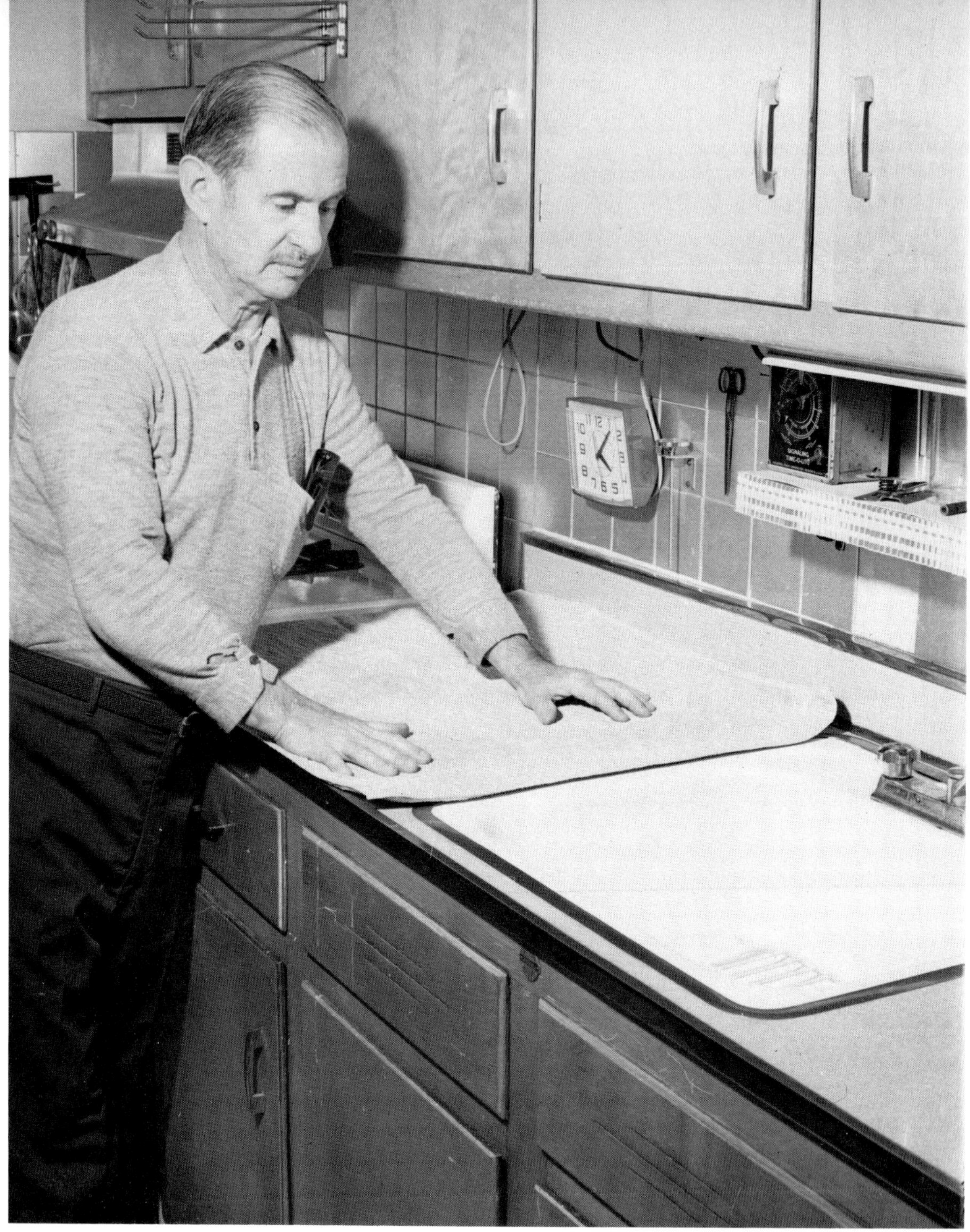

Fig. 1-5. To soak up possible spills of developer, fixer, and other chemicals from trays, spread a couple of old bath towels over the drain boards. These make a very good work surface.

Try opening a bridge table in your bathroom and see if you can even move around it. Remember also that the bathroom is quite likely to be needed by someone else at any time.

It is possible to build or adapt an existing table to fit either inside the tub or half in and half out, and to use the sink as a print washer. However, a table of adequate size would necessarily be heavy and cumbersome, and even if it had folding legs you would have trouble finding storage space for it.

A PLACE IN THE BASEMENT

If you live in a private house with a clean, warm basement, you can easily organize a corner of it for the equivalent of a darkroom in which you can leave your paraphernalia set up more or less permanently. For black-and-white processing you do not need a formal, fully-enclosed chamber because you will probably do all or most of your developing and enlarging at night. Since the windows of most basements are small and are easily fitted with lighttight shades, and since the whole area is completely independent of the living quarters upstairs, merely turning off the lights is usually enough to turn it into a workable darkroom.

While film developing absolutely necessitates a short period of utter blackness, enlarging can tolerate an astonishing amount of leakage of weak outside light. (A simple test of the safety of any work area is described in the chapter on enlarging.) This means, for example, that if inclement weather or personal indisposition keeps you at home during the day, you can spend it profitably by loading exposed film into its tank upstairs in the lighttight kitchen or closet and then descending to the basement for all the remaining steps to finished enlargements.

You will naturally gravitate toward the laundry section of the basement because you must have running water, both hot and cold, for photo processing. A couple of old tables about four feet long suffice for the equipment. Two short tables are better than one long table. Use one for the dry items such as the enlarger, printing paper, and so on, and the other for the wet trays. Experiment with the positions of the tables. A popular "L" arrangement has them forming a right angle, with the edge of the wet one next to or slightly overhanging the laundry tub to allow for drainage in case of spills from the trays. Thus you can stand or perch on a high swivel kitchen stool and have everything within easy arm's reach.

There is always an electric outlet near the tub for laundering machines; a cube tap plugged into it converts one outlet into three, taking care of the enlarger and a couple of safelights. Some extra shelving might be needed for bottles and supplies.

If the floor is concrete, cover the area in front of the tables with linoleum mats or discarded pieces of old carpeting. Concrete is hard, and becomes progressively harder on your feet the longer you stand on it. A little scrounging through neighbors' garages is bound to turn up usable "junk" that they are glad to donate to a worthy cause!

Don't plan a permanent darkroom until you've accumulated a winter of experience with a temporary one. You'll know the time is ripe when you start thinking of color processing.

TOOLS FOR THE JOB

As a hobby, photography is a gadgeteer's paradise because of the number and variety of devices sold for darkroom use. Before you buy anything, study the detailed illustrations in this book to learn what is important, and look around your kitchen or home workshop for existing objects you might be able to use.

For instance, a 0–15-minute egg timer of the wind-up type or an electrical timer built into a stove is excellent for timing film processing because the individual developing, fixing, and washing cycles run from about 5 to 15 minutes. Interval timers of more sophisticated design are more accurate, but the others will do the job nicely, except for the critical timing required by some special developers.

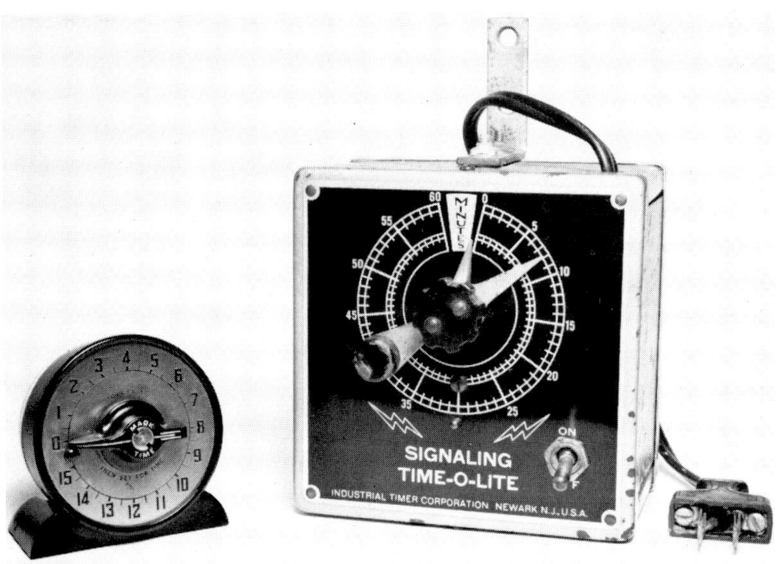

Fig. 1-6. (Above) Two types of minute timers suitable for film processing purposes. Left: familiar kitchen wind-up model. Right: electrical model. These produce audible signals at the end of a timing cycle: the first. a bell sound; the second, a raucous buzz.

Fig. 1-7. (Below) Print timers are automatic switches that turn an enlarger off after a preset interval. Here are two representative types. Left: fully electronic, with accurate timing from 1/10 to 90 seconds. Right: electric clock mechanism, 1 to 60 seconds.

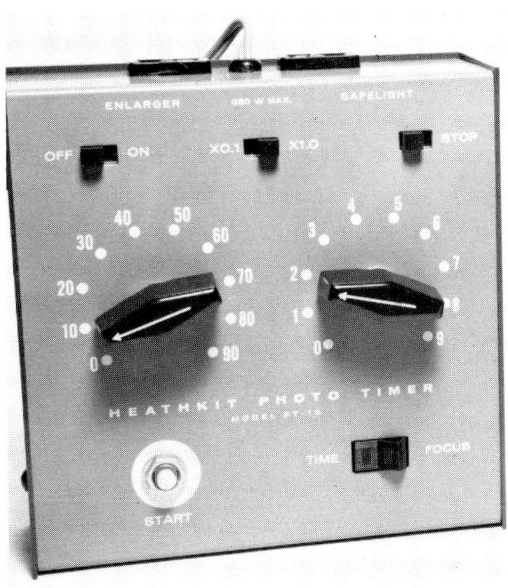

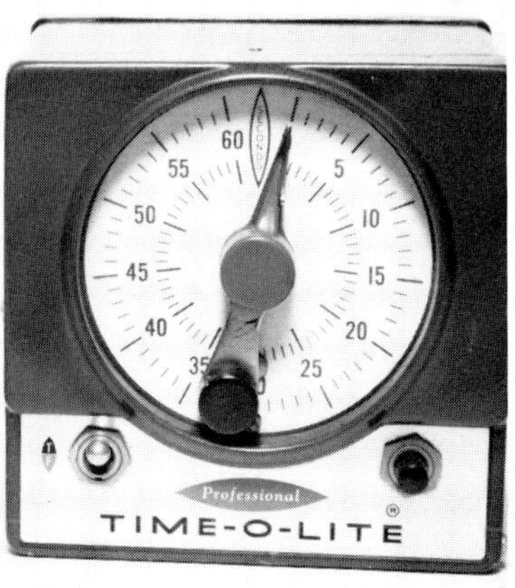

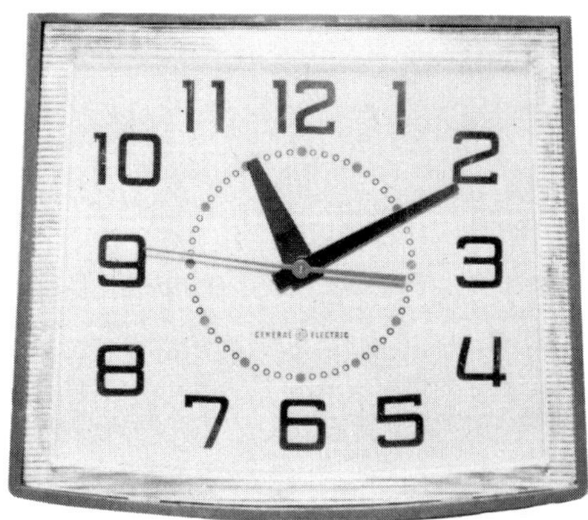

Fig. 1-8. (Above) For approximate timing of prints in the developer tray you only have to follow the sweep second hand of an ordinary kitchen clock.

Fig. 1-9. (Below) The best print tongs are of the spring-loaded type, made of stainless steel. They hold wet prints securely, yet release them quickly when the handles are squeezed slightly.

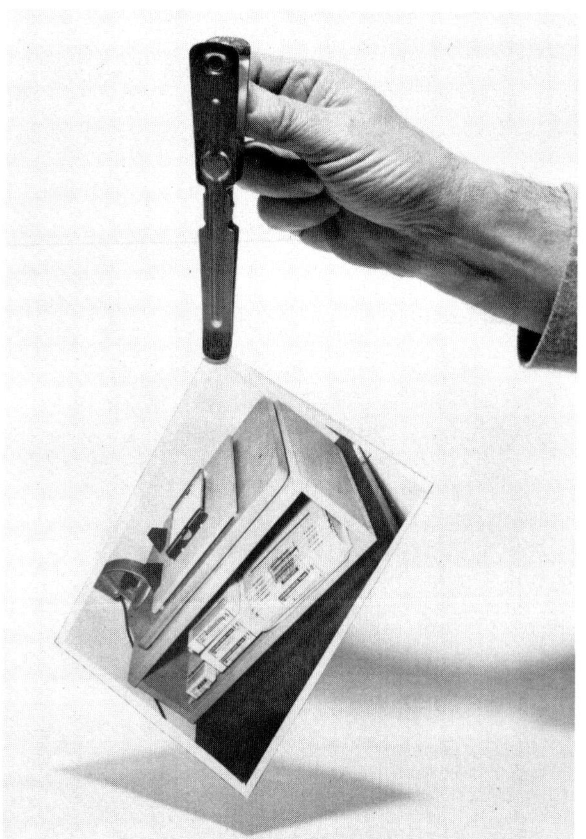

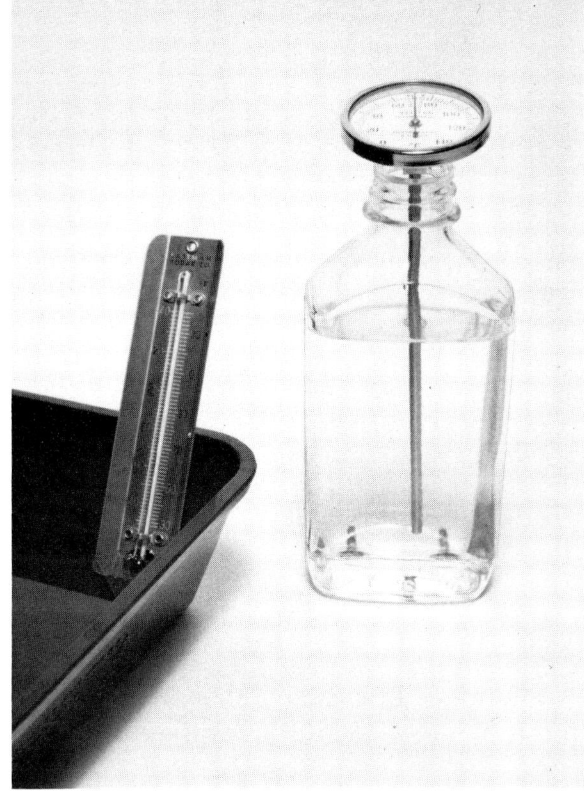

Fig. 1-10. Accurate thermometers are important. Get a small one that clips against the side of a tray, and another of the stem type with a round indicator dial.

Fig. 1-11. Essential measuring vessels. Left to right: stainless steel graduate, with markings inside, 1 liter capacity; plastic graduate, 5 ounce (150 milliliters); kitchen measuring cup, 1 quart, with tape marker for solution amounts needed for two sizes of tanks.

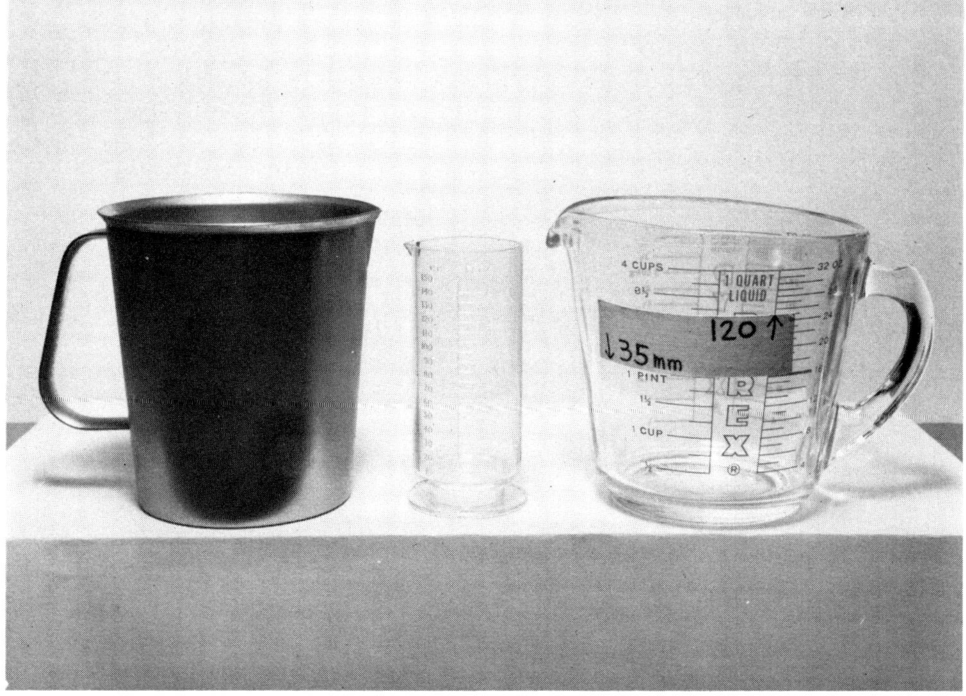

What kitchen doesn't have an open-faced clock with a sweep second hand? If yours is too high up on a wall for observation with the room darkened, buy another and hang it behind the developer tray. Clocks of this type in plain bodies are quite cheap. Many darkroom workers snip off the hour and minute hands and are thus able to follow the single sweep second hand without confusion. The clock mechanism is usually held to the case by a couple of small screws in the back, and can be easily taken apart, adapted, and reassembled in a few minutes.

There is no ready substitute for the print timer, which turns the enlarger on and then off after any preset number of seconds up to 60 or 90. This provision for exact exposure time is such a great convenience and will save you so much wasted under- and overexposed enlarging paper that you definitely should figure on buying a print timer along with the enlarger.

Temperature control of all film developers and of most of the subsequent baths is fairly critical. Neither kitchen nor bathroom thermometers are satisfactory for the purpose. Your best bet is a brand-name meter with a round dial attached to a thin stem that slides into bottles or other containers. Most such instruments have special markers for 68° F., the ideal temperature for black-and-white films, and 75° F., for certain color operations. The dial usually reads up to 140° F., which takes care of the 90 – 125° F. water required for the mixing of dry chemicals. No processing is ever done below the 60's because everything literally goes numb.

While temperature is much less critical in print processing than in negative processing, it is still advisable to check the various baths, particularly the developer. For this purpose there are special little thermometers that clip onto the inside of a tray and can be left there for periodic monitoring.

There is much mixing and measuring of solutions in the darkroom. A regular Pyrex kitchen measuring cup is fine for both purposes because it easily withstands the hottest water that comes out of any house tap. For mixing larger quantities use a stainless steel bowl. For all mixing use a stainless spoon or egg beater. (This metal does not contaminate photo chemicals.)

You should also have a one-liter stainless graduate and a much smaller 100ml or 150ml glass or plastic graduate.* For adjusting solution temperature by the immersion method, a stainless cup is better because metal conducts heat much more rapidly than glass. The small graduate is handy for the small amounts of liquid stock solutions that are added to water to make working baths. For example, only 16ml of stop-bath concentrate makes a full liter of working bath.

POWDERS AND POTIONS

The most important thing to know about photographic processing baths is that they consist largely of water. The basic chemicals are packaged in either powder or concentrated liquid form, for quick and easy mixing in hot water. The solutions must be allowed to cool down before use to the standard 68° F. or 70° F. specified by film and paper manufacturers.

For storing the liquids nothing beats clear glass bottles with secure screw caps of plastic, *not metal.* The latter corrodes in the presence of most solutions, with certain damage to them. Almost any household yields a goodly supply of bottles in an assortment of shapes and sizes. The sizes best suited to photographic preparations are pint, quart, half-gallon, and gallon. Wash them thoroughly with soap and hot water until they lose their original odors.

---

*In the metric system, which is universally used in technical and scientific circles, the unit of volume is the liter. (This is a trifle larger than the U.S. quart.) Smaller quantities were formerly expressed as "cc," for cubic centimeter, but the newer standard is "ml" for milliliter. (Metric abbreviations do not take a final "s" for plurals, nor a period.)

In the United States the metric system has been legal since 1866 but not obligatory; yes, 1866. It has always been used in some fields. For example, movie films are 8mm, 16mm, or 35mm, never anything else; radio transmissions are designated either in meters for wavelength or kilohertz, megahertz, gigahertz, and so on, for frequency.

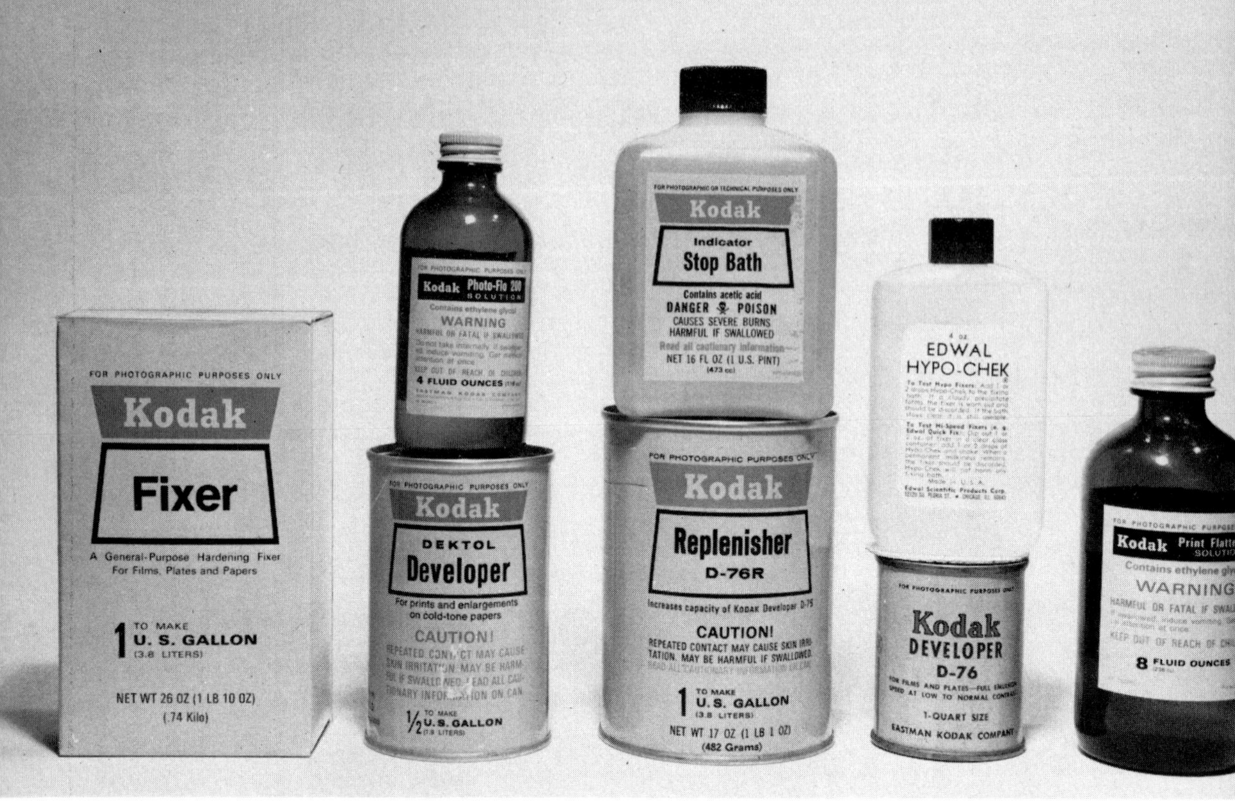

Fig. 1-12. The common developers and fixers are usually sold in powder form, for mixing with water. Other preparations are bottled in concentrated liquid form, for quick dilution.

Avoid the pretty colored plastic containers that are popular for detergents and similar liquids. They vary greatly in composition, and their resistance to photo chemicals is uncertain. There's no point in speculating with them when absolutely safe glass bottles are available for the saving.

Many camera stores offer dark amber "photo bottles" at rather fancy prices. If you ask a salesman the reason for this color, he'll probably answer, "Oh, that's to keep light from affecting what's inside."

This unfortunate half-truth is so widely believed that dealers don't even sell clear bottles, which are not only cheaper but more practical because you can observe the quantity and condition of

20

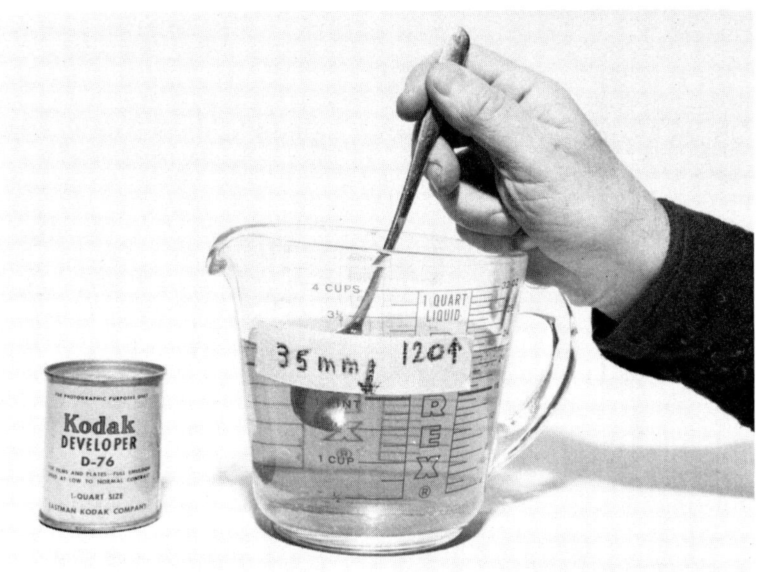

Fig. 1-13. (Above) Easiest way to mix small quantities of powders is with a stainless steel jam spoon in the glass cup.

Fig. 1-14. (Below) For gallon quantities, a stainless steel mixing bowl and a slotted spoon (both found in many kitchens) make the job quick and simple.

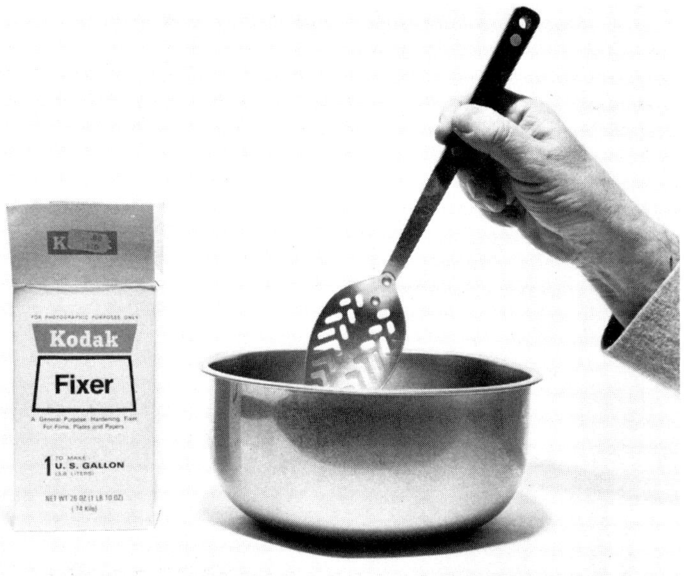

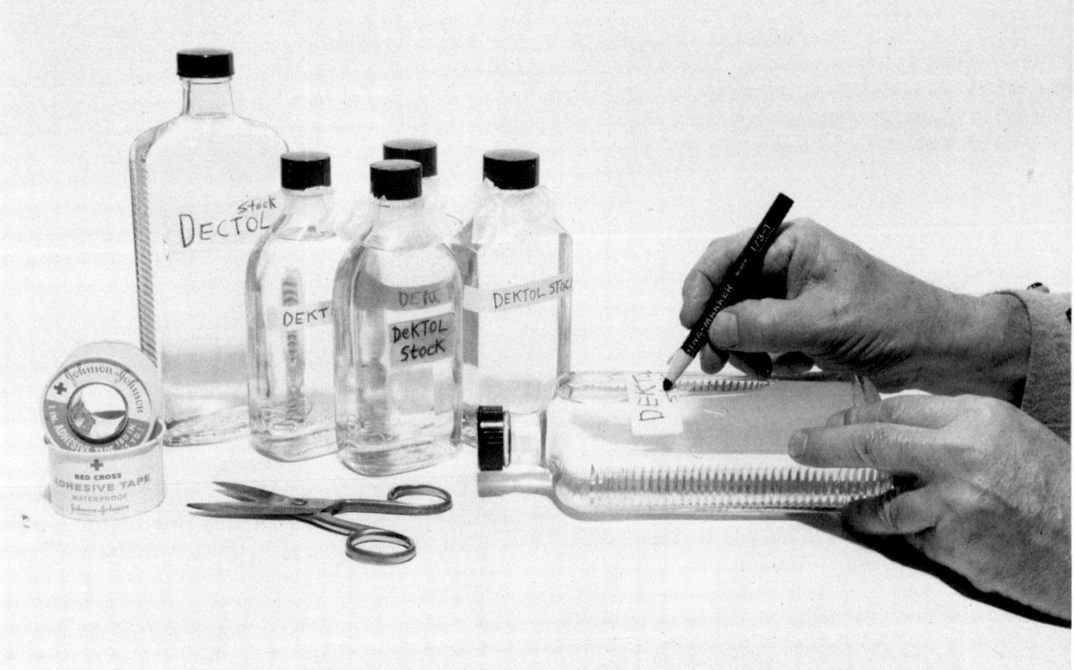

Fig. 1-15. (Above) To avoid deterioration by exposure to air, it's better to keep a half-gallon of developer stock solution in several small full bottles rather than in one large partially empty one. This is a good assortment: four eight-ounce and two pint sizes. For waterproof labels, use adhesive tape and a grease pencil.

Fig. 1-16. (Below) Small graduate is needed to measure small quantity of stop-bath concentrate, 1/2 ounce in 32 ounces of water (16ml in one liter), as an example.

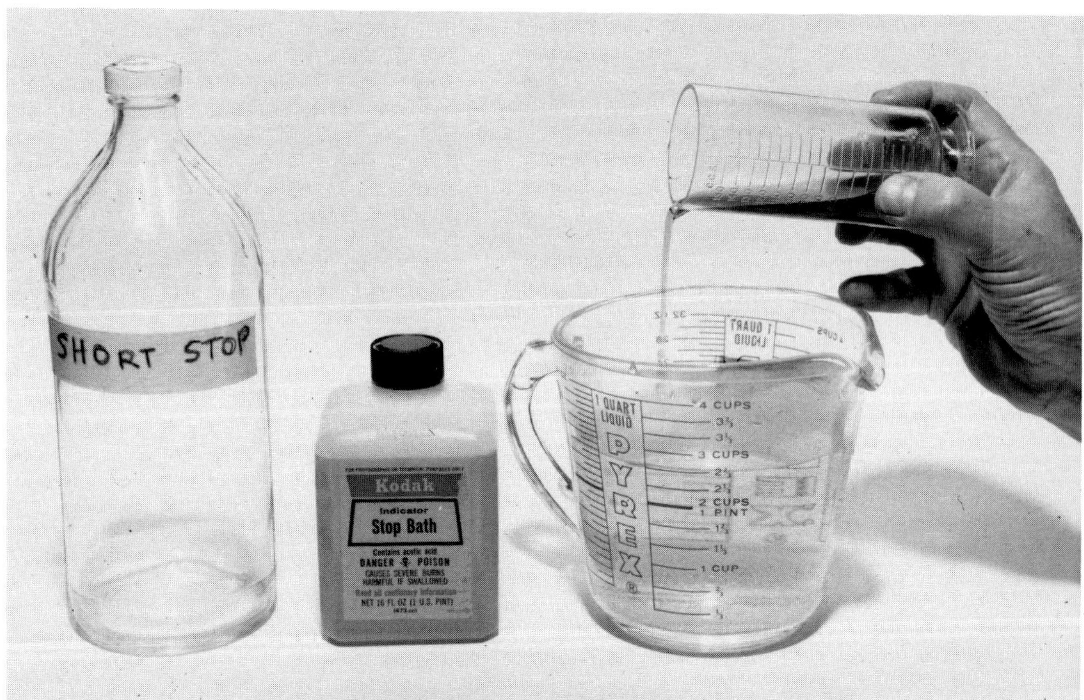

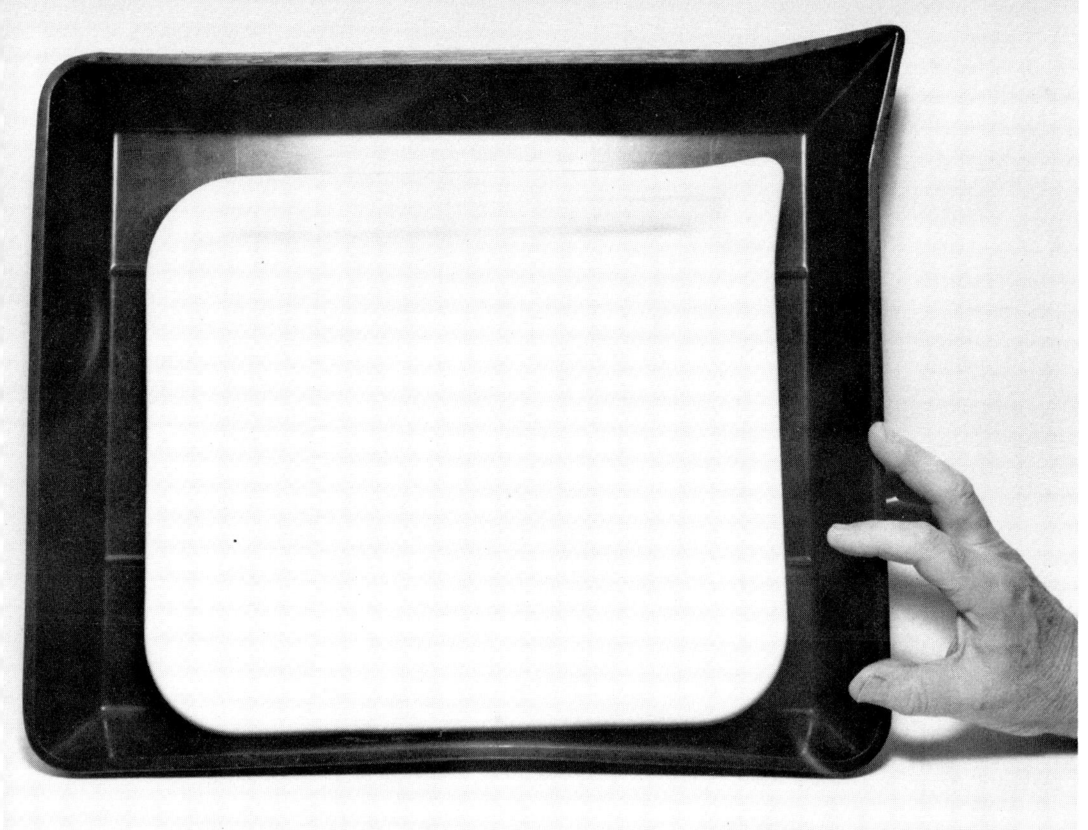

Fig. 1-17. Trays are made of hard rubber, plastic, or stainless steel. Most commonly used sizes are the 11" × 14" (the black one here) and the 8" × 10" (the white). Actually, they measure slightly larger, to allow leeway for print movement in the solutions.

the contents at a glance. The fact of the matter is that some photo chemicals do tend to deteriorate slightly *if exposed to the ultraviolet light of sunshine for several months.* However, under what imaginable circumstances would bottles of developer and fixer be left out in sunshine? Their natural resting place is a darkened room, or a closet in a normally light room. The Eastman Kodak people, who know about these things, sensibly recommend clear containers for the positive advantages they present.

Of all photo chemicals, paper developer is the most vulnerable to deterioration, from exposure to air, not light. A simple way to preserve it is to distribute a half-gallon of concentrate, for example, among two 16-ounce and four 8-ounce medicine

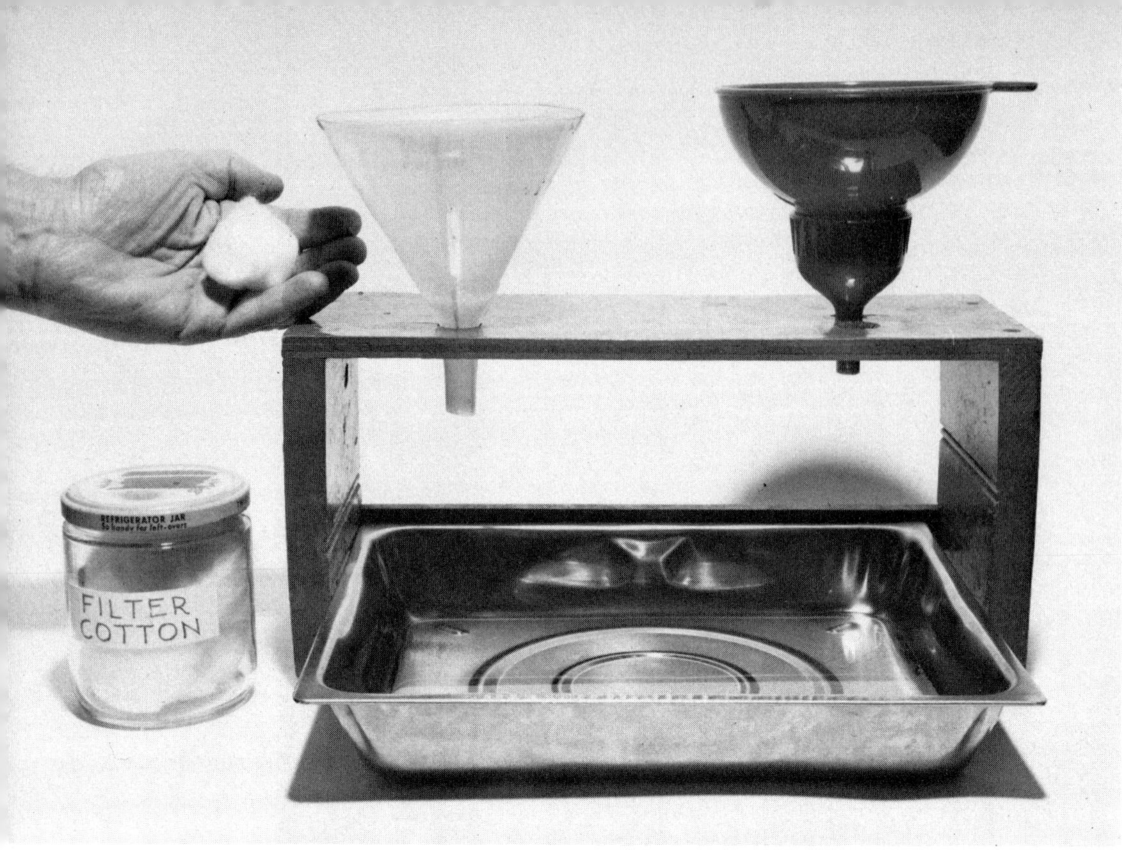

Figs. 1-18a and b. Filtering of solutions directly into trays is greatly accelerated by the use of *two* funnels and this sturdy stand, made of some scraps of wood. Wads of ordinary absorbent cotton about the size of a golf ball will trap a surprising amount of impurities from seemingly clean developer, fixer, etc. Rubber-headed nails on the bottoms of the upright pieces are a worthwhile addition to steady the trays.

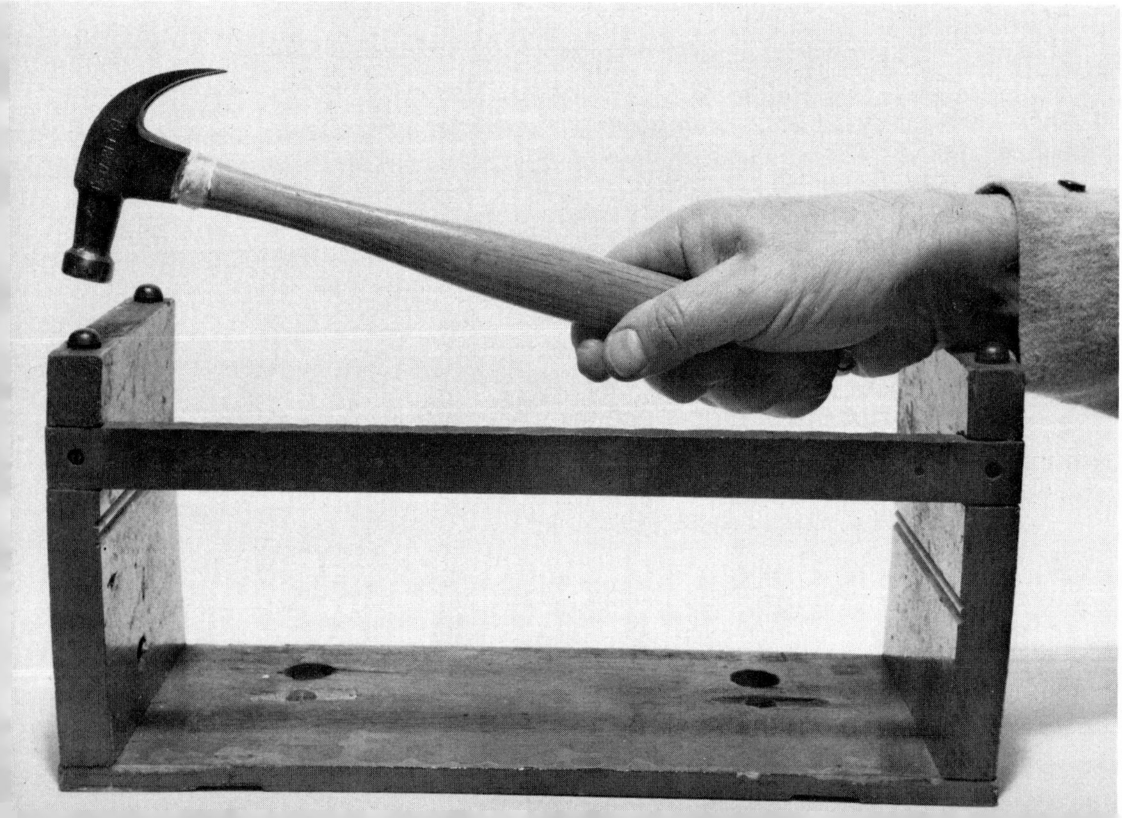

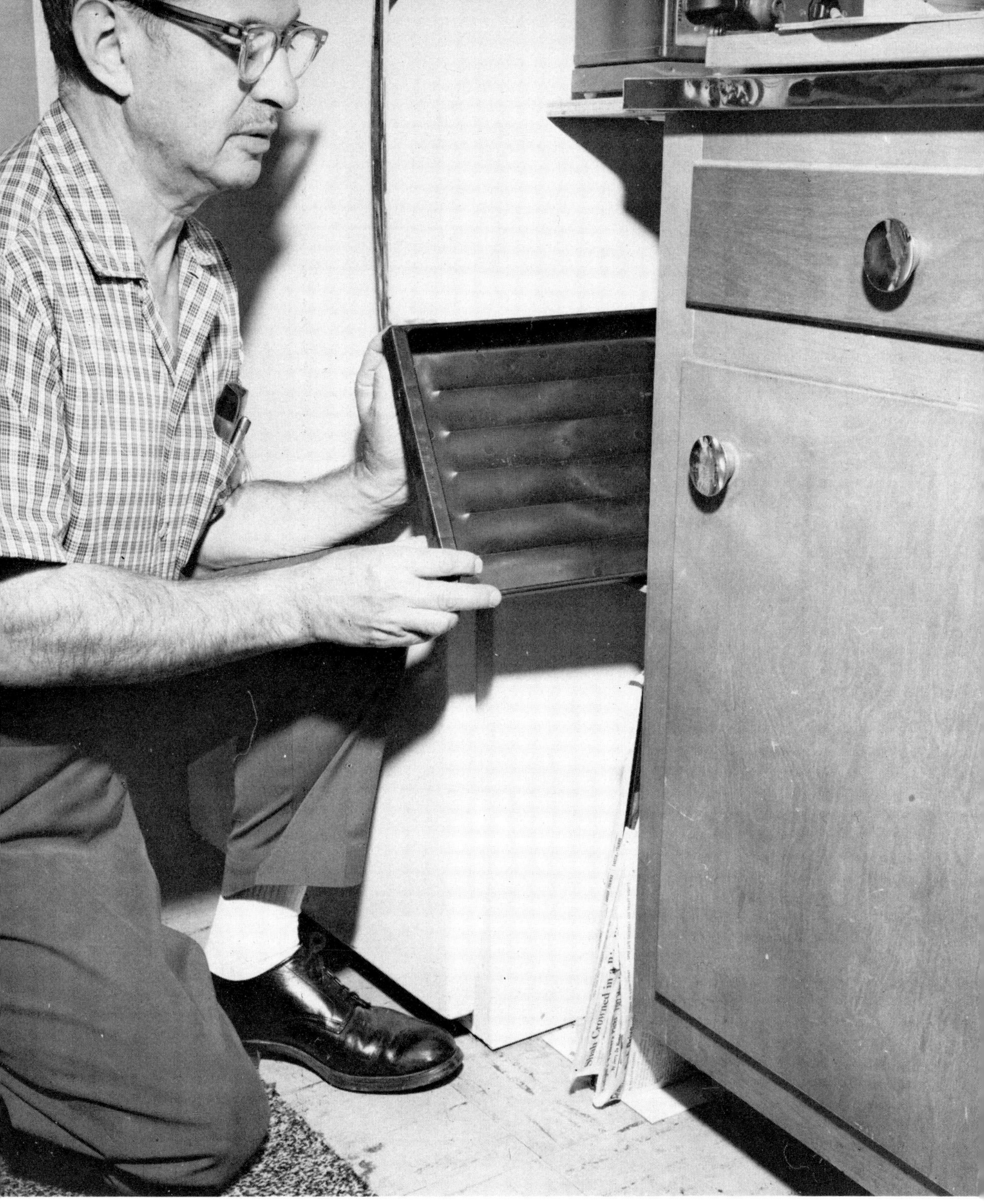

Fig. 1-19. Narrow spaces between the kitchen cabinet and the stove or refrigerator are just right for storing trays, the enlarger baseboard, and other flat objects.

bottles, filled to the top and tightly stoppered. You can buy these for very little in any drugstore. When you are setting up for enlarging, empty one bottle into a tray and add the required water (usually twice the amount of the concentrate), and you are in business. This mixture will last through the evening, but not much longer. If you rebottle it and try to use it a couple of days later, you will see that it has turned almost black.

KEEP IT CLEAN

The importance of filtering all solutions *before* use cannot be overemphasized. This is a slow operation, but it can be speeded up considerably by the use of two funnels at a time in a simple stand made as shown in the accompanying illustration.

2

DEVELOPING

Only good negatives can make good prints. The process is foolproof if you follow the instructions herewith.

WHY DO YOUR OWN?

To assure yourself of better pictures. Can there be a better reason?

Undoubtedly you understand that rolls left for processing in pharmacies, stationery stores, supermarkets, luncheonettes, and even camera stores are not done in back rooms there, but are picked up daily and sent to large commercial laboratories where they are developed in bulk. Regardless of whether the films came from $25 Instamatics or $500 Nikons and Leicas, they go through a series of common baths of uniform temperature for a uniform time. This kind of machine processing is of necessity a compromise; the developer itself and the temperature/time combination are chosen to accommodate films shot under greatly varying conditions.

The experience of knowledgeable customers indicates that many labs tend to overdevelop a little, to compensate in part for underexposure in the camera. In this way it is often possible to obtain fairly satisfactory prints from incorrectly exposed negatives that otherwise might be hopeless. However, forced developing sometimes seriously degrades correctly exposed films that happen to be going through the same baths.

Another risk of "drugstore" processing is that some of those anonymous labs might try to save themselves a few dollars by stretching the useful life cycle of their chemicals. The result can be weak negatives that print poorly and turn brown, or fade away, after a few weeks.

If you do your own developing you can experiment with developers, temperature, and time until you establish a combination that produces perfect negatives from your own camera. This processing requires so little equipment and space and is so simple and foolproof that it is undertaken as a matter of insurance even by photographers who are not complete "do-it-yourselfers" but are interested mainly in the artistic side of the hobby. If they don't want to set up their own darkrooms for printing, at least not right away, they can send their finished negatives to custom labs for enlargements. Prints can always be remade if necessary, but once a roll of negatives is spoiled no subsequent treatment can reclaim it.

THE NEGATIVE — BASIC PROCESSING

If you open a new roll of film and inspect it under a white light, you will note that one side of the flexible plastic base is shiny while the other is dull gray. The dull surface is actually a thin layer of chemicals in which certain compounds of silver predominate; this is called the "emulsion."

When a scene is "shot" with a camera, the lens projects an image onto the film. The parts of the scene that are bright reflect the most light and make a stronger impression on the emulsion than those that are darker. However, the image remains altogether invisible until the film is passed through a series of chemical baths. The first is the "developer." This attacks the silver component of the emulsion and causes it to blacken, to a degree depending on the relative brightness of the various areas of the scene. What was light in the original becomes dark on the film, and what was dark remains light. This is why film is called "negative." The extreme example of the reversal of tone values on a negative is a shot of a black-and-white checkerboard.

The second bath is the "fixer" (also known as hypo) and has the job of removing the undarkened parts of the emulsion. If you hold a fixed film up to a light you will see that it is clean, with no sign of the original grayness. However, processing is not quite finished; for permanence, the developed and fixed film must be washed thoroughly in plain water to remove all traces of chemicals.

Exposing a film to unwanted light is called "fogging." You fogged the new roll when you opened it for inspection. If you developed it, the entire surface would turn a dense, uniform black. On the other hand, a roll that hadn't been exposed at all would develop out perfectly clear.

(An interesting characteristic of the "latent" image projected onto light-sensitive emulsion is its long life. Exposed negatives that have lain dormant in cameras for years and years often develop nicely and produce good prints.)

In practical processing several desirable steps are usually added to the basic three-stage procedure just described. Between developing and fixing there is the "short stop." This is commonly a weak acid that arrests the developing action quickly and prevents overdevelopment of fast-acting developers that require only four or five minutes. For slower developers having a cycle of 10–15 minutes, overdevelopment is not quite such a hazard and a water wash is satisfactory. This doesn't neutralize the developer chemically as the acid does; it merely rinses away most of it. Both short stop and water rinse greatly lengthen the useful life of the fixer.

The normal washing time recommended for thorough removal of fixer is about 30 minutes at a nominal water temperature of 70° F. However, if the fixed film is first given about two minutes in a "fixer-neutralizer" the time can be reduced to five minutes and the water can be as cold as 35° F.

After coming out of the wash, films are usually hung up anywhere in the clear and swabbed down with a double viscose sponge to remove excess water. During this step there is some danger of scoring the film with fine lines, which show up like tire tracks when enlargements are made. After just one experience with this sort of damage most photographers discard the sponge and instead give the washed film a 30-second immersion in a valuable preparation called "Photo-Flo." This not only eliminates the need for wiping but also greatly accelerates drying and leaves the film spotlessly clean.

THE IMPORTANCE OF THE DEVELOPER

By far the most important chemical in film processing is the developer. There are dozens of different concoctions on the market, and you can spend lots of time and dollars playing with them without producing any worthwhile pictures. Without question you should start with the developer recommended by the film manufacturer. If your exposures in the camera are anywhere near correct, you will at least be certain of visible negatives. The chemicals that follow the developer are of more or less standard composition, regardless of make.

KEEPING DOWN THE GRAIN

Virtually all developers intended for roll films are of the "fine-grain" type; some are merely more so than others. By this term is meant the ability of the chemical to minimize its granulating action on the emulsion. Grain is not visible to the naked eye, but like scratch marks it shows up horribly in blow-ups. Grain is an inherent quality of the film itself. It is relatively low in films with low exposure ratings, in the neighborhood of ASA 32—64, and is much more noticeable in high-speed films rated upward of ASA 200—300.* If you want to make really big enlargements from small negatives, obviously you should use the slowest

---

*In much photographic literature, film speed numbers are preceded by the letters ASA, for "American Standards Association." Actually, the name of the organization has been changed to "American National Standards Institute," but ANSI is scarcely recognized by many people in photography. The likelihood is that ASA will continue in use for some time because it is shorter and easier to remember.

available film. This is no great handicap because the high speed
of many common lenses often compensates for it.

DEVELOPER VS. FILM SPEED

The developer determines the effective speed of a film as well
as its grain pattern. Some ultra-fine preparations reduce the
published ratings; this is a small price to pay for the favorably
tight grain. On the other hand, moderate-grain developers are
quite likely to increase the speed, often considerably. Manufacturers cheerfully admit in their instructional material that the
ratings assigned to their films are only a guide, a starting point
for experimentation.

Assume for purposes of discussion that you use the recommended developer at the proper time and temperature, and that
your film is rated at ASA 64. You set your exposure meter for
this number, shoot a couple of rolls, and process them. Suppose
all the negatives look thin. What to do? Lower the meter setting
to ASA 40 and try again; there is sure to be an improvement in
negative quality. (Film is cheap, and any rolls you burn up now
will save you from wasting more film in the future.)

Or suppose the first negatives come out as dark as coal. Boost
the meter to ASA 80, shoot one roll; raise it to ASA 125, shoot
another. Then process, always at the previous time and temperature to eliminate the developer as a variable. The results of
these trials will probably surprise you.

You might be able to pep up an underexposed roll by
increasing the developing time or the temperature, or both, but
this is highly inadvisable because forced processing of *any* film
in *any* developer invariably coarsens the grain structure.

CHOOSING A TANK

Film developing tanks are made of either a hard, smooth
plastic or a particular stainless steel known as type 18/8. Both
materials are impervious to the action of photo chemicals.

Since a tank must be loaded in complete darkness, its film reel must be absolutely foolproof. In the simplest and cheapest plastic tanks, the reel consists of one fixed and one adjustable spirally grooved member, to take film from 35mm to 6cm. To load it, you start one end of the film into the open end of the spiral at the outer edge of the reel, and push in slowly. Don't take a tank of this type as a gift! After a few inches of the film have gone in, the rest usually jams in the grooves, and you are left swearing and sweating with a real problem.

The better plastic tanks have a semi-automatic loading action. The two reel halves are still grooved, but the outer one can be twisted back and forth on its mounting post through about 15 degrees. After the film is started in the grooves, this motion causes it to wind steadily into the reel.

Stainless steel tanks use one-size reels of stainless wire. In these, one end of the film is clamped to the *inner* core and then it is supposed to wind outward between the spiral grooves formed by the wire as you turn the reel. Without some sort of a guide or loading mechanism this is generally a difficult and frustrating job even in full room light. A loader should be part of the tank package, but it isn't; tank manufacturers sell it as a separate accessory.

Although stainless steel runs into some money, the equipment made from it is widely favored by experienced photographers for several reasons: the tanks themselves are virtually indestructible; the reels are rigid and accurately spaced; several reels can be piggy-backed in a single tank for simultaneous processing; the surfaces remain clean and shiny.

Learning to load any reel is simply a matter of doing it. Start in a light room. On a table, lay out the open tank and its cover, a reel with its loader attached, a pair of scissors, and a trial roll of film. Put them all in the same relative positions each time you practice. With stainless reels the main trick is to get the end of the film under the center clamp; once this is done the rest rolls on smoothly and quickly. After a few practice sessions, shift to the actual darkened room of your choice and get accustomed to the feel of it with more practice.

What can you do if you fumble a stainless reel and its loader when handling a "live" film and then find that it's stuck? It usually sticks only the forward direction, so pull it out carefully, roll it up loosely in your palm, drop it into the tank, and put on the cover. Now turn on the light, reassemble the loader to the reel, and try again. If the film is in a plastic reel, simply pull off the movable half; the film then comes loose.

The entire process of film developing is shown in detail in the accompanying pictures. Study them well before you do your first roll, duplicate the steps faithfully, and you will be rewarded with a strip of clean negatives.

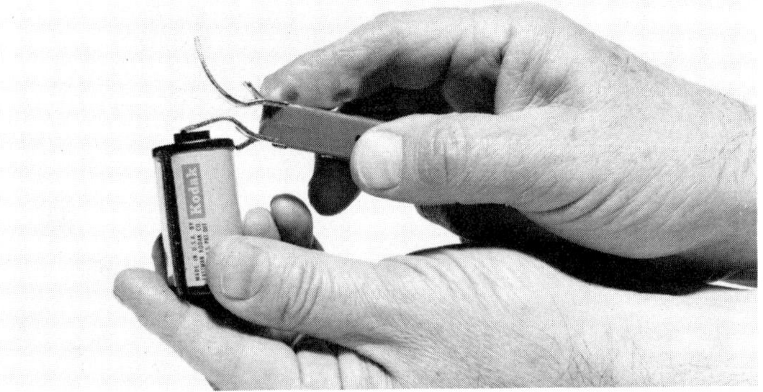

Fig. 2-1. An ordinary bottle opener is an excellent tool for opening a roll of 35mm film. Hold the magazine firmly and dig the small prong of the opener under the rim; then lift off cap with a strong upward pull. Remember, this and the following operations are all done in the dark-darkroom.

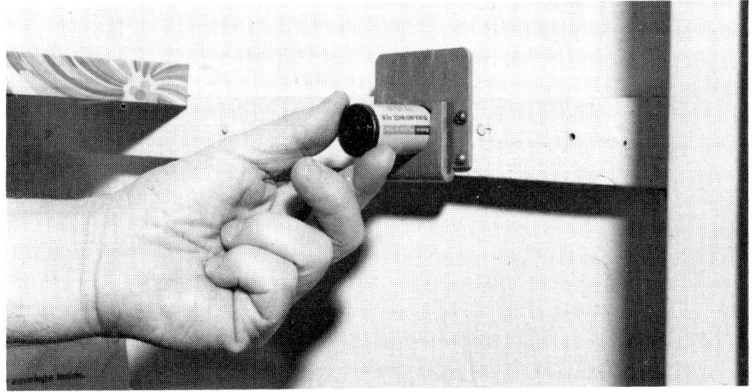

Fig. 2-2. If you fix up a permanent darkroom or have a good film-loading area in a comfortable closet, this Kodak wall-mounted de-capping jig is a good investment. You simply jam the bottom of the film magazine into the U-shaped opening and push down.

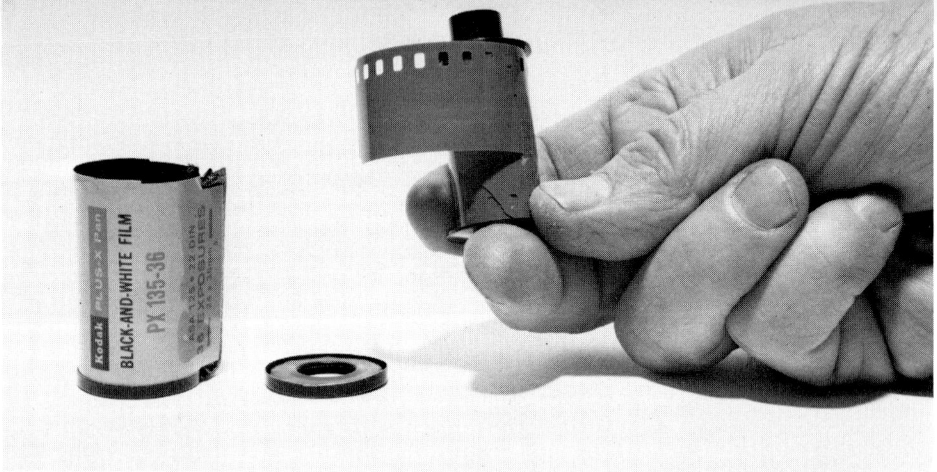

Fig. 2-3. Extract the spool of film carefully to avoid scratching it. The end you see here is the tongue-shaped leader that went onto the take-up spool of the camera. The film is somewhat springy and unwinds easily.

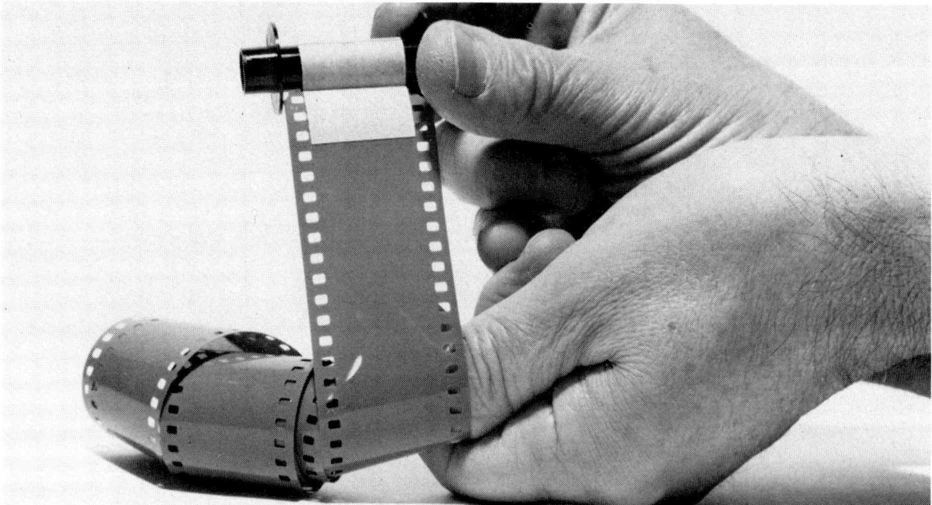

Fig. 2-4. The inner end of the film is securely fastened to the spool by tape; Peel the tape off slowly. If you rip it too quickly, a very visible discharge of static electricity occurs. This might register like a small lightning flash on the negative.

Fig. 2-5. Some film developing tanks load more easily if one end of the negative is trimmed on an angle at the corners, as shown. Trim the other end square. Hold the film by its edges, as much as possible, to avoid finger marks on the emulsion.

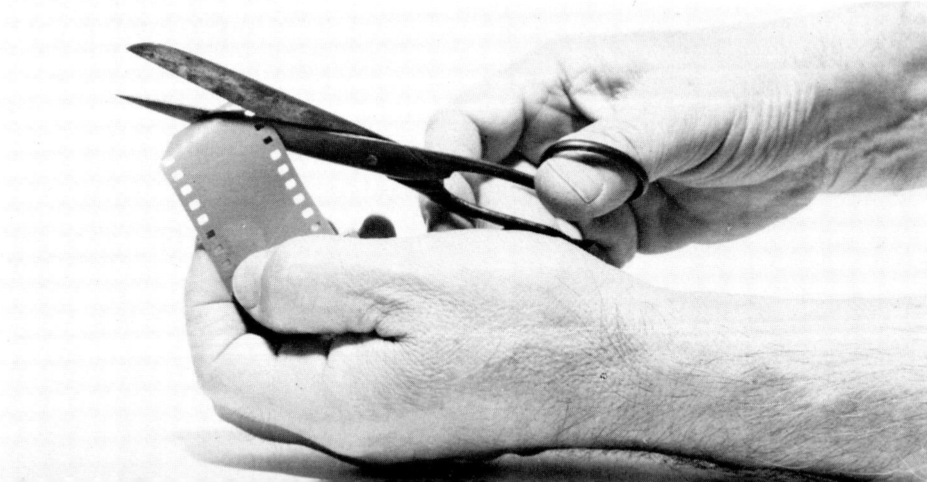

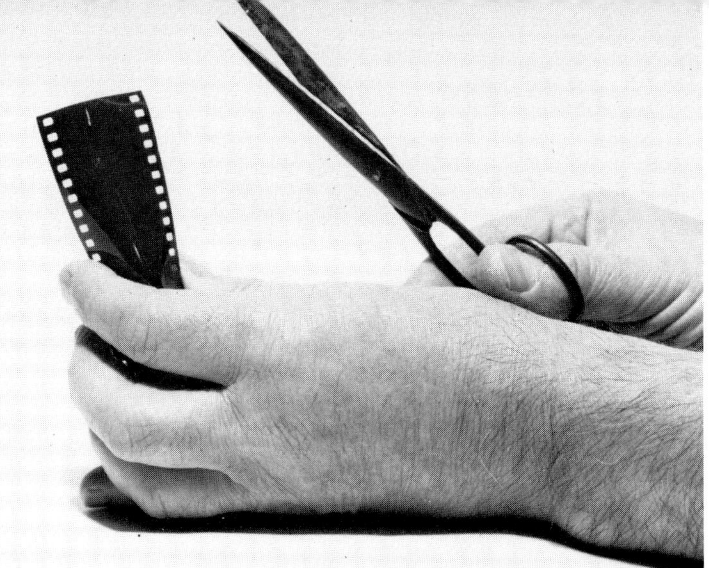

Fig. 2-6. The instructions for some tanks specifically call for a square cut, preferably between sprocket holes. In the dark this isn't easy, but with a little practice you can feel for the right spot to apply the scissors.

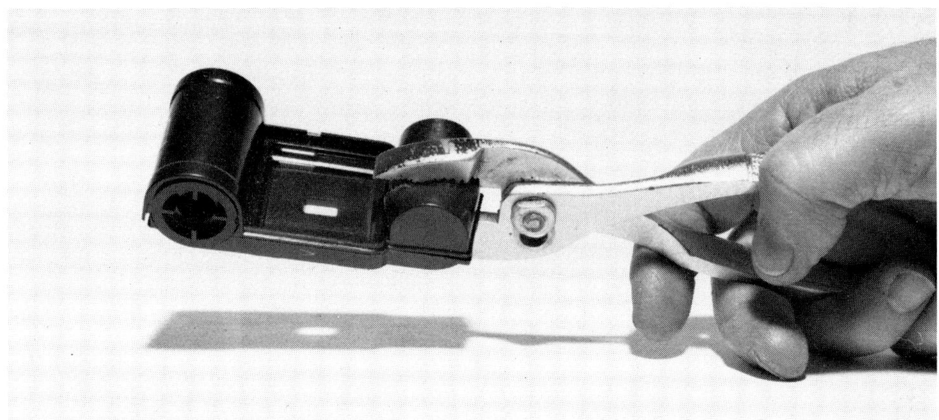

Figs. 2-7a and b. The two-section plastic cartridge for 126 film used in Instamatic-type cameras must be destroyed to release the exposed film. When you crush one part of the case, the cartridge comes apart readily. In the dark a pair of pliers does the job quickly. There is a smaller version of the Instamatic cartridge, with the type number 110, for use in flat pocket-size Instamatics. The film is a trifle less than 16mm wide, has the same sprocket arrangement as in the 126 size, and is packaged in a scaled-down cartridge of identical shape. Processing procedure remains unchanged except for the use of smaller reels for developing tanks.

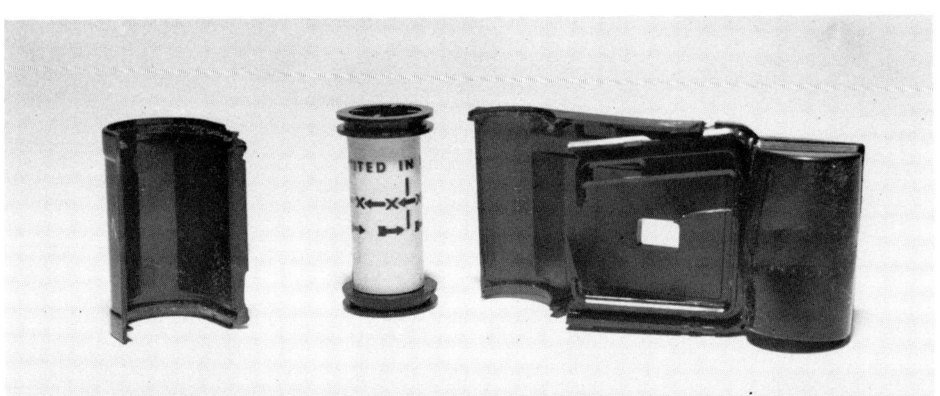

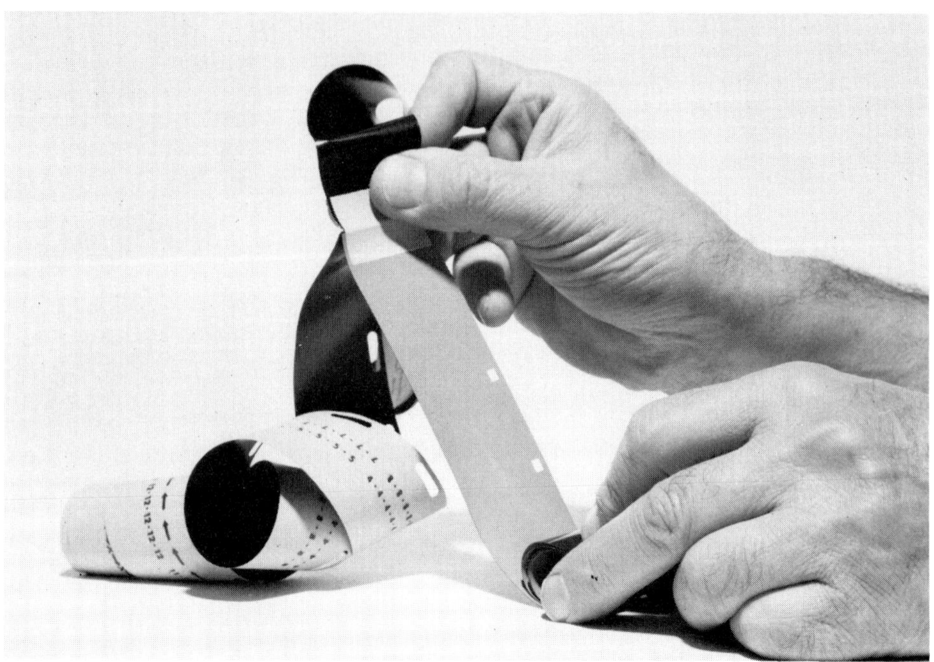

Fig. 2-8. Unlike 35mm film, 126 has a paper backing that must be removed and discarded. Note the single sprocket holes on only one edge. Although it looks wider, 126 is exactly 35mm wide, just like the double-perforated film.

Fig. 2-9. Loading film into a reel — especially long strips of 35mm — can be an exasperating experience in the dark. The film must be arched slightly as it is run into the spirals. This must be done delicately between thumb and forefinger, unless a loading guide of some sort is used. This Kinderman model loads a roll in about 15 seconds without jamming.

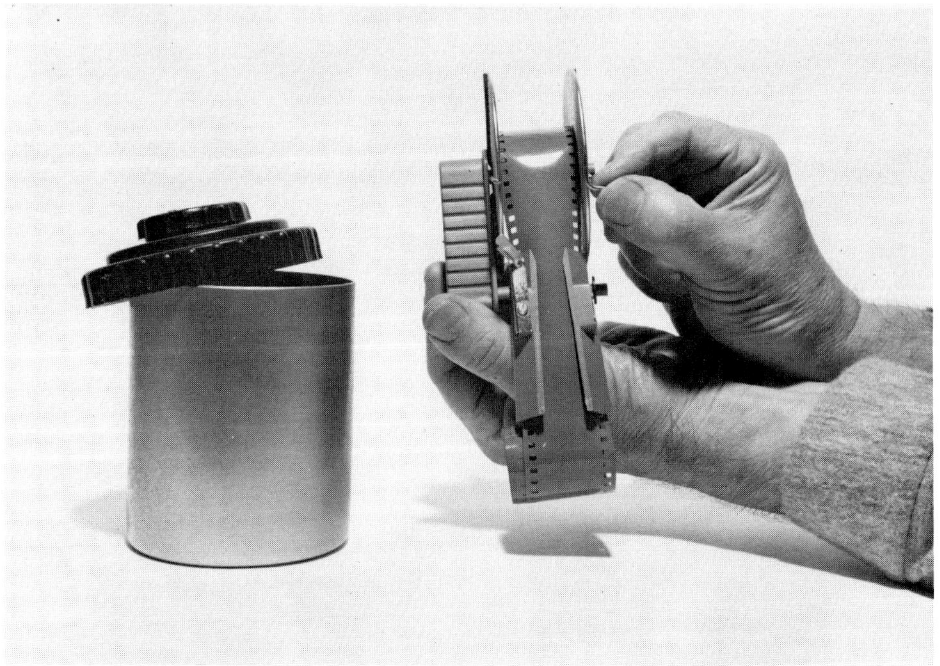

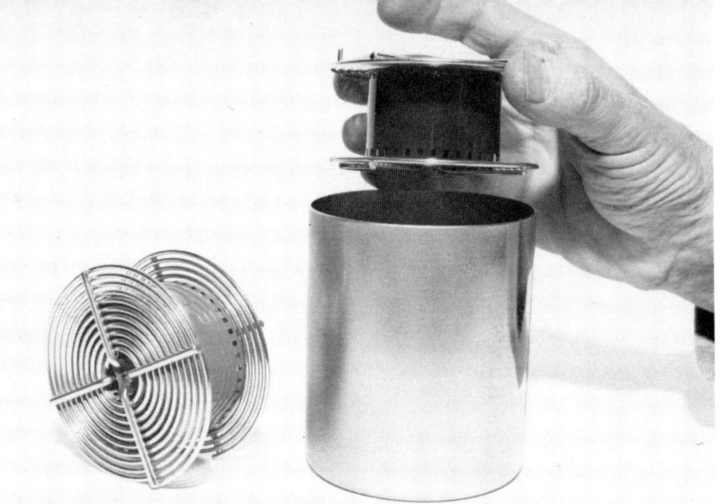

Fig. 2-10. A stainless steel tank that takes two 35mm or 126 rolls is a convenience. It also accommodates a single 120 roll.

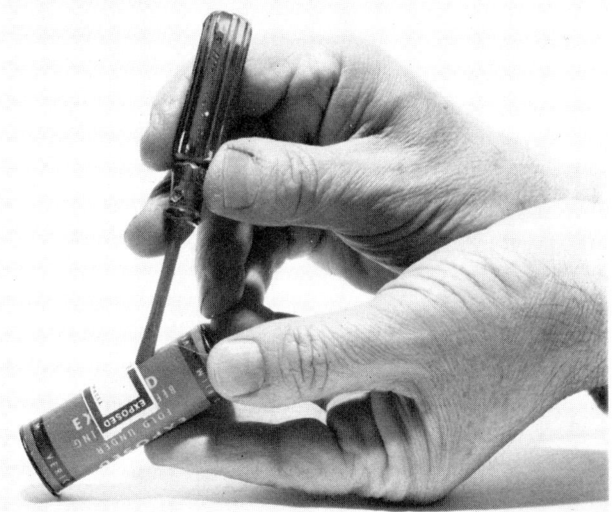

Fig. 2-11. When a roll of 120 film is removed from a camera it must be taped over to prevent it from unravelling and becoming fogged. In the dark, therefore, the first step in preparing for the developing process is cutting the tape.

Fig. 2-12. Like 126 film, 120 film has a paper backing. Instead of pulling apart the taped joint, cut it off completely with scissors. This will prevent a troublesome static build-up and discharge.

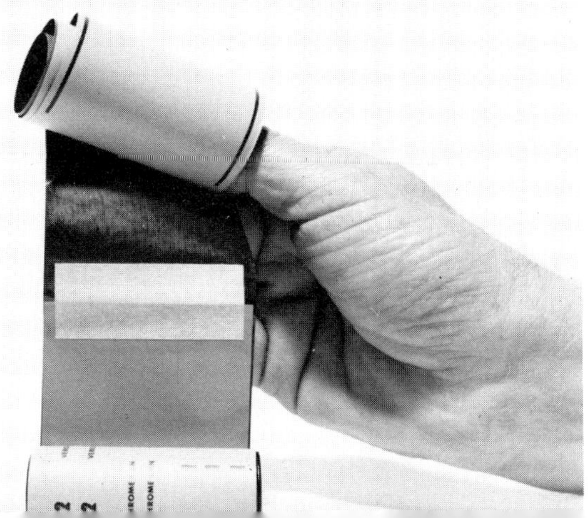

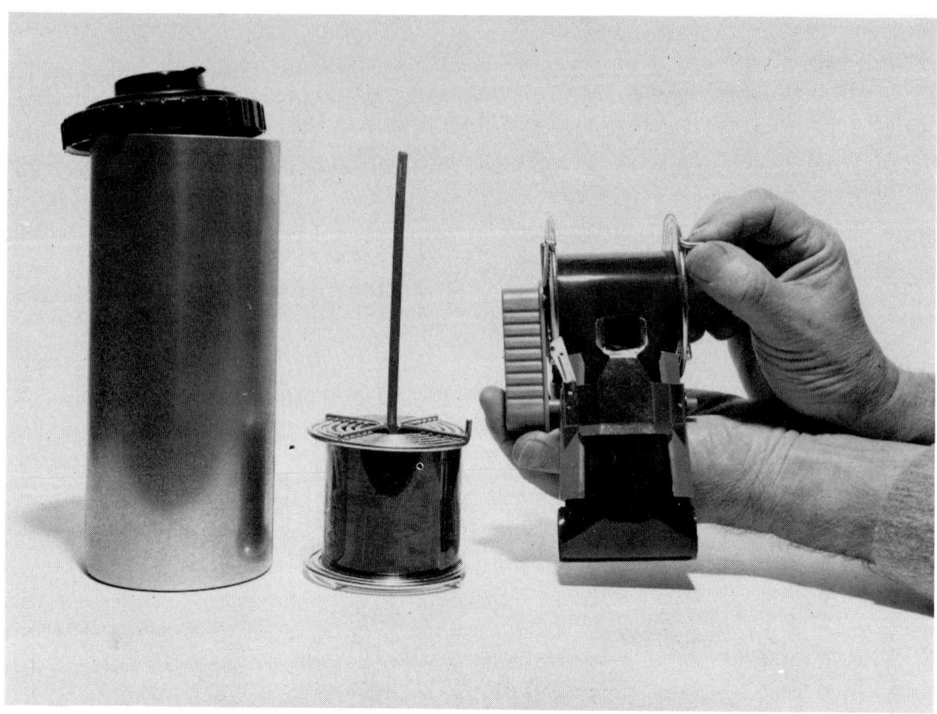

Fig. 2-13. Film loader at right eases 120 roll into stainless-steel reel with winding motion. Loaded reel, center, is on lowering rod that puts two reels, piggy-back, into large Kinderman tank.

Fig. 2-14. Self-loading Ansco reel uses ratchet motion of light colored section to feed film into grooves. The assembly is adjustable and takes films from 35mm to 6cm (120 film).

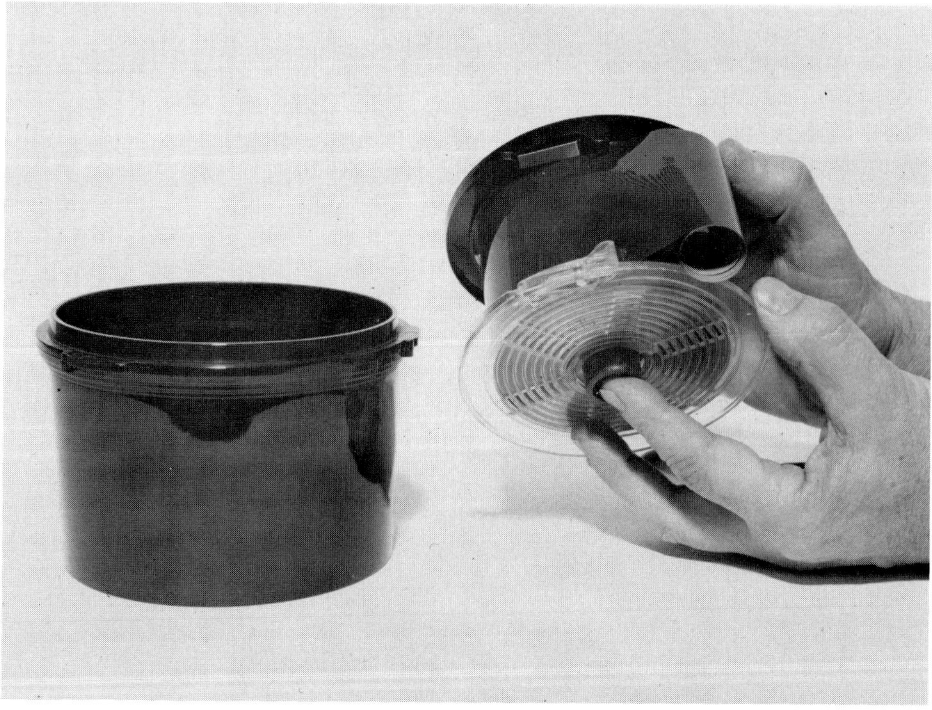

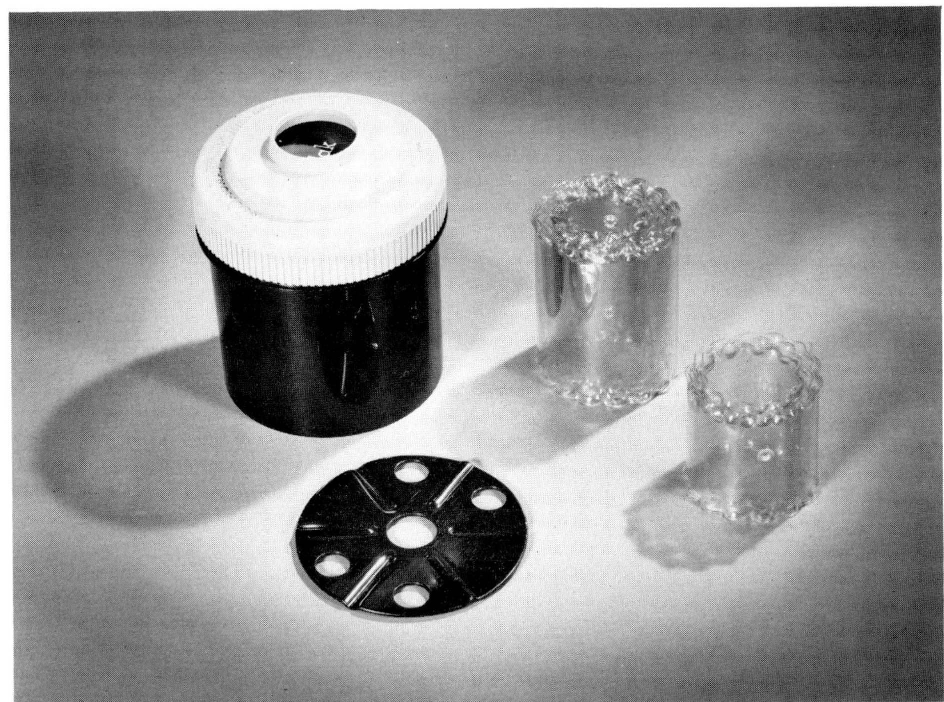

Fig. 2-15. Kodak's Kodacraft tank and easy-to-load transparent film aprons can be used for both 35mm and 120 roll film. With the apron unrolled, place the end of the film next to the looped end of the apron and carefully roll the film into the apron. Be sure to always hold the film and apron by the edges. The metal weight is used to hold the aprons down in the developing tank.

Fig. 2-16. Spool for 120 film (left) is made of metal; 35mm and 126 spools are made of plastic. Don't throw them away; children love to play with them.

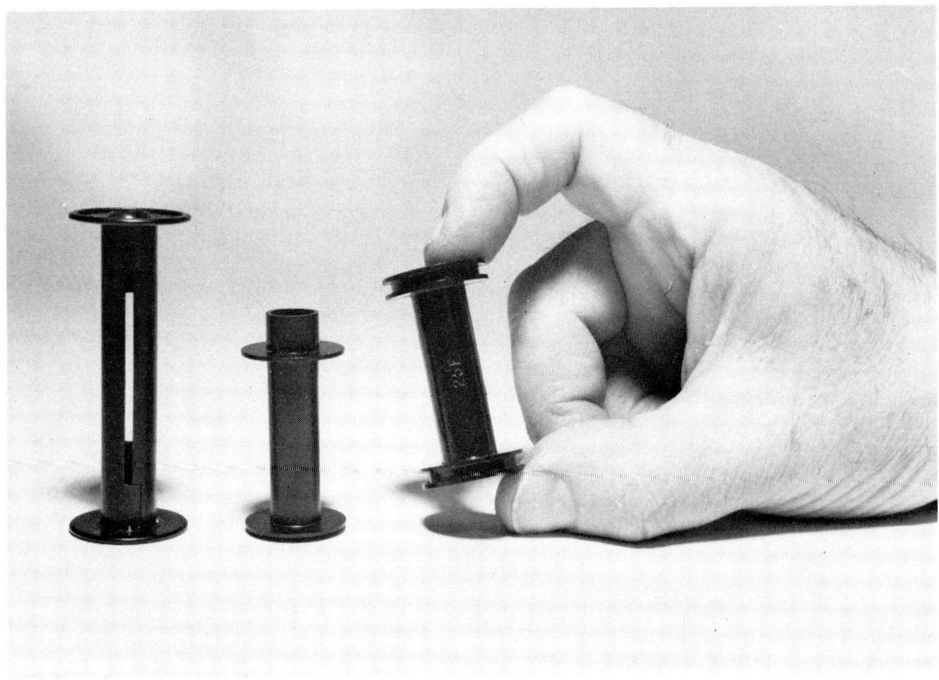

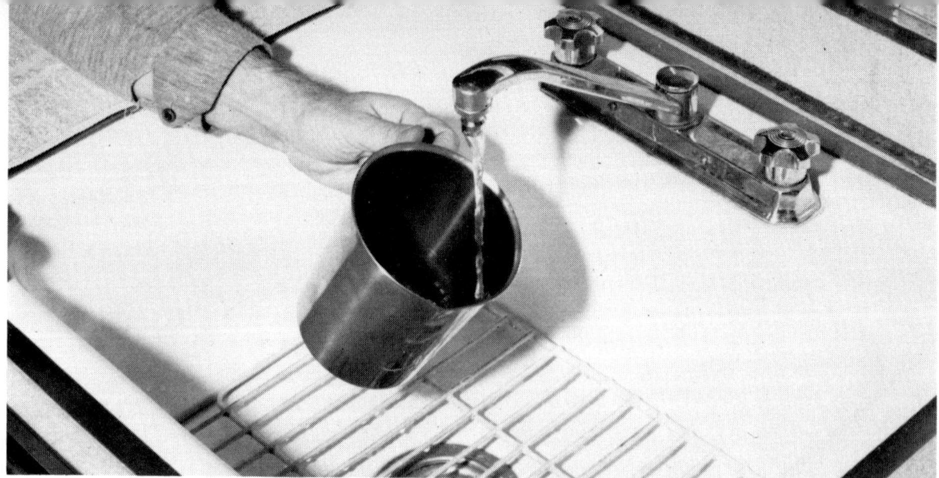

Figs. 2-17a and b. With the tank loaded and capped, the room lights can be turned on and the developing process can begin. Rinse graduate and funnel under running water.

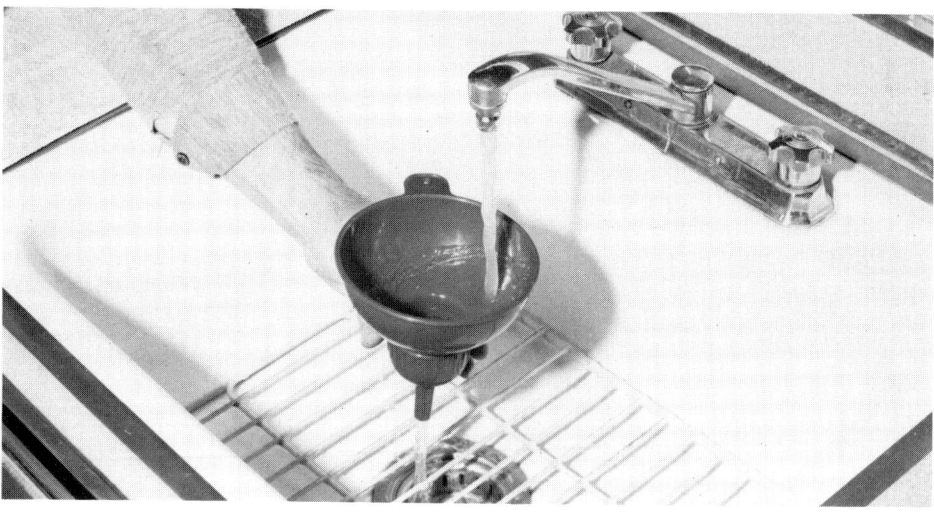

Fig. 2-18. This simple stand is virtually spillproof. Put a wad of cotton in the neck of the funnel and filter through the amount of developer prescribed for your tank.

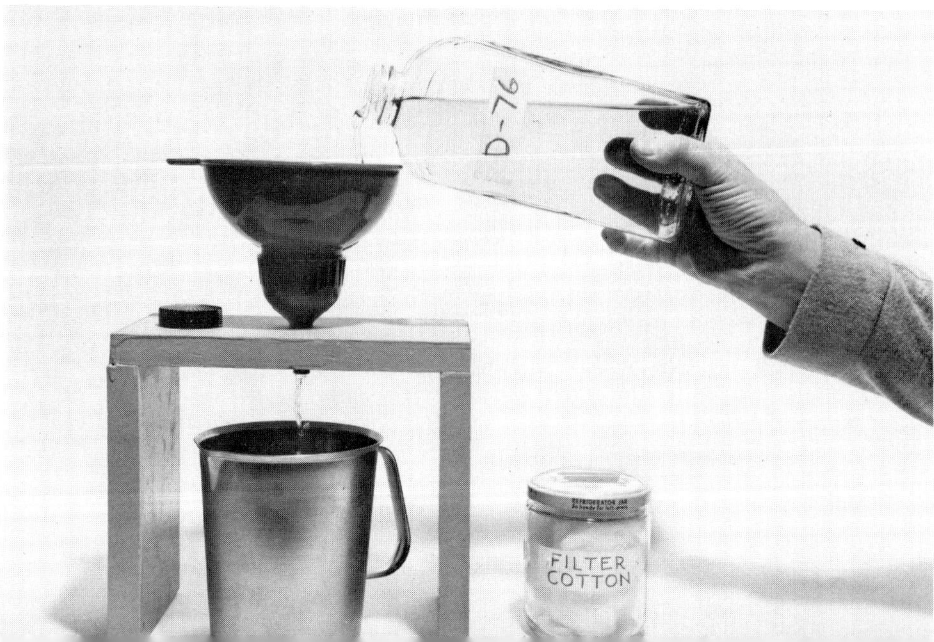

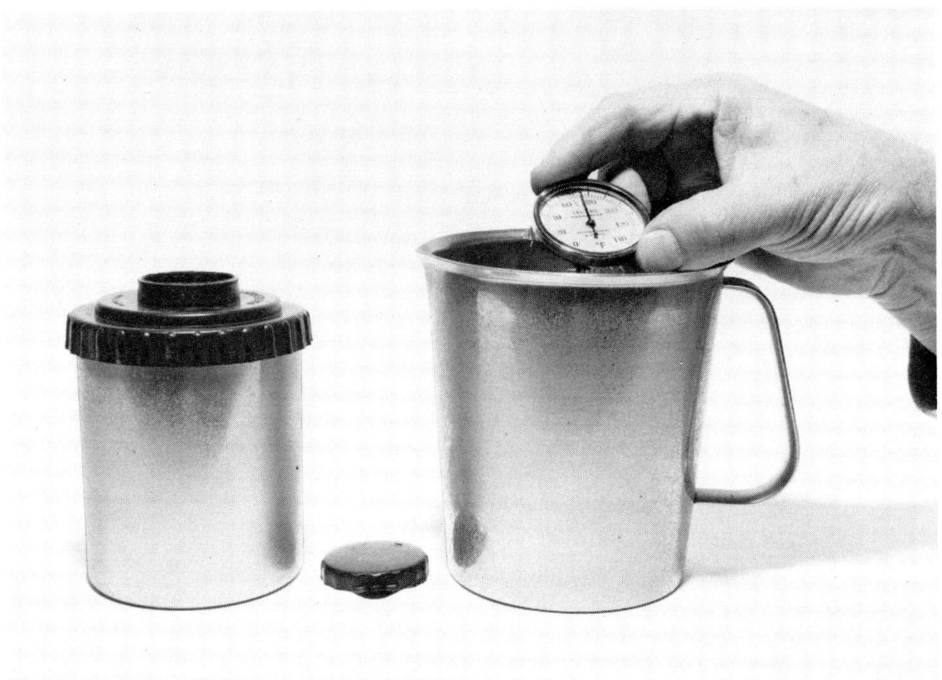

Fig. 2-19. Ideal developing temperature is usually given as 68° F, but anything up to about 75° F. is acceptable. It's better to be a couple of degrees above 68° F. than below, as chemical action becomes sluggish when solutions are cold. Leave thermometer submerged for ten seconds or so and then observe reading.

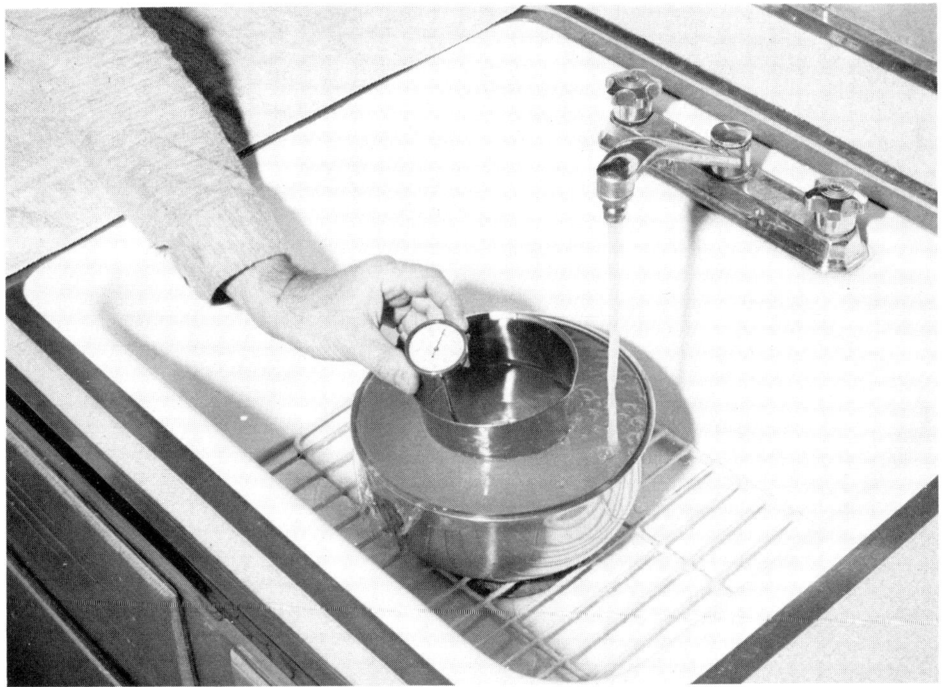

Fig. 2-20. Adjust developer temperature up or down by immersing graduate in large bowl and letting warm or cold water flow around it. Be careful not to let this water splash into the graduate.

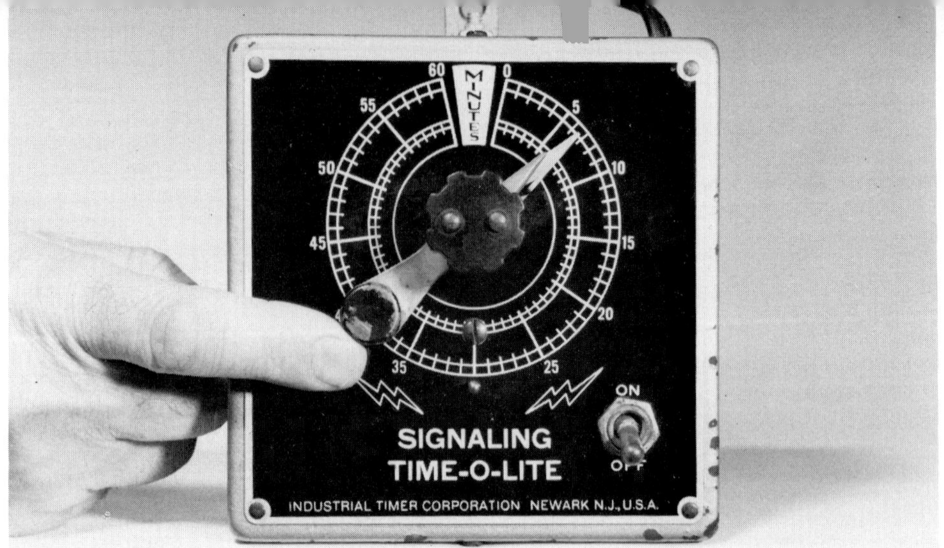

Fig. 2-21. Set the timer for the number of minutes prescribed by the film manufacturer for your developer at a specific temperature, minus about half a minute.

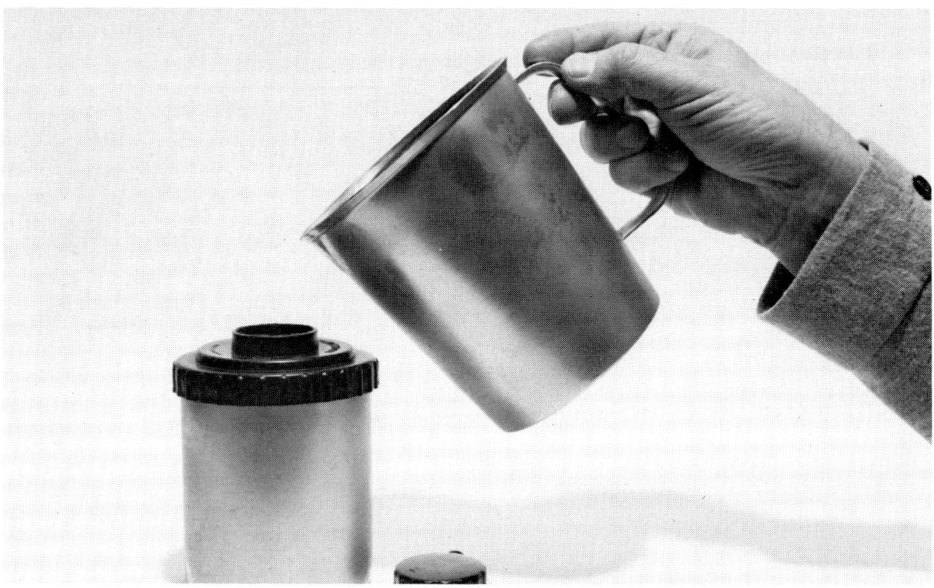

Figs. 2-22a and b. Turn the timer on and immediately start pouring the developer into the tank. Then place the small cover tightly on the tank.

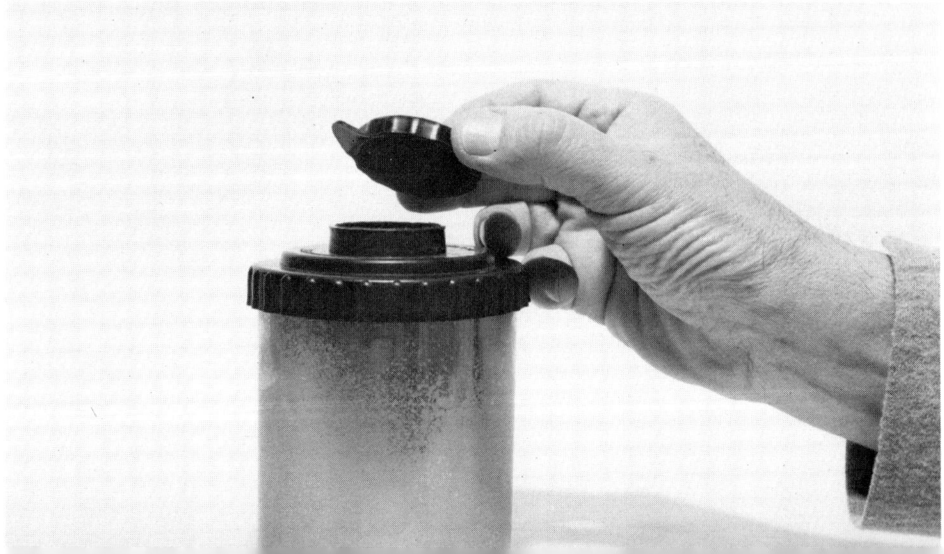

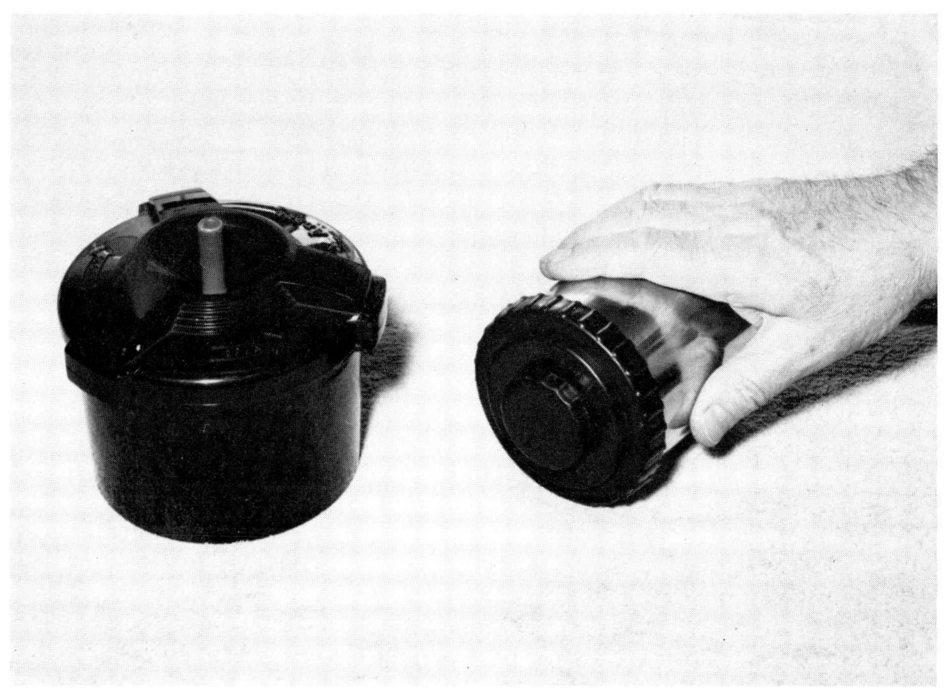

Fig. 2-23. Roll the tank back and forth gently a couple of times to dislodge air bubbles and to distribute the developer around the film evenly. Repeat this agitation every minute or so.

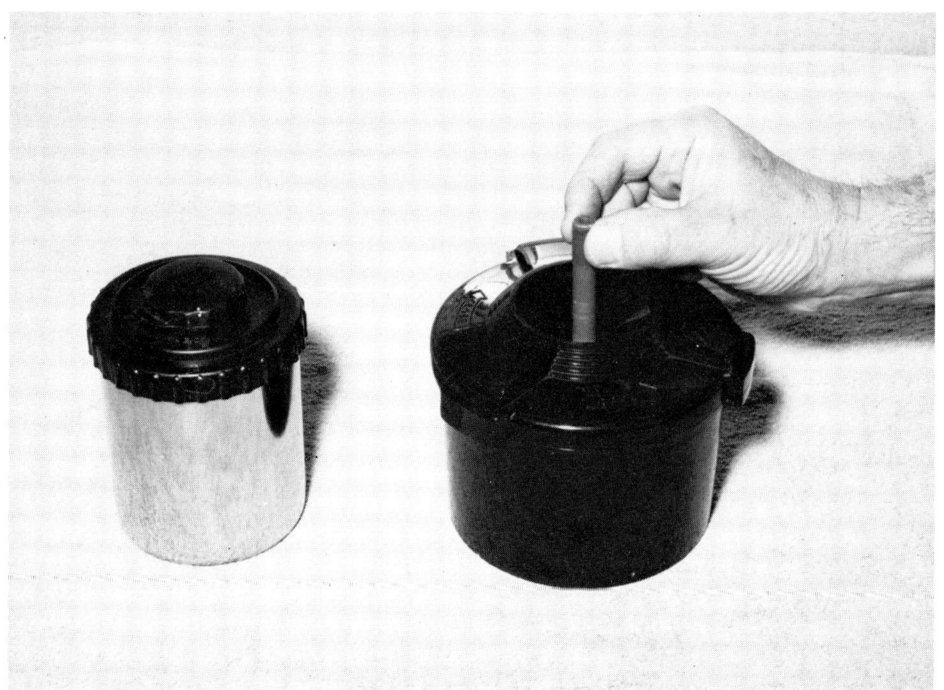

Fig. 2-24. If your tank is of the plastic type with a central opening, agitate the film by means of the twirling rod that comes with the unit.

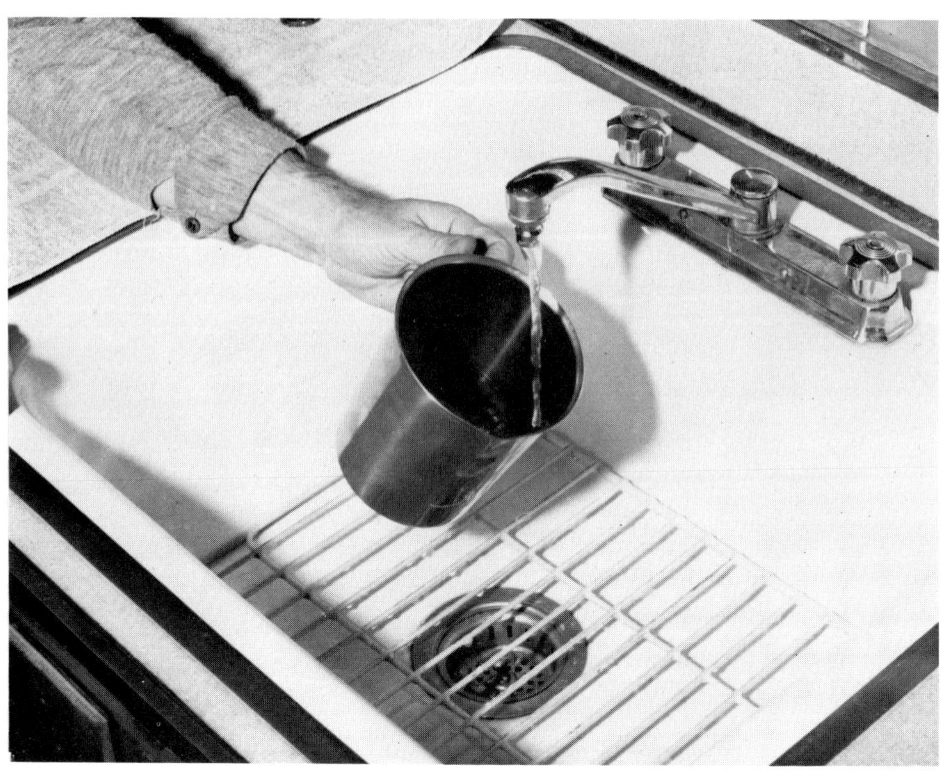

Figs. 2-25a and b. With the developing process under way, again rinse the graduate and the funnel.

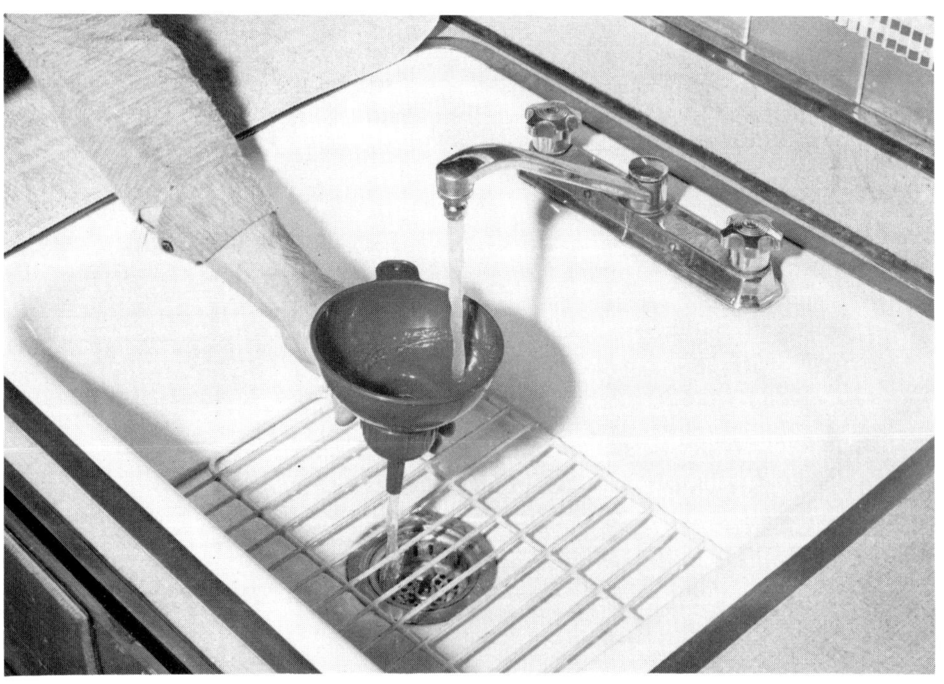

44

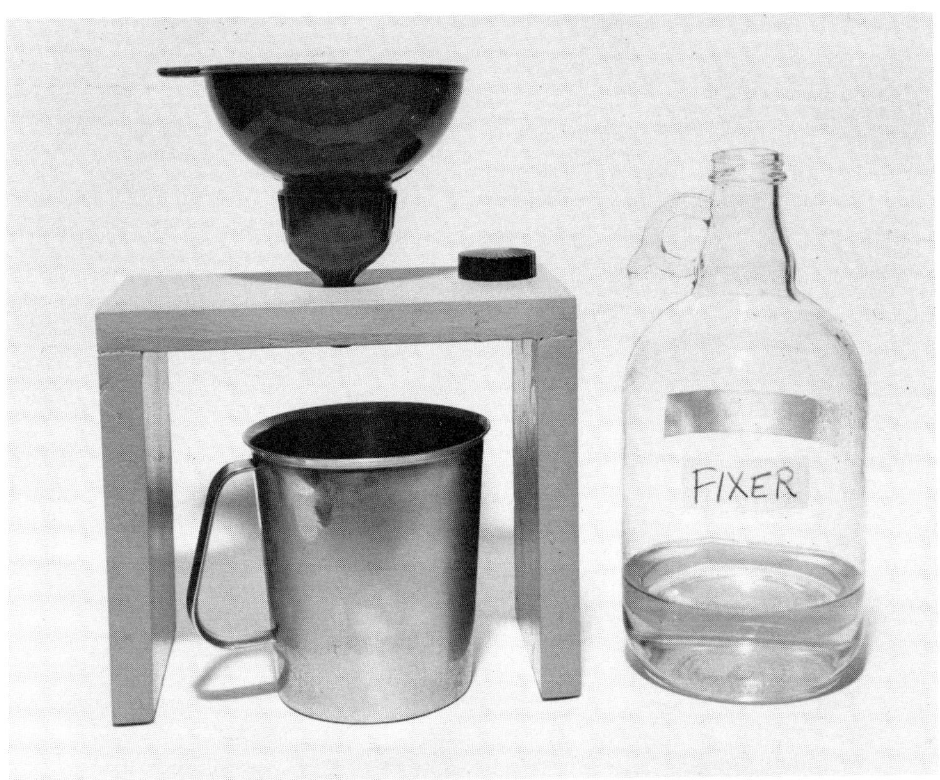

Figs. 2-26a and b. Repeat the filter step, this time with fixer. Take its temperature and adjust it to that of the developer. Put the graduate aside, and remember to agitate the film again.

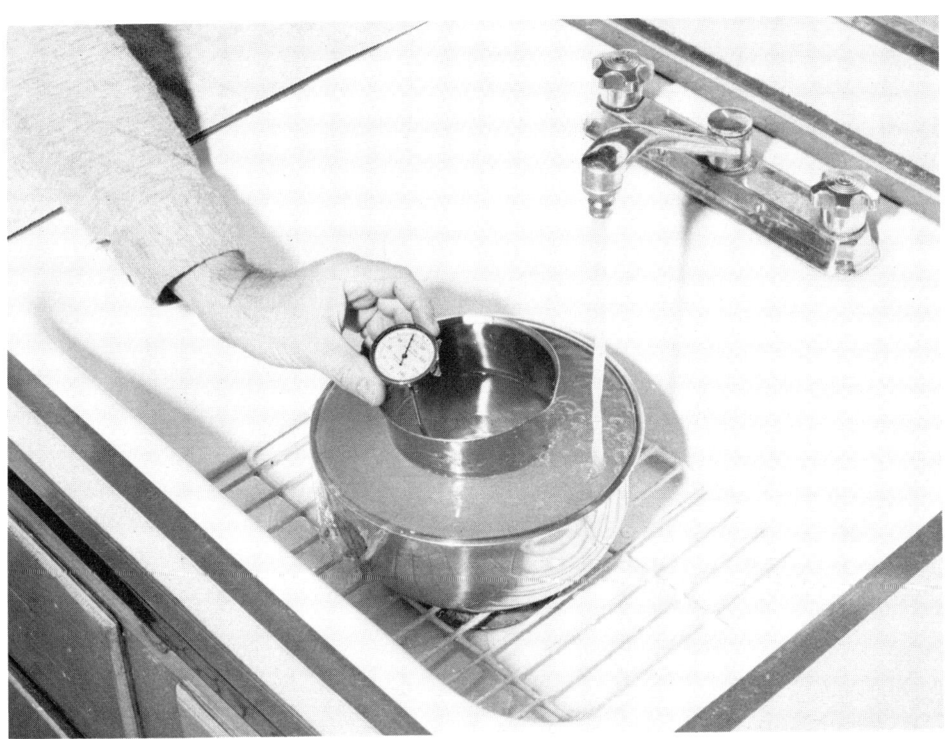

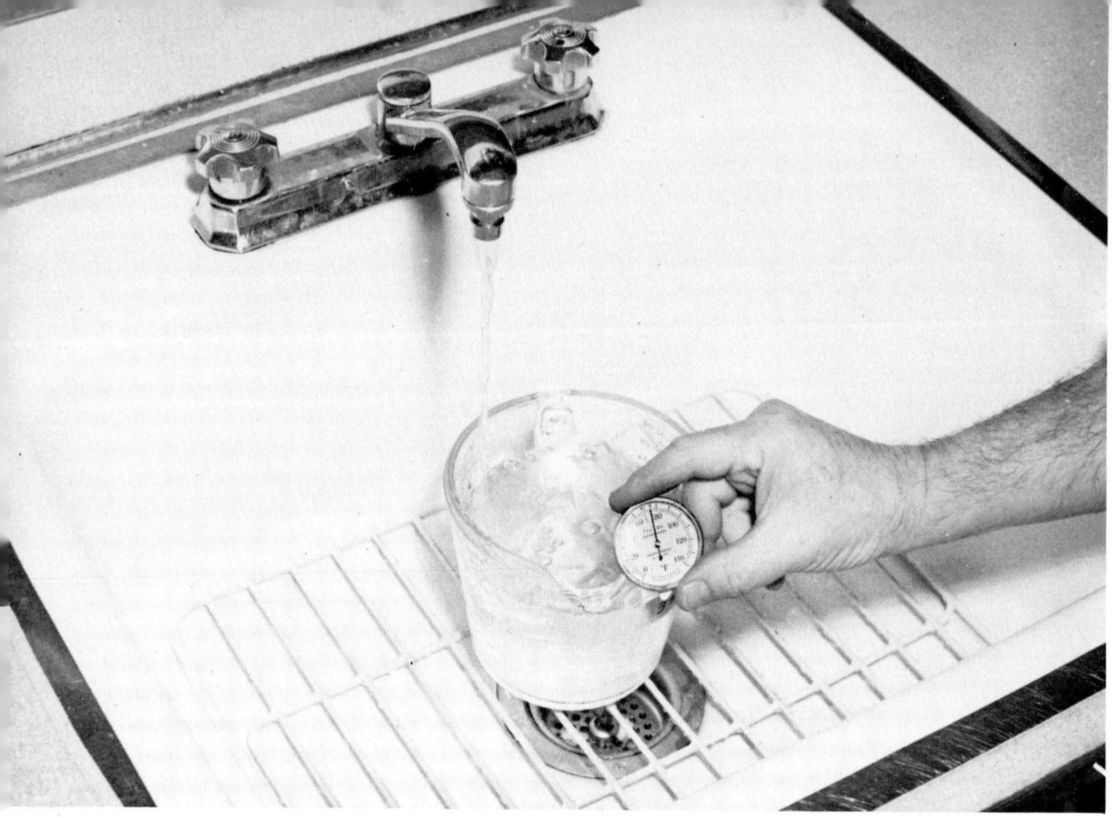

Fig. 2-27. You'll need some plain rinse water to follow the developer in the tank. Use another graduate and adjust the temperature as before. Put this container aside for a moment, and again agitate the film.

Fig. 2-28. If your developer can be replenished, now is the time to add the replenisher by means of a small graduate. Rinse the latter after use and put away to dry.

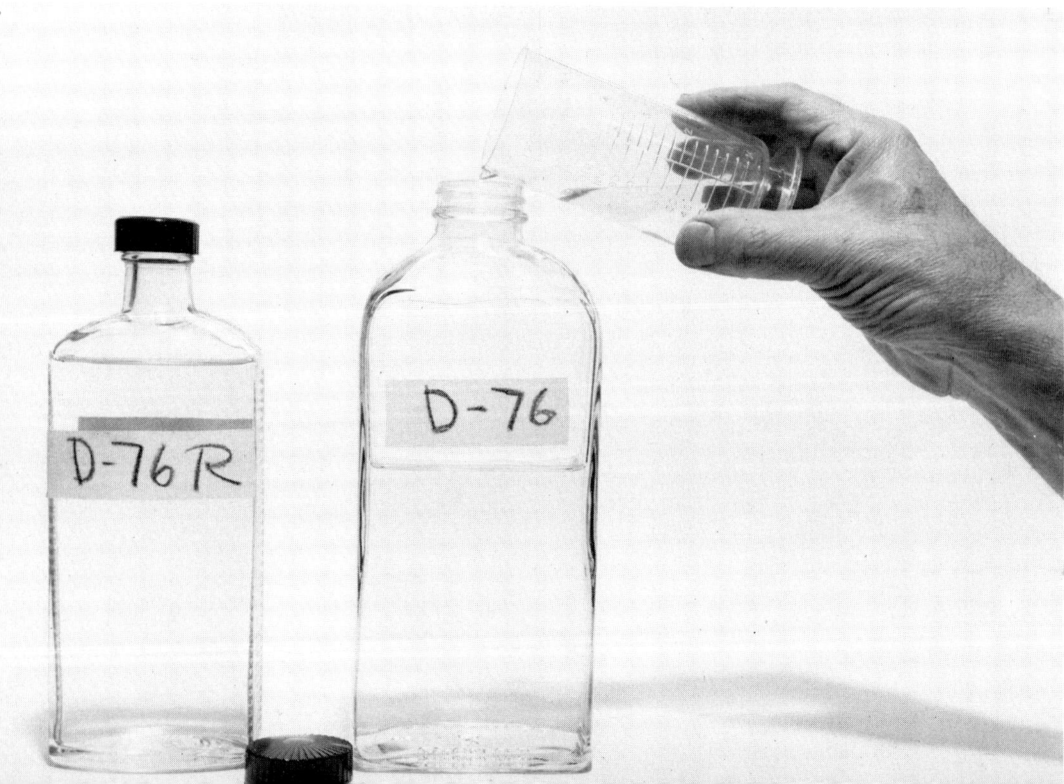

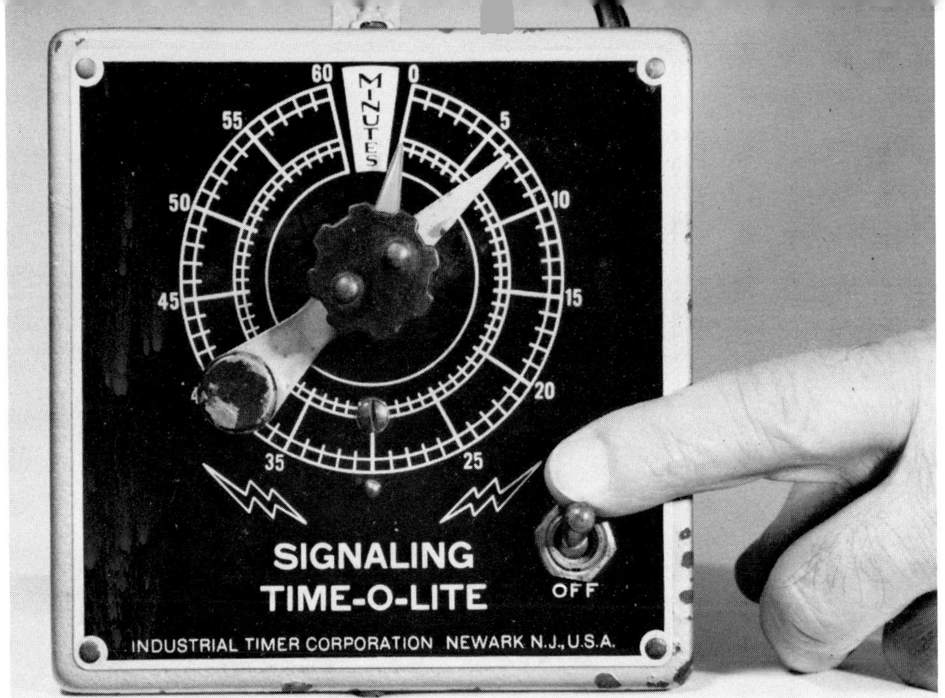

Fig. 2-29. BUZZ! The loud noise from the timer can't be ignored. Turn it off.

Fig. 2-30. Remove the tank's cap and pour the developer back into its bottle. This takes about half a minute, and meanwhile the film is wet and still developing, but you allowed for this when you set the timer.

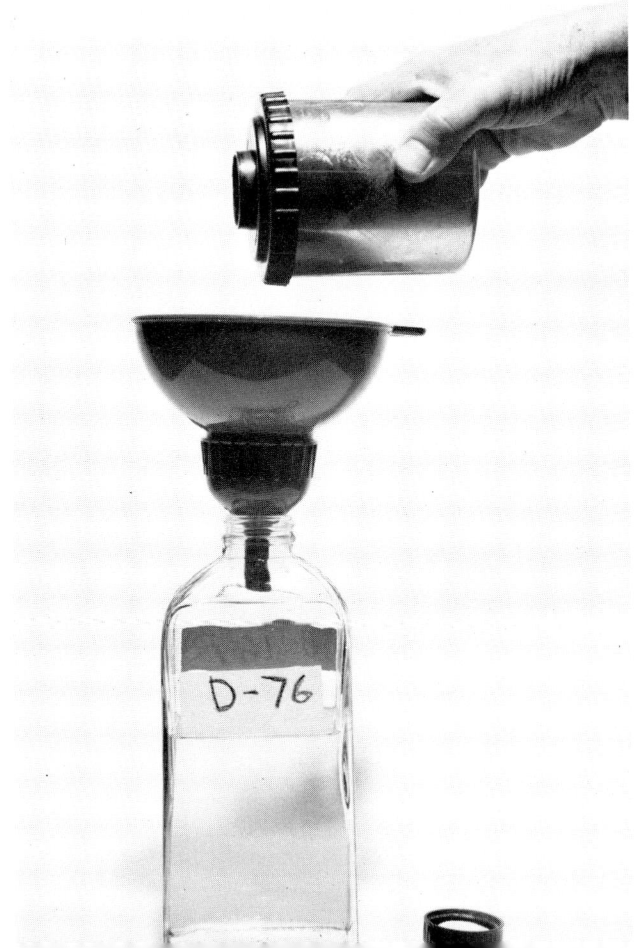

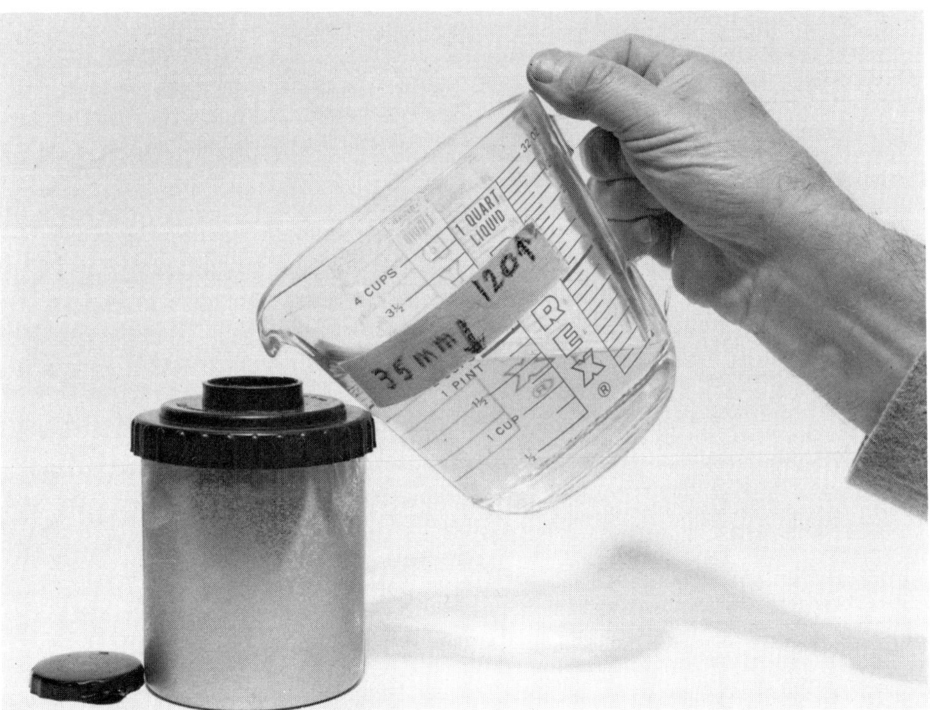

Fig. 2-31. With the developer drained, pour the rinse water into the tank. Put the cap back on and roll the tank for about a minute to let the water absorb some of the remaining developer.

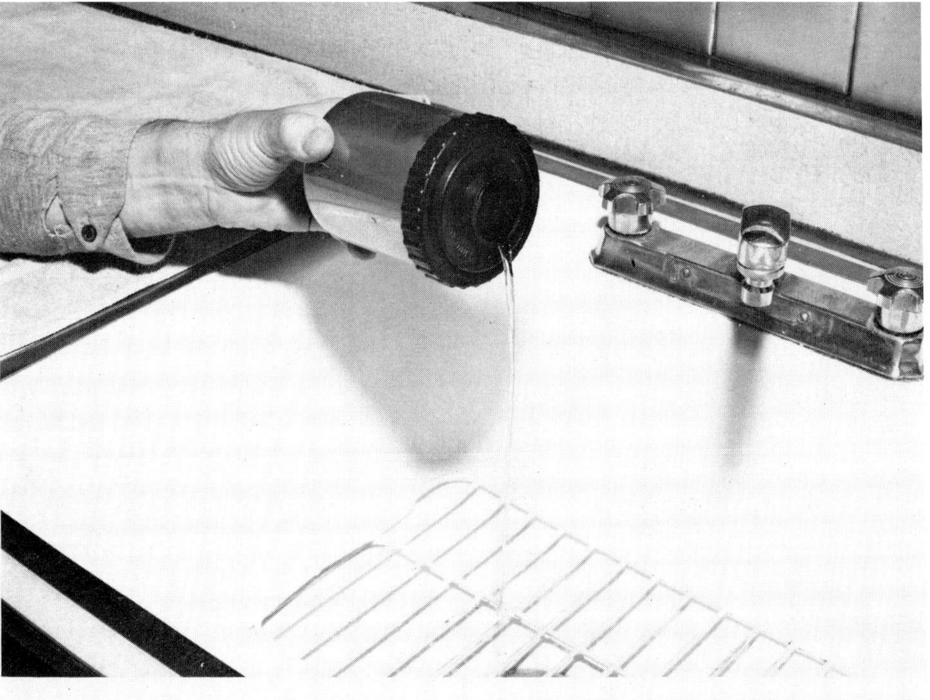

Fig. 2-32. Remove the cap and pour the water into the sink. Drain the tank out quite thoroughly.

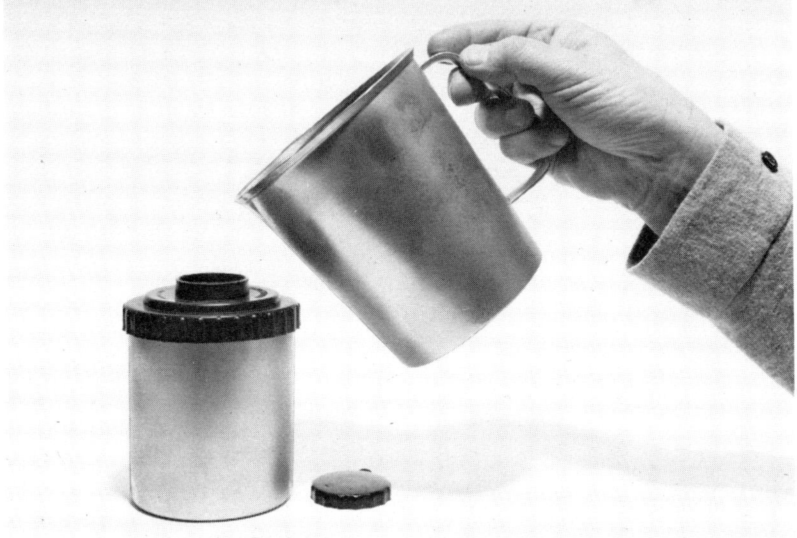

Figs. 2-33a and b. Now pour in the previously filtered fixer. Put the small cap on and roll the tank or use the stirrer to distribute the fixer.

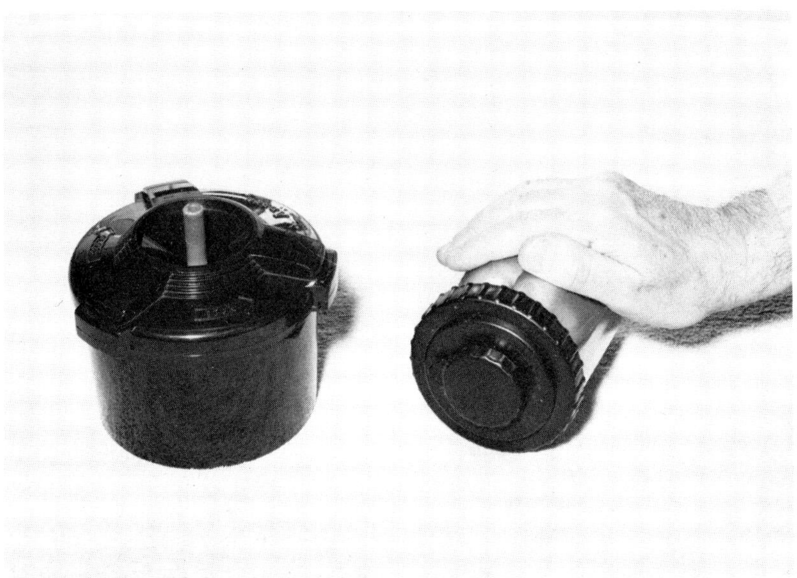

Fig. 2-34. Reset the timer for the fixing stage. Depending on the type of film, this can run from as little as 2 to 15 minutes. It is not critical; a minute or two more is better than one or two less. Agitate tank a bit.

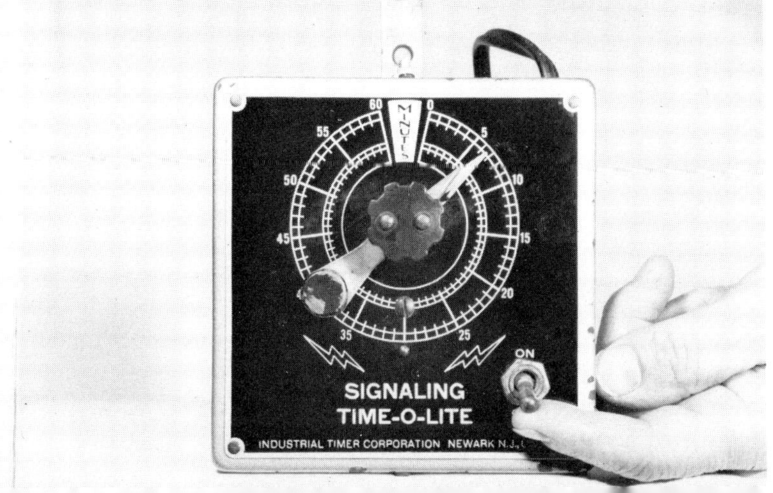

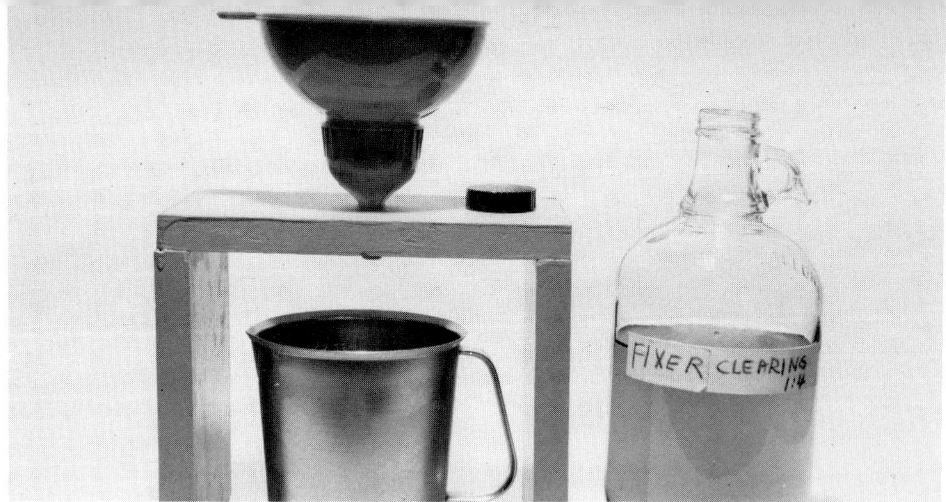

Fig. 2-35. With fixing underway, filter some fixer neutralizer (hypo clearing bath) into the graduate and adjust its temperature as with the developer and fixer.

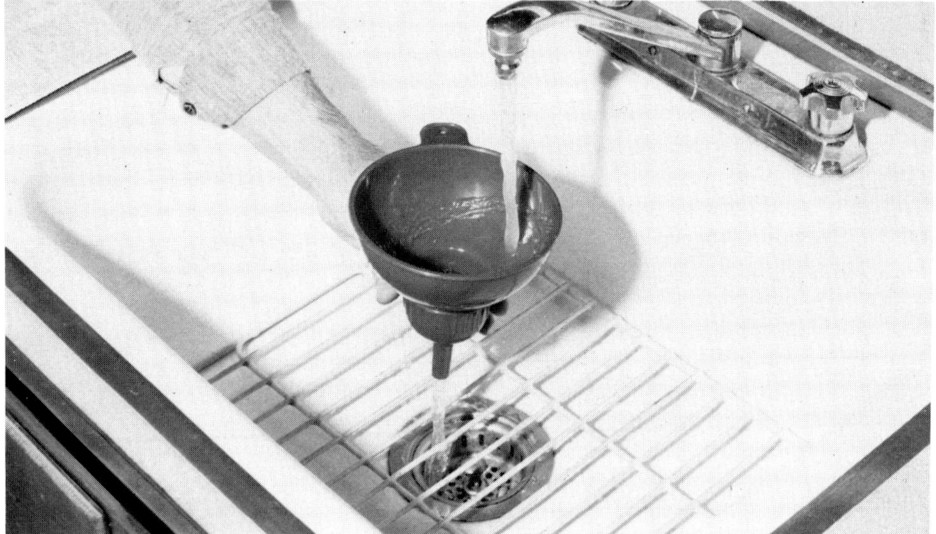

Fig. 2-36. Rinse the funnel. This frequent washing eliminates any danger of cross-contamination of solutions.

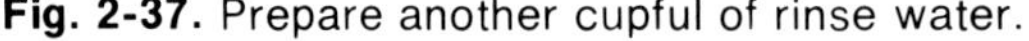

Fig. 2-37. Prepare another cupful of rinse water.

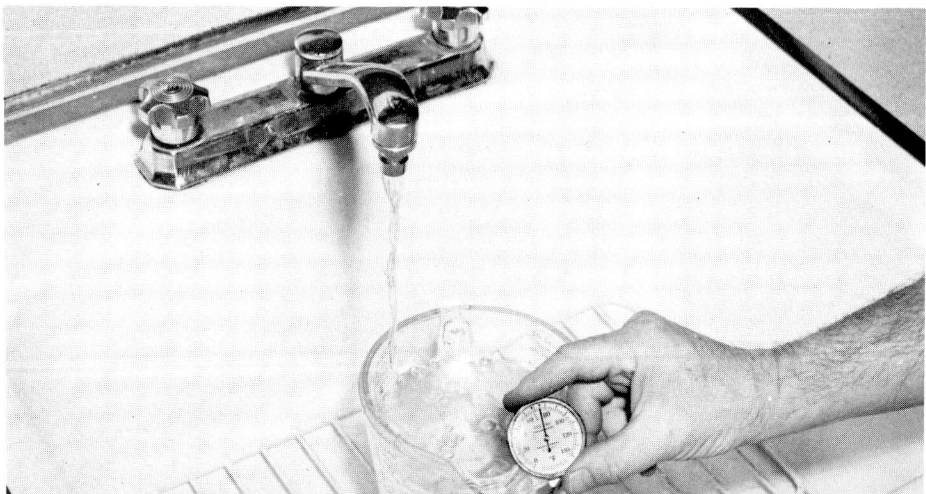

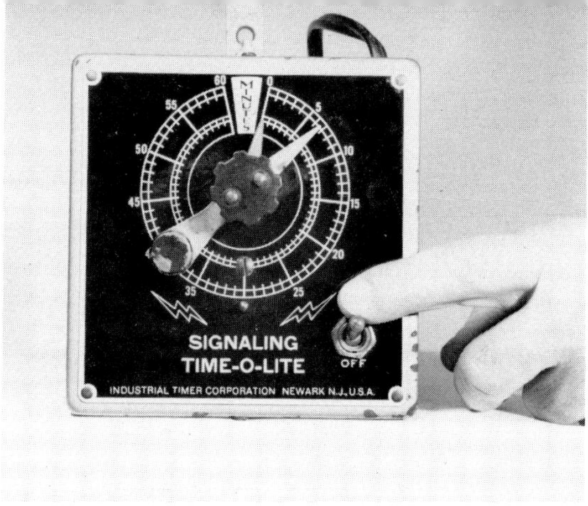

Fig. 2-38. The timer signals the end of the fixing cycle. Shut it off.

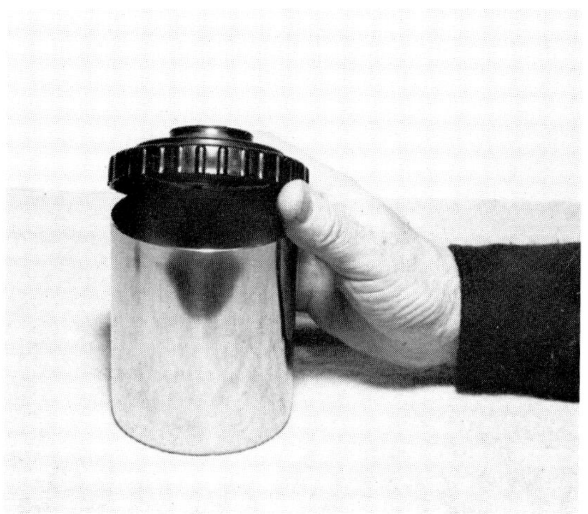

Fig. 2-39. Remove the cover of the tank. This is now safe, as the film has been developed and fixed and is no longer sensitive to light.

Fig. 2-40. Return the fixer to its bottle. Keep a thumb on the reel to prevent it from dropping into the funnel and possibly upsetting the bottle.

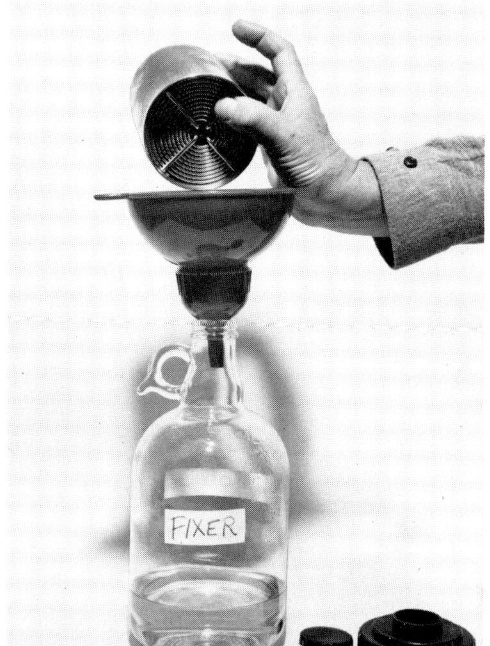

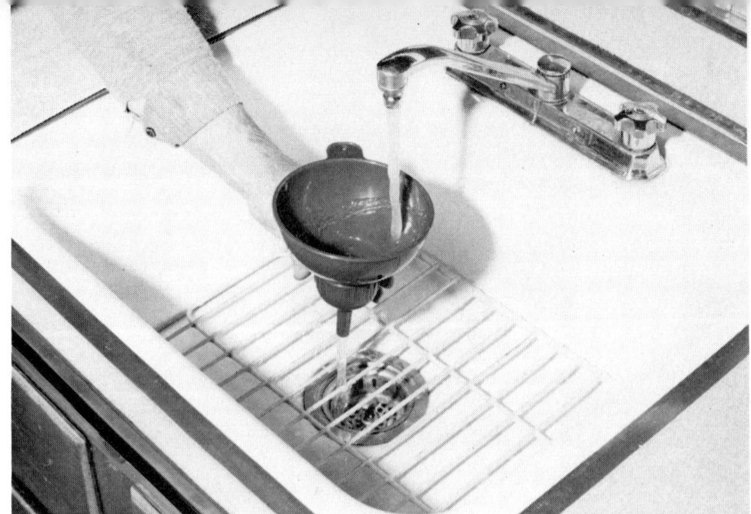

Fig. 2-41. Wash again!

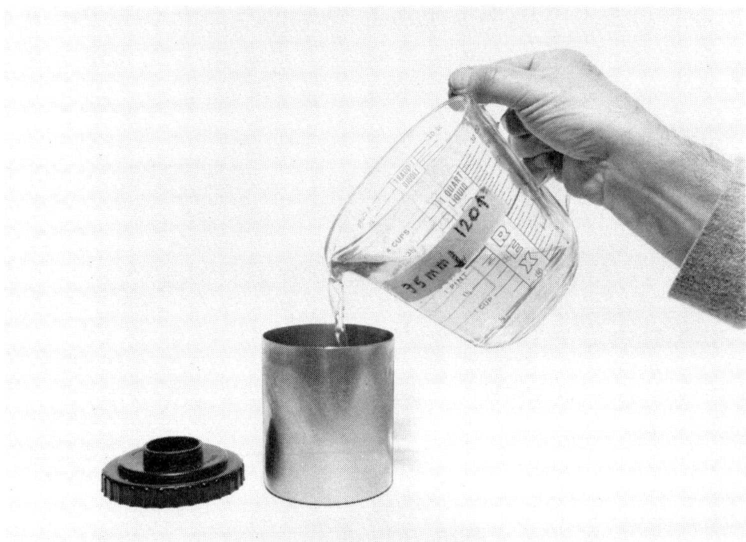

Fig. 2-42. Pour in the rinse water, turn the reel inside a few times, and then pour out the water.

Fig. 2-43. Pour in the fixer neutralizer, agitate the tank a little, and let it stand for about a minute.

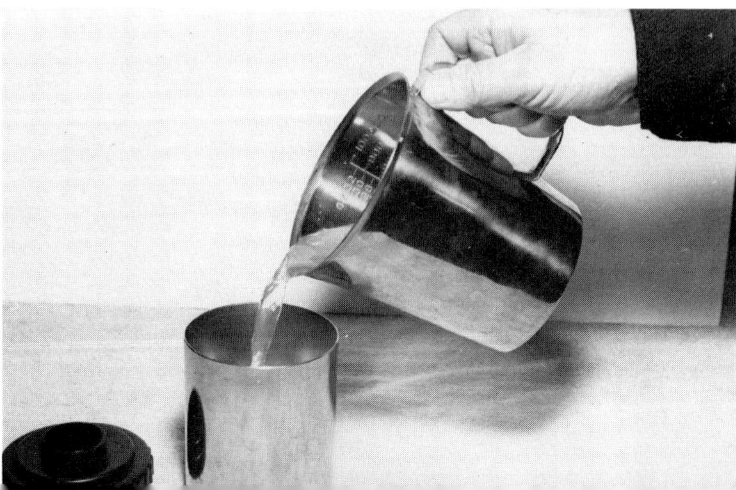

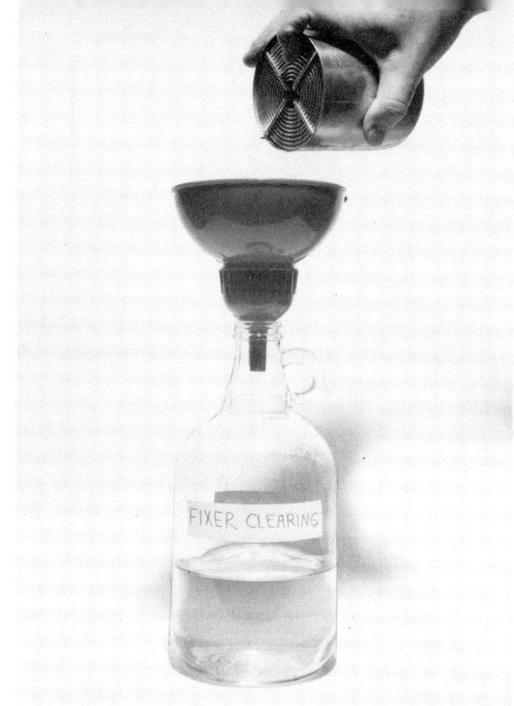

Fig. 2-44. Then return the fixer neutralizer to its bottle.

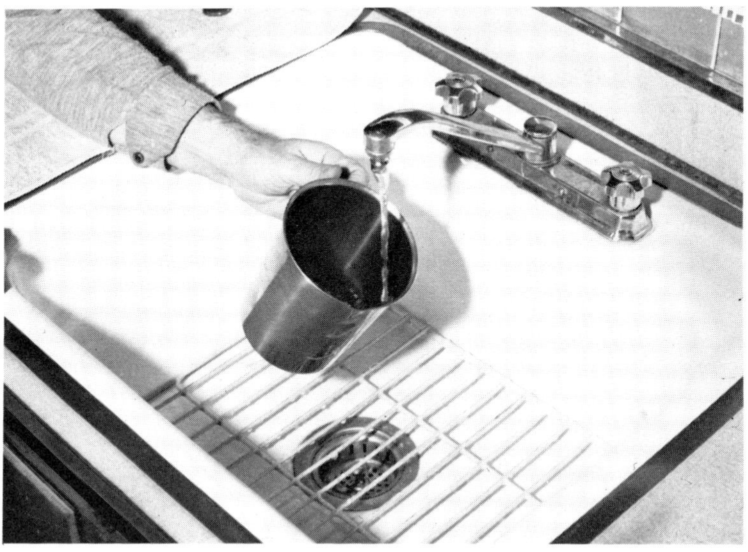

Figs. 2-45a and b. Rinse the graduate and the funnel.

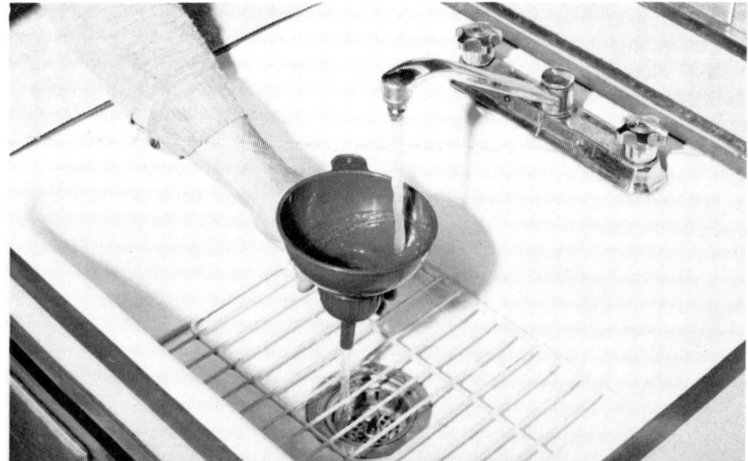

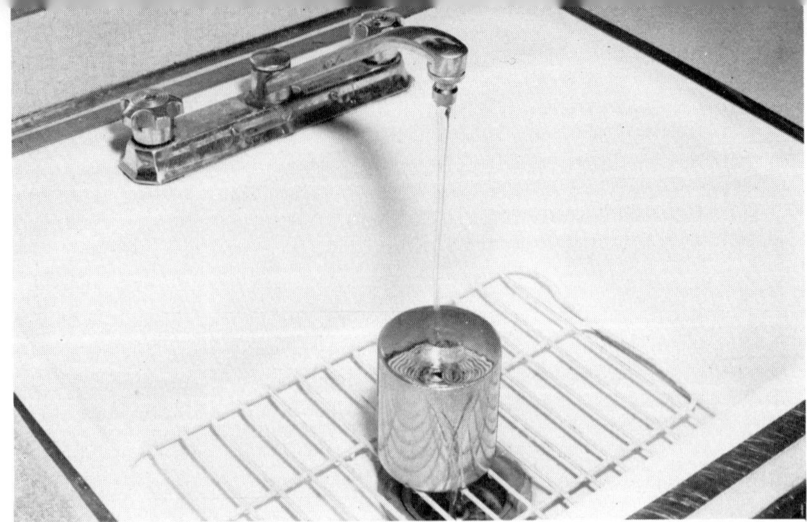

Fig. 2-46. Film that has been treated in fixer clearing solution need be washed for only about five minutes in a strong stream of water.

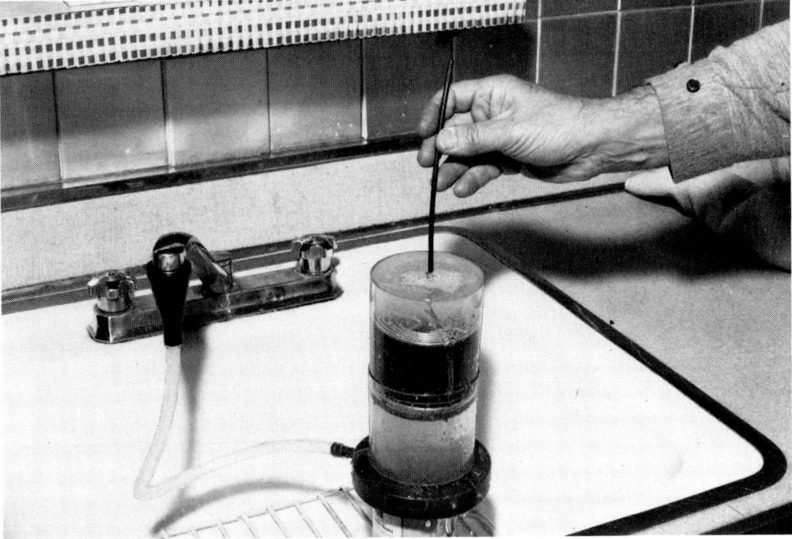

Fig. 2-47. In this Kinderman jet-action film washer, the water enters at the bottom and gurgles out over the top. It is very fast and effective. Two reels can be washed at the same time.

Fig. 2-48. While the film is washing, filter the Photo-Flo into the glass measuring cup.

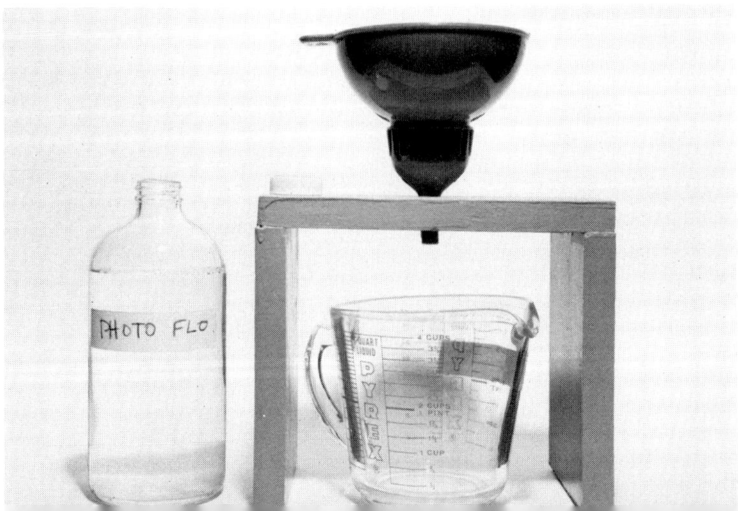

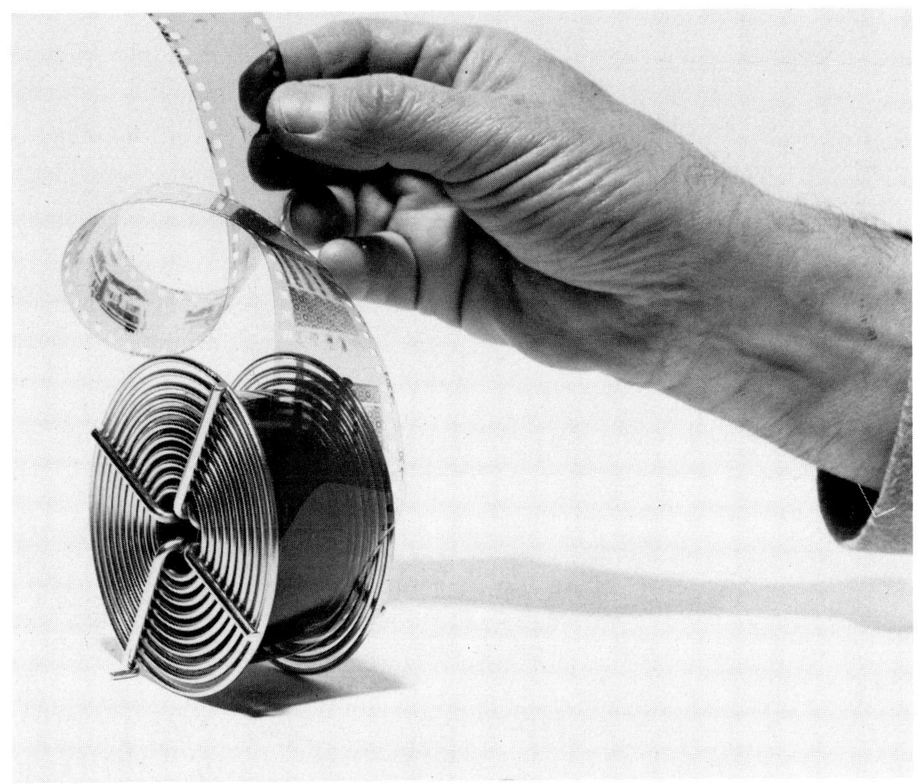

Figs. 2-49a and b. With the washing completed, carefully unfurl the film from its reel, and dunk it for about a minute in the Photo-Flo.

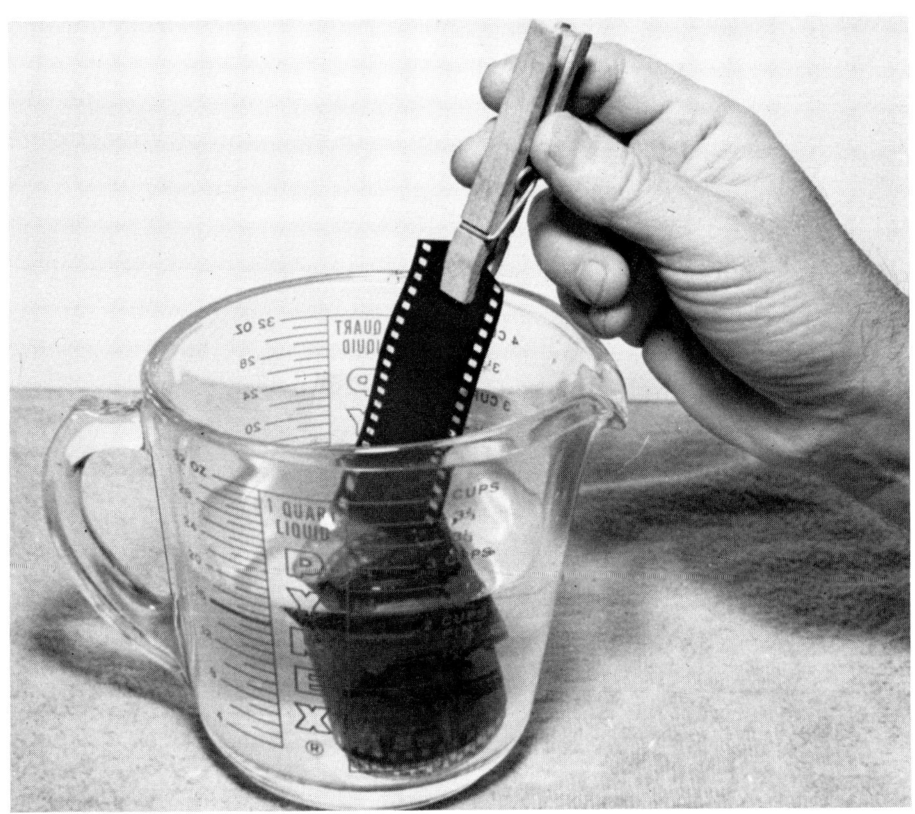

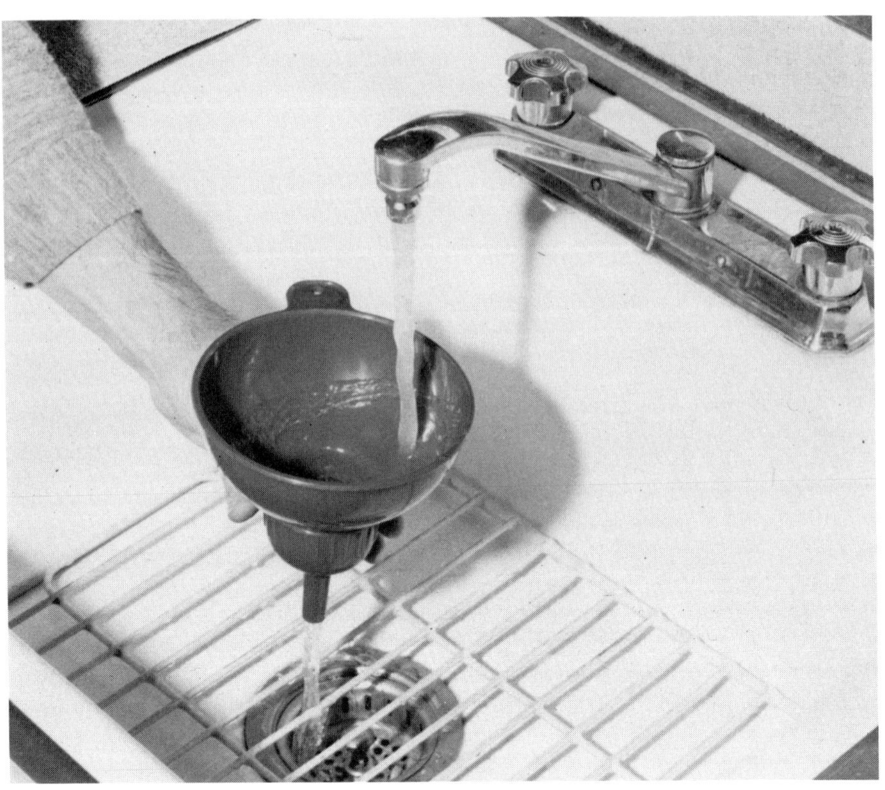

Figs. 2-50a and b. While the film is in the Photo-Flo, rinse the funnel and the glass cup.

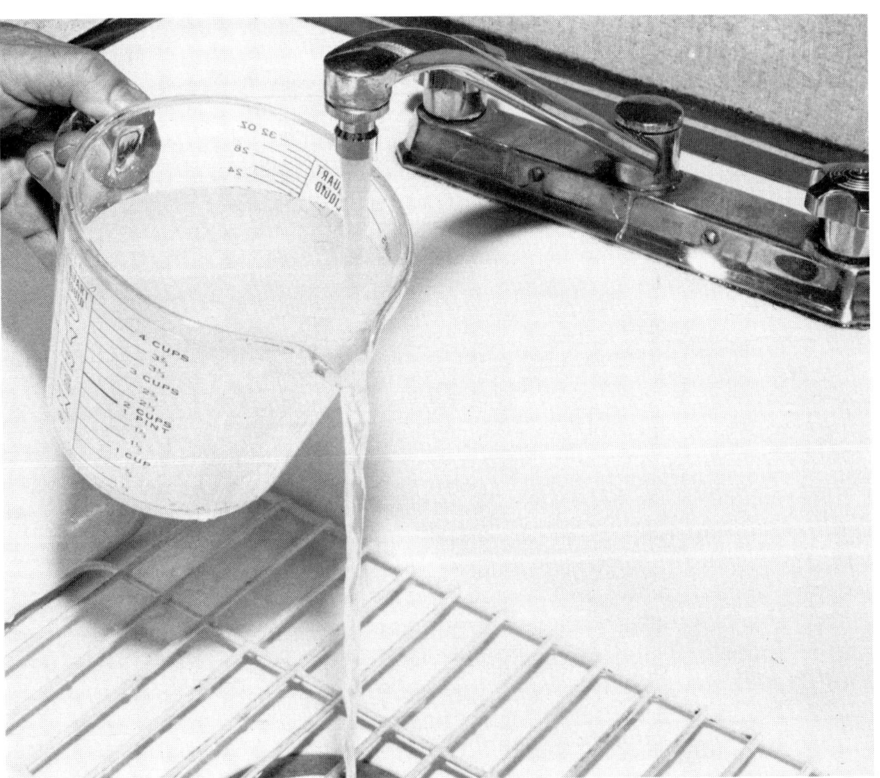

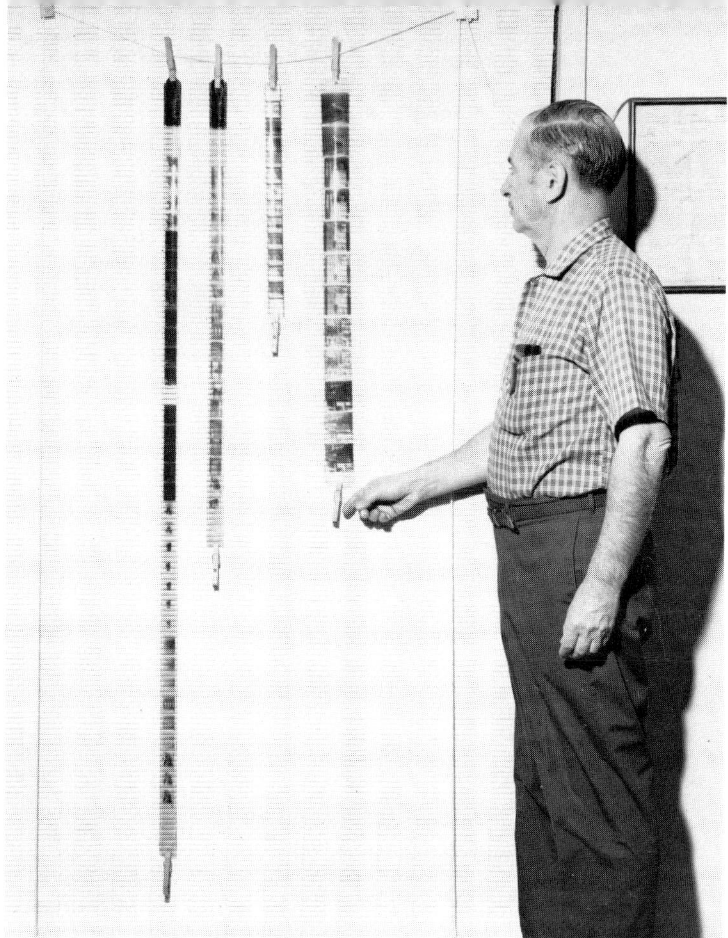

Fig. 2-51. Hang the film up to dry in any clean spot. If treated in Photo-Flo it *does not* have to be swabbed down with a sponge; it will dry quickly without streaks or other marks. This picture shows the four most common black-and-white film sizes: (left to right) 35mm, 36 exposures; 35mm, 20 exposures; 126 Instamatic; 120 roll.

Fig. 2-52. To keep negatives clean before printing them, cut them into strips about nine inches long and put them in a No. 10 envelope.

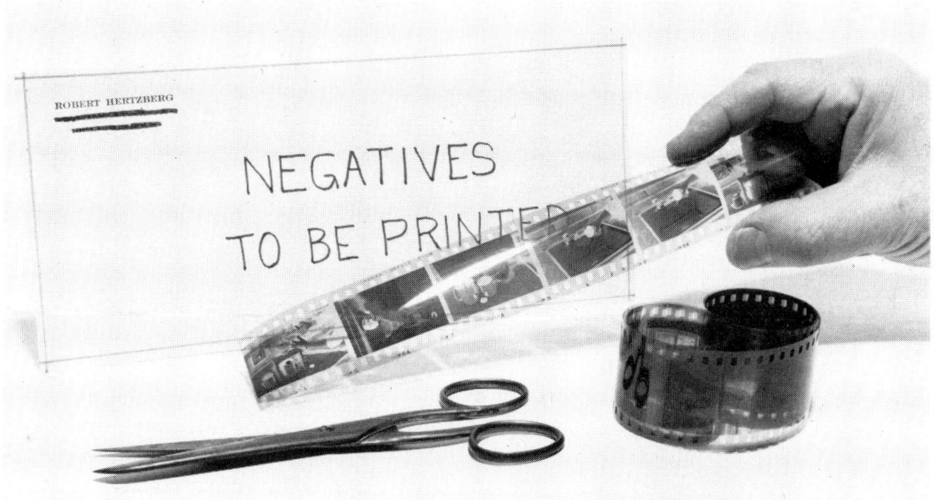

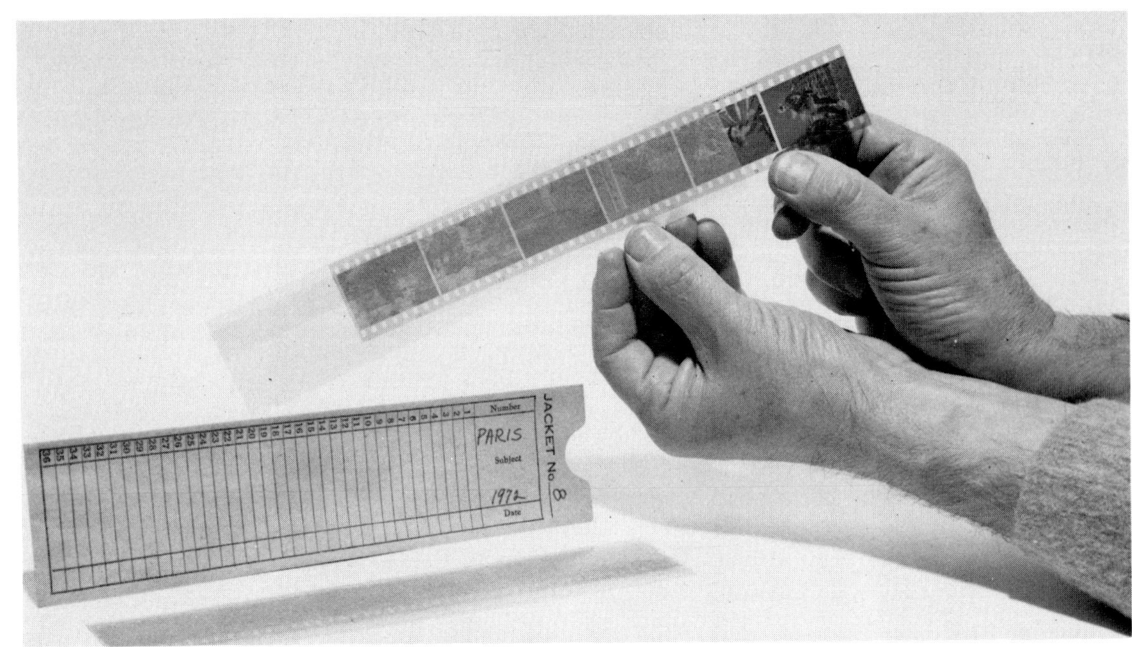

Fig. 2-53. You can also put them in glassine sleeves that fit inside manila file jackets.

Fig. 2-54. Full-size reproductions of three standard sizes of films: (top to bottom) 126 Instamatic; 35mm; 120 roll.

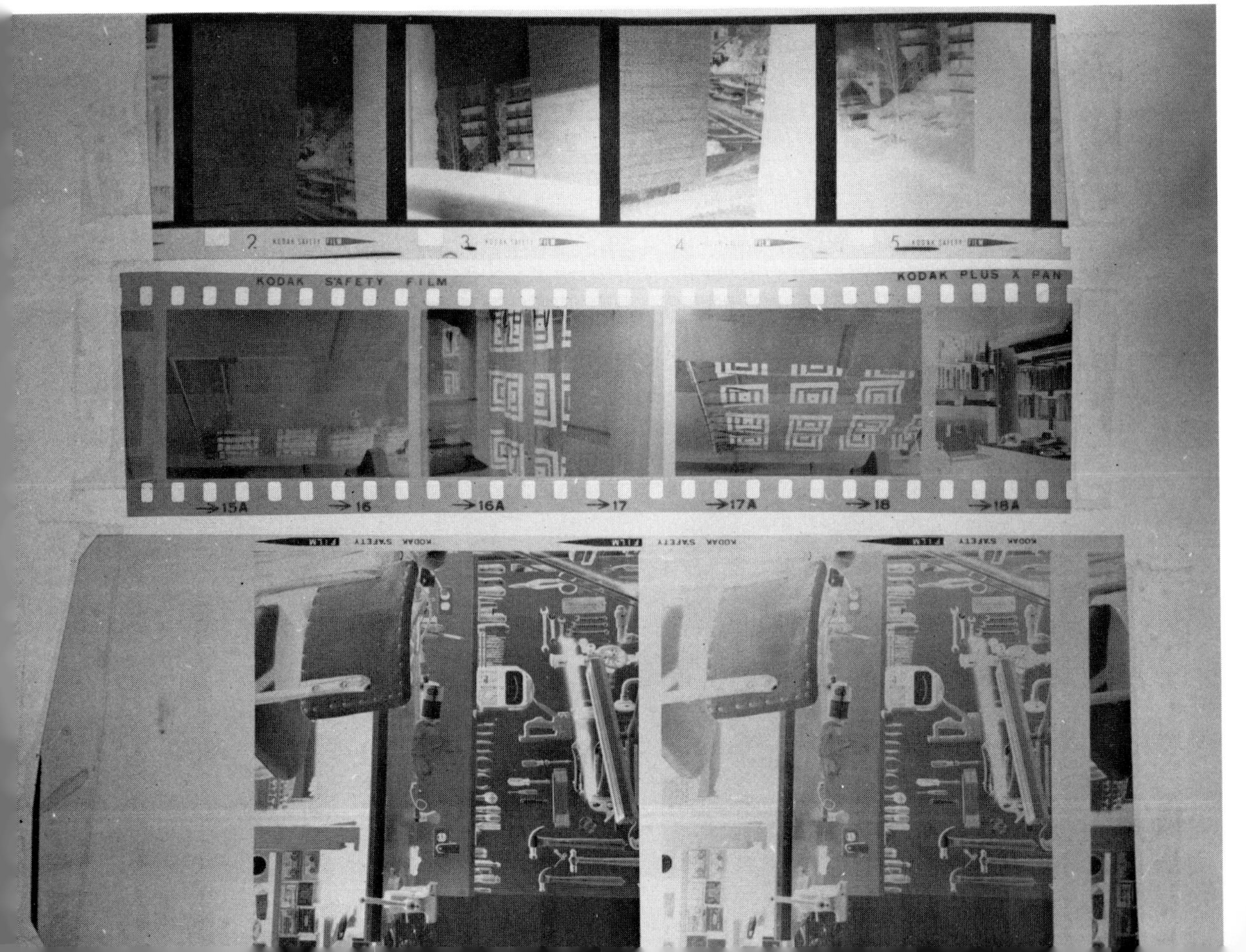

3

CONTACT PRINTING

It means making same-size pictures from negatives.

As the name of the process implies, contact prints are made by direct positioning of sensitized paper against the negative. A strong white light is directed through the exposed film, thus exposing the paper. The routine of developing, fixing, washing, drying, and so on is then carried out precisely as described in the section on enlarging (Chapter 4).

Contact printing is usually done on a simple plastic or metal box with a glass top, on which the negative/paper sandwich is placed. This is secured by a hinged platen, which, when fully flattened down, turns on an electric bulb inside the box, which shines up through the negative exposing the paper.

Contact paper develops more rapidly than enlarging paper; 40–60 seconds is about normal time in the developer.

A contact printer is of some value to the owner of a camera using 120 film, for the occasional production of 6 × 6cm (2¼″ × 2¼″) or slightly larger prints. For the owner of a 35mm camera a different printing device called a "film proofer" is more useful. This looks like a hinged picture frame. The film is cut into strips and laid out edge-to-edge, dull side up, on the glass. A single piece of contact paper is put over the film, the frame closed against the sandwich, turned glass-side up, and an exposure is made with light from an electric bulb above.

The single contact sheet or individual 2¼″ × 2¼″ prints provide a quick and simple way to see everything you've shot on a roll of film. You can then study the contact prints to determine which frames are worth enlarging.

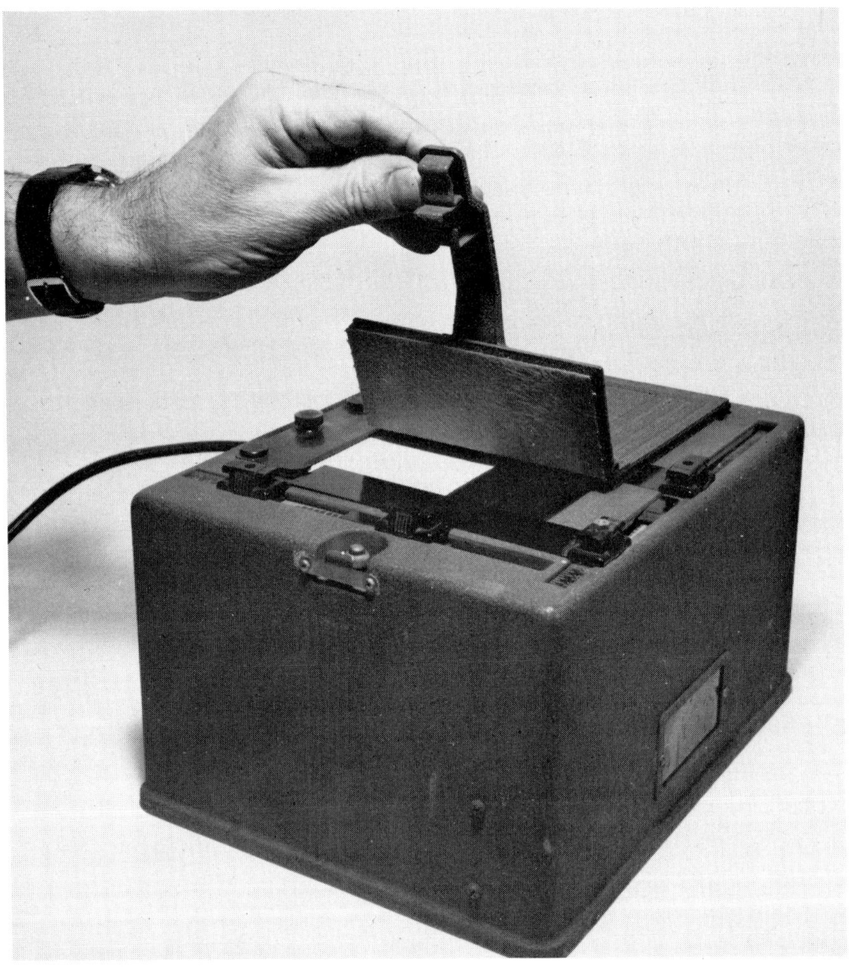

Fig. 3-1. Representative contact printing box (Kodak) of metal construction. The white area shows a piece of contact paper partially held by the hinged platen. When the handle is lowered it actuates a light switch.

60

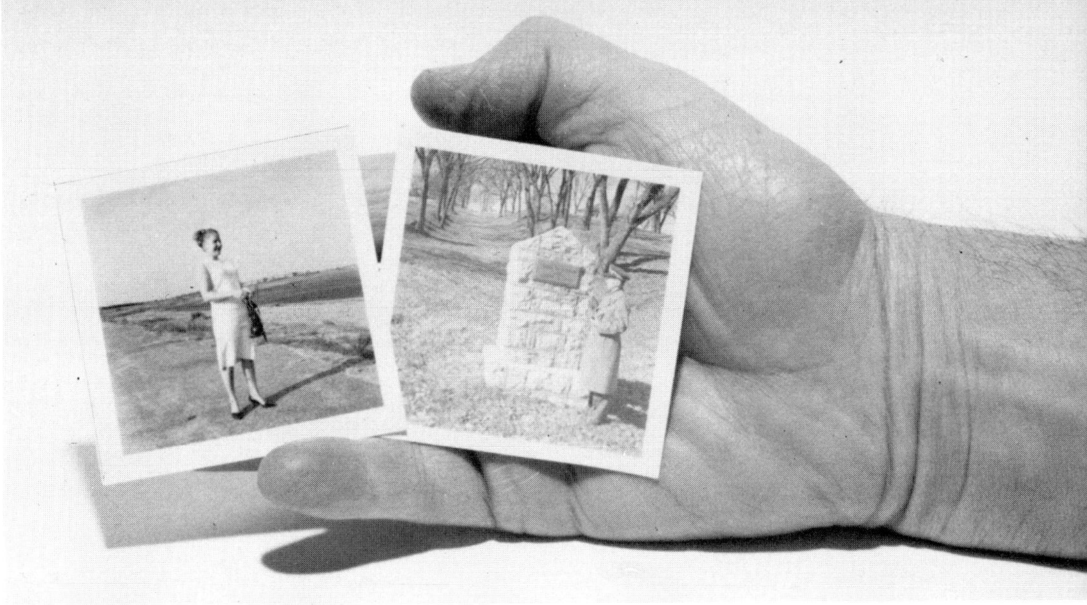

Fig. 3-2. Contact prints from 6 × 6 cm (2 1/4'' × 2 1/4'') negatives are just big enough for comfortable viewing.

Fig. 3-3. Entire roll of 35mm film can be contact-printed on single sheet of paper with this typical film proofer (Spiratone). Film strips, emulsion side up, are held to glass plate by clips along front edge.

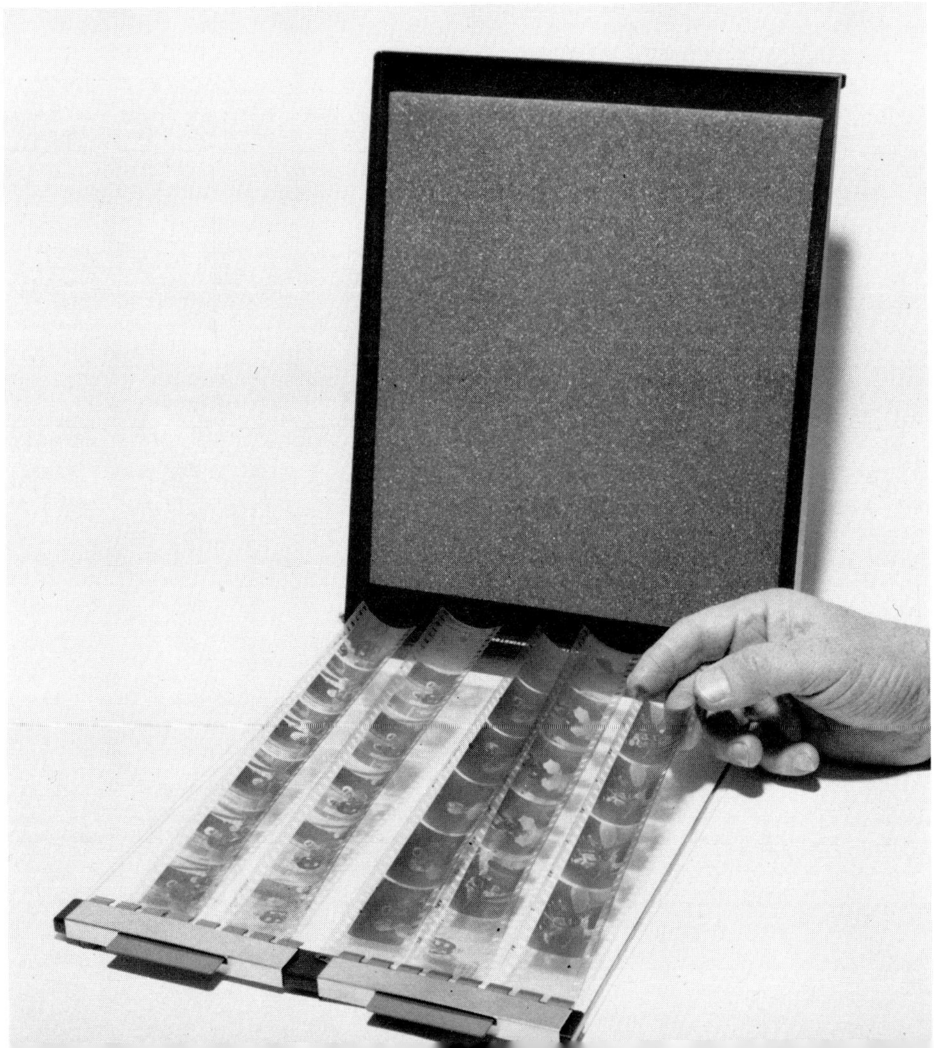

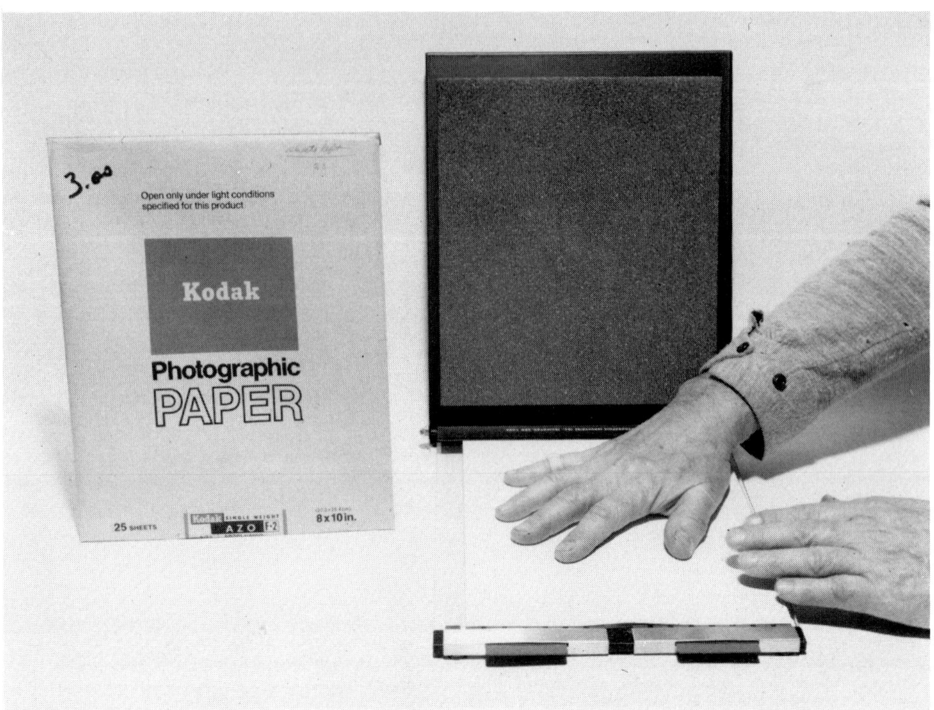

Fig. 3-4. Shiny side down, sheet of contact paper is placed over negative strips: in the dark, of course! Sponge-rubber coated back section of frame will flatten out the assembly.

Fig. 3-5. With the proofer closed, the negatives and the paper are in smooth contact and ready for exposure to bright light. Film of 120 size can be proofed in the same manner.

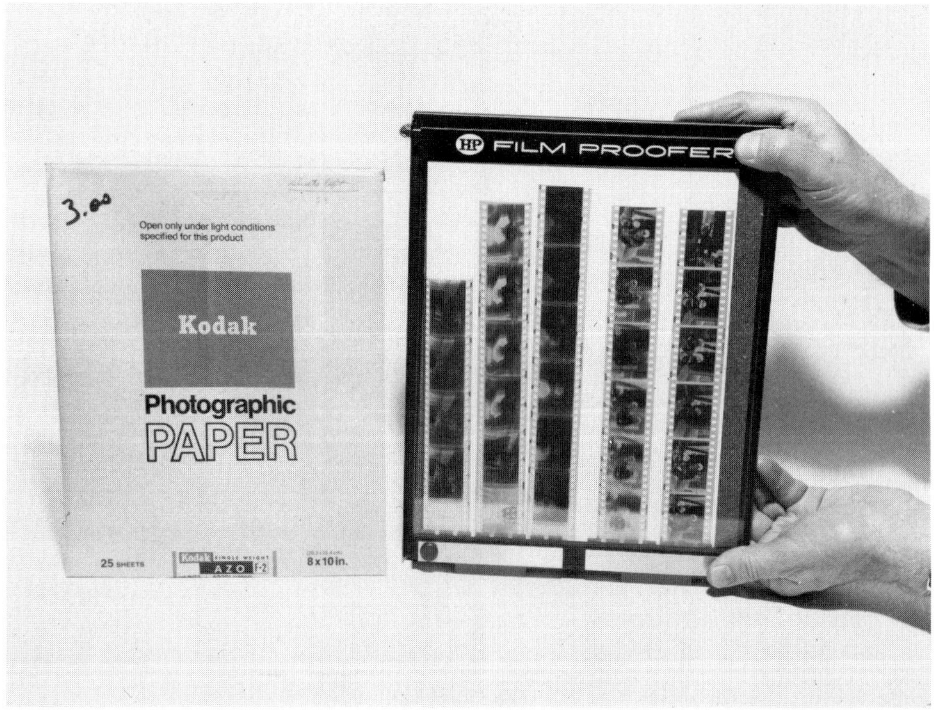

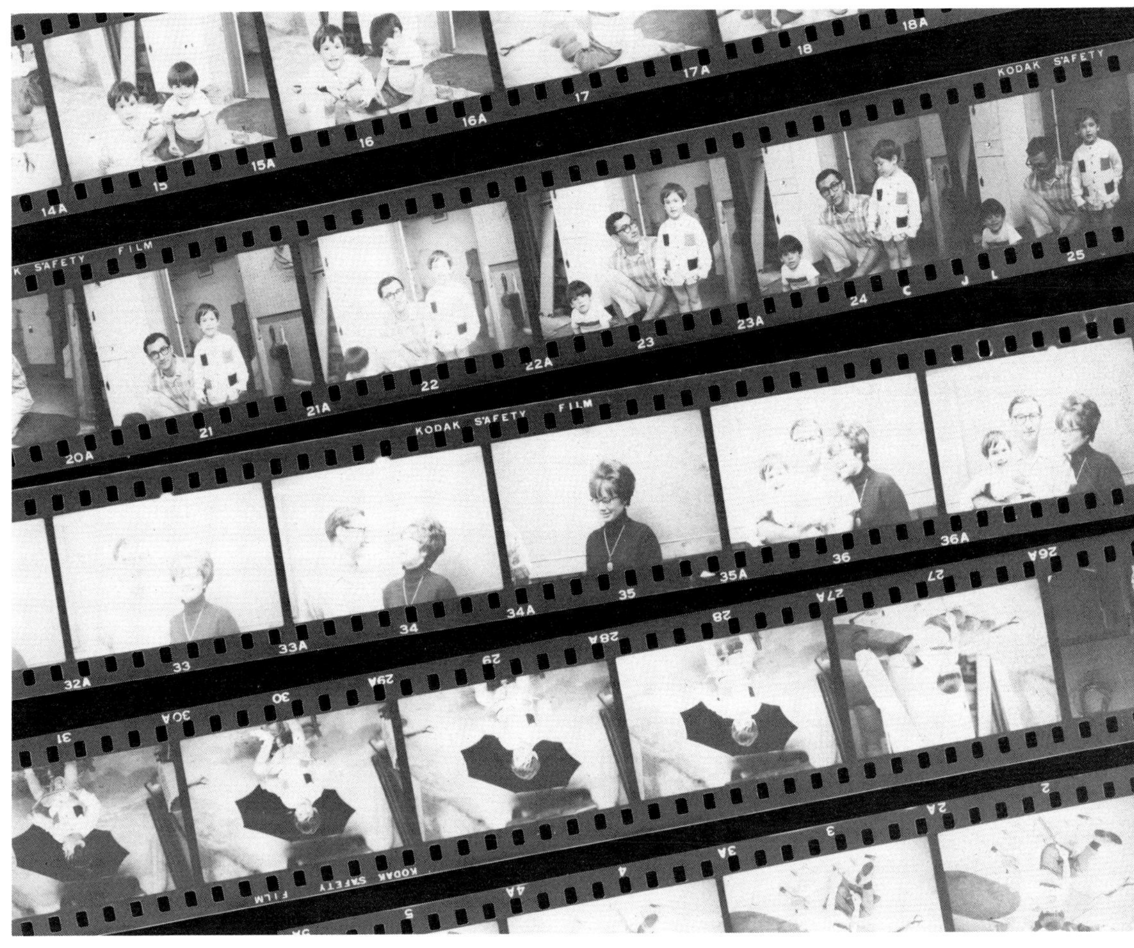

Fig. 3-6. Because frame numbers show clearly on the edges of the film, it is easy to identify negatives selected for enlargement.

4

ENLARGING

How to make big pictures from little films. The equipment you need, and how to use it.

THE ENLARGER IS NO. 1

The enlarger is the most important piece of equipment in a darkroom. It is a sort of camera in reverse, and it should be equal in quality and precision to the camera whose negatives you will use in it. Consider the following features when you start shopping for one in supply stores:

Size: This refers to the largest negative the machine can accommodate. If you expect to use 35mm film for all of your picture taking, as many professionals do, you won't have to look far. The market offers a wide choice of 35mm models, and they are compact and readily storable.

If you own a 6 × 6cm (2¼″ × 2¼″) camera in addition to a 35mm, or expect to enjoy this excellent combination in the near future, you should look for a 6 × 6cm enlarger. This is easily the most popular of all sizes because it is only slightly larger than a 35mm model, takes both film sizes, and is still small enough for storage in an apartment.

During the early 1970's the 6 × 7cm negative (2¼″ × 2¾″) was adopted for certain new cameras because this format blows up to 8″ × 10″ without cropping. That extra centimeter caused some initial unhappiness among users because the negative could be handled only in a 4″ × 5″ enlarger, the next standard size beyond 6 × 6cm. If the extra centimeter of negative length was snipped off to make the film fit in a 6 × 6cm enlarger, shooting in the 6 × 7 cm. format lost its one and only advantage. Manufacturers quickly revamped some of their machines to take the new size and a bit more: 6 × 9cm (2¼″ × 3¼″).

Construction: If an enlarger trembles when a refrigerator in the same room turns on or a truck passes the house, a picture being exposed at that time will be fuzzy. Therefore, look for a sturdy center column or truss or girder construction for your enlarger.

Lenses: Lenses for enlargers are made in simple barrel mounts, and do not need shutters because the exposure through them is controlled electrically by a timer in the lamp circuit. Lenses are usually sold as accessories rather than as original fittings; the buyer determines for himself what quality he can afford and what focal length he needs. Enlarger manufacturers make the choice easy by offering a wide variety of lenses already mounted on lens boards that can be attached to the machines in a few seconds.

For 35mm film, a 50mm enlarging lens, usually with a speed of $f/4$ or $f/4.5$, is more or less standard. For 6 × 6cm film the longer focal length of 75mm is required; for 6 × 9cm film, 100mm. You can use 35mm film with either of the longer lenses, but with a smaller degree of enlargement than is possible with the 50mm.

Super-Enlargement Capability: The maximum print size with any enlarger in its normal position is determined by the maximum height of the head above the baseboard. If the whole column assembly can be turned around to project over the edge of the table to the floor, or turned sideways to project on a wall, much bigger enlargements become practical. Then the only limitation is the size of available trays for processing the prints. If the head assembly is turned for floor projection, the baseboard must of course be clamped or weighted down to balance the unit.

The main advantage of super-enlargement capability is that very small but important areas of a negative can be enlarged to fill 8″ × 10″ or 11″ × 14″ paper, which can be processed without difficulty.

Means of Focusing: With the manual method, you raise or lower the main head assembly to produce the picture size you want, and then you fine-adjust the lens for focus. With the automatic method you move only the head, and regardless of the latter's position the lens keeps track and stays in sharp focus. Auto-focusing is a desirable but expensive convenience.

Color Capability: Many high-grade black-and-white enlargers can be adapted for color printing. An enlarger with built-in color capability can be used without change for black-and-white. Obviously, then, the second type is the one you should consider if you intend eventually to take up color printing, and if you are in a position to build a fairly elaborate darkroom with proper plumbing, temperature control, and work space. Some typical enlargers from recognized manufacturers are shown on these pages.

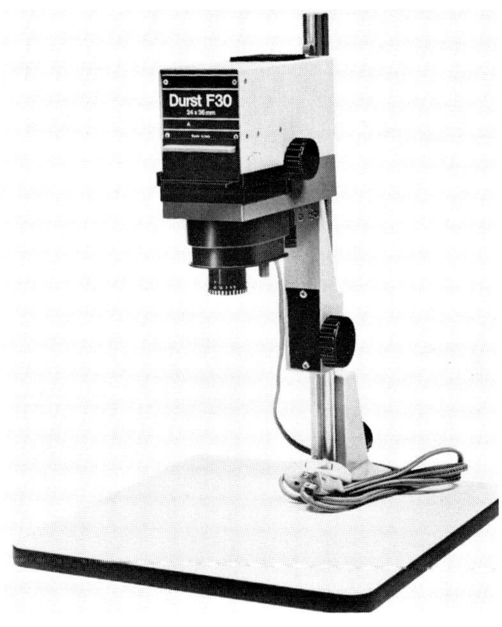

Fig. 4-1a. The Durst F30 is a modest, compact enlarger for 35mm film. In spite of its simplicity it works smoothly and makes excellent enlargements up to 11″ × 14″. For bigger prints the head swivels for projection onto a wall or the floor. The whole assembly disassembles quickly and can be stored on a shelf or in a drawer.

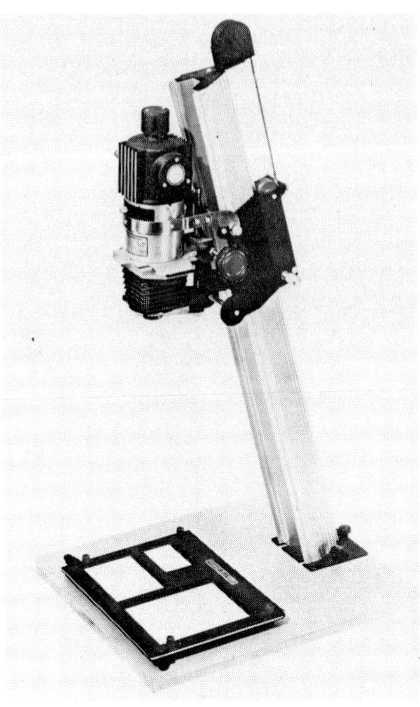

Fig. 4-1b. The Simmon Omega B-22 takes both 35mm and 6 × 6 cm (2 1/4" × 2 1/4") negatives. It features a rock-steady cantilever girder and a head assembly that rides up and down on a counter-balanced track. Lenses are changeable. In the lamp housing is a drawer for color filters, for color printing. The girder reverses for floor projection of giant prints. Loosen some thumb screws at the base of the girder, and the column and the baseboard come apart for storage.

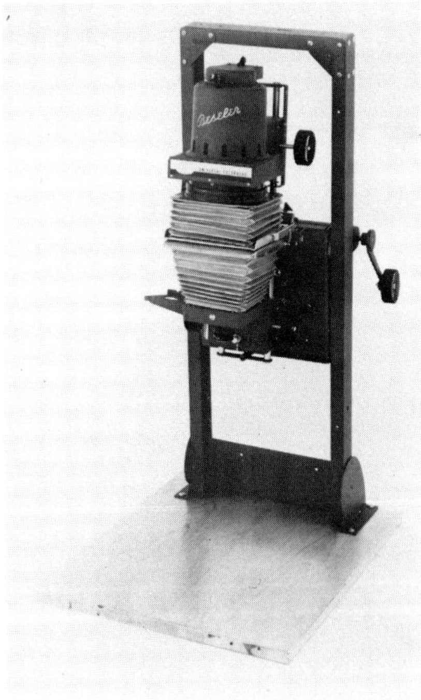

Fig. 4-1c. The Beseler Model 23C handles all negative sizes from sub-miniature to 6 × 9 cm (2 1/4" × 3 1/4"). The lens stage tilts for distortion control. The sturdy double-post construction is an assurance of fuzz-free prints. A concealed compression spring counter-balances the head assembly for easy movement. There is also a lighttight drawer for color printing filters. This is a real piece of professional quality machinery.

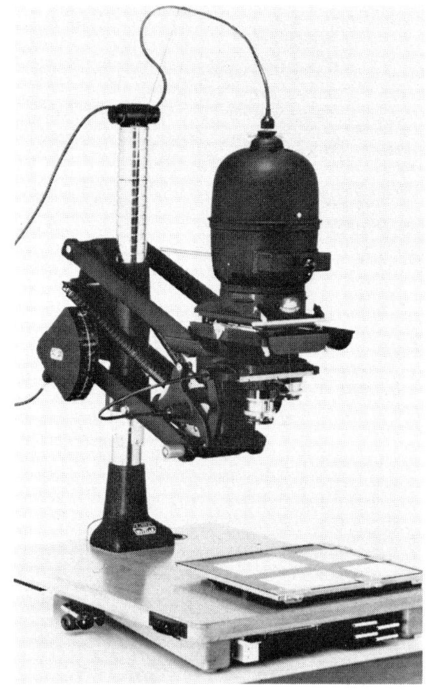

Fig. 4-1d. The Leitz Focomat IIC, made by the Leica people. is a highly sophisticated auto-focusing enlarger. It only looks complicated; actually, its operation is almost effortless because of the auto-focus feature and also because of the balanced parallelogram support of the lamp head. It is supplied with two lenses, of 60mm and 100mm focal length, to cover negatives up to 6 × 9 cm (2 1/4" × 3 1/4"). They are mounted on a sliding changer, and can be flicked back and forth in an instant; the focusing system adjusts itself to them automatically.

BUYING USED EQUIPMENT

Used enlargers are generally safe buys because you can check their controls and condition right in the store. Lenses are not usually included, but with the money you save over the price of a new machine you can afford to splurge on a couple of high-grade optics.

ENLARGING PAPERS

Chemically, photographic paper is closely related to film in that it is coated with a light-sensitive emulsion. A latent image forms on it under exposure in an enlarger, and becomes visible immediately upon development. The developed print then goes through fixing, washing, drying, and other stages, as with film.

Paper is available in more than a dozen surface finishes, ranging from plain glossy through fancy tapestry luster, and in sizes from about 4″ × 5″ sheets to large rolls four feet wide. The most popular sizes are 5″ × 7″, 8″ × 10″, 11″ × 14″. For anything larger you need a large darkroom to accommodate the necessary trays.

Sheets of paper are packaged 25 to a double envelope and 100 or 500 to a box. There is a considerable saving in cost with the boxes, but this is tangible only if you use up the contents before the expiration date printed on the label. Beyond this date the condition of the paper becomes suspect because of a tendency of chemical fog to form on the emulsion.

Start with some 25-sheet packages of plain glossy, in all the contrast grades, as this paper is the easiest to dry quickly. You'll undoubtedly experiment with the other types as you build up experience.

In the darkroom, paper can be handled very comfortably under a yellow safelight. At first this illumination looks rather weak, but after a few minutes you'll be able to see everything in the room quite clearly. It is helpful to have two safelights; one over the dry table, and the other over the trays in the wet area.

IS THE DARKROOM DARK ENOUGH?

You are now prepared for actual printing, but before you proceed take a few minutes to check the safety of the darkened room. Place a test strip of any contrast number in the center of your dry work table under a yellow safelight, cover half of it with a black envelope, leave it there for about 30 seconds, and then transfer it to the developer tray. Watch it closely. If there is still no change in the overall whiteness of the strip after about 30 seconds development, it has not been fogged; that is, the room is safe. If the uncovered half darkens unmistakably, while the covered half remains white, the room is not safe.

The fogging indicated by the darkened strip can be caused by white light leaking into the room from the outside, by an overly bright bulb in the safelight, or by a combination of these factors. The safelight bulb should be 15w, no larger. Run another test strip with the safelight off. If this one shows no evidence of exposure, the fault is with the safelight; if it does, the trouble is with outside leakage. Turn off all the lights in the room, sit quietly for a while to become accustomed to the darkness, and look for tell-tale streaks from a window or a door.

FIGURING THE EXPOSURE

Okay ... the enlarger is focused. Before you go any further, consider these questions: What lens opening to use? What timer setting? What paper grade?

With no previous experience to go by, you simply have to make some wild guesses. You could leave the lens wide open at $f/4.5$, but most lenses produce sharper images at smaller than maximum apertures, so compromise for $f/8$. For the timer, pick an easy number like 10, for 10 seconds. With four or five grades of enlarging paper available, pick No. 2 without hesitation as the starter, because it is rated as "normal" for properly exposed and developed negatives.

Exposure on the paper is determined by the combination of lens opening and enlarger "on" time. Just as in exposing film, a large opening and a short time represent the same exposure as a relatively small opening and a long time. For example, $f/8$ at 10 seconds is the equivalent of $f/11$ at 20 seconds, and of $f/5.6$ at 5 seconds. If you find that your initial exposure on a test strip makes it turn black too fast (an indication of overexposure), you have the option of decreasing the exposure by either a smaller aperture or a shorter time. It is good policy to stick to $f/8$ as the basic opening and to experiment first with the timing.

It is entirely possible to encounter a thin negative that overexposes at $f/8$ at the minimum setting of the timer, usually about two seconds if the device is of the clock-motor type. In this case simply close down the lens another stop to $f/11$, or further to $f/16$ or $f/22$, and try again. On the 50mm and 75mm focal-length lenses used for enlarging 35mm and 6 × 6cm films, respectively, the smallest opening is generally $f/16$ or $f/22$, depending on the make.

With most enlarging papers the developing image starts to appear after about 15 seconds and ideally reaches completion at about 90 seconds ... that is, if the exposure was correct. If it flashes almost black in 20 or 25 seconds, it was overexposed and must be discarded. If it seems to be complete at about 60 seconds, you can preserve it by switching it quickly to the short-stop tray. On the other hand, if only a faint image, or none at all, is evident after about 30 seconds, the paper was underexposed. If you try to force the development by keeping the print in the developer for long periods, you will observe that it takes on an overall gray appearance; this is called chemical fogging.

Figs. 4-2a and b. All enlargers have two basic adjustments: one for moving the entire head assembly up and down the supporting column, and one for moving the lens, at the bottom of the black bellows, up and down in relation to the negative, which is inserted above the bellows. With this particular enlarger the head assembly can swing to a horizontal position for projection onto a wall or other vertical surface.

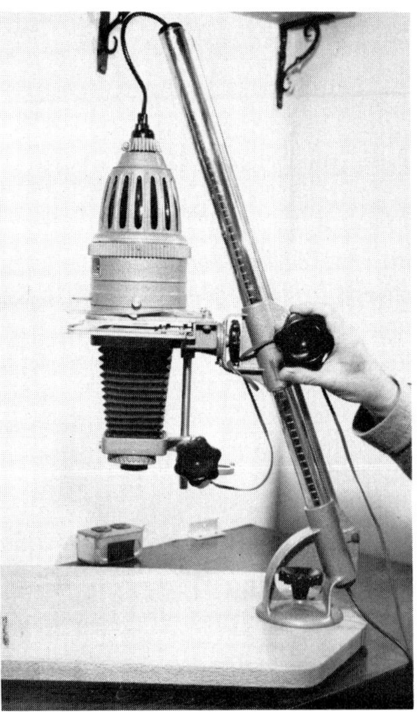 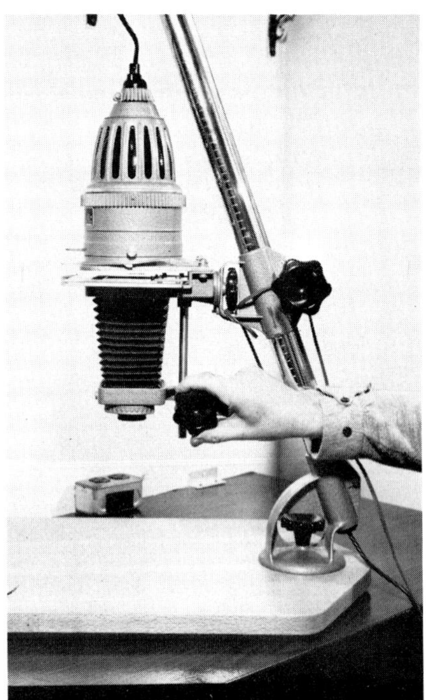

While No. 2 paper is normal for normal negatives, there are many negatives that aren't normal at all. If they are very contrasty, they might print better on No. 1, which is called a "soft" paper. If the negatives are thin and flat, they call for No. 3, No. 4, or No. 5 paper. These are progressively harder "hard" papers, with built-in contrast that helps to compensate for the lack in the negatives.

There are no formulas or rules in enlarging. Try all five grades of paper with a variety of thick and thin negatives, and you may well come up with some startling pictures.

You're set; get going on some prints!

Figs. 4-3a and b. For small enlargements, the enlarger is moved down toward the paper easel. on the baseboard, and the bellows is somewhat extended. For larger prints, the head is raised and the bellows is moved upward.

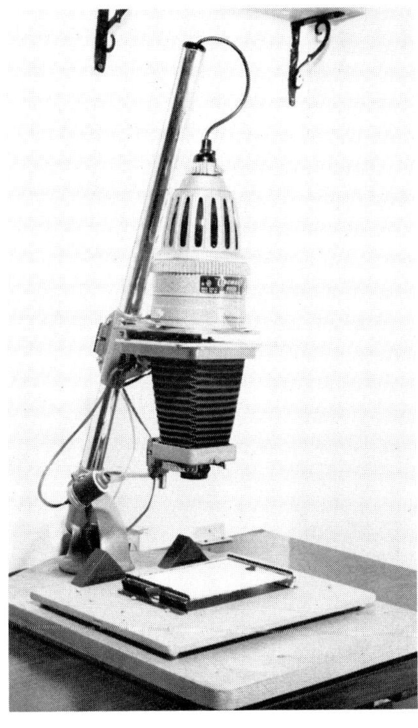
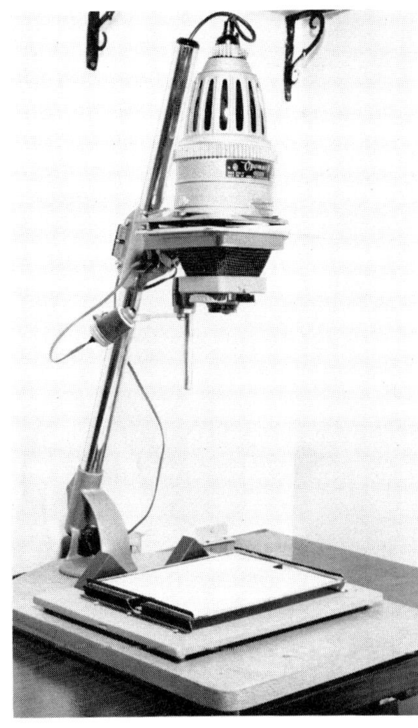

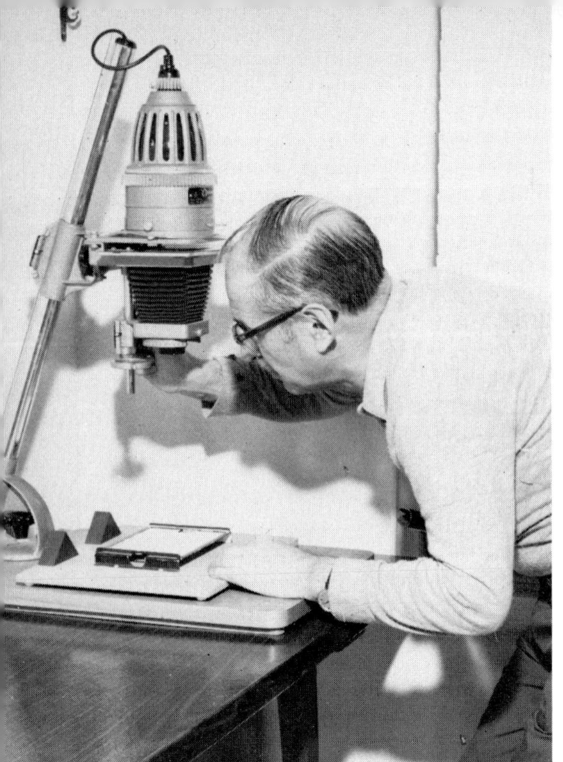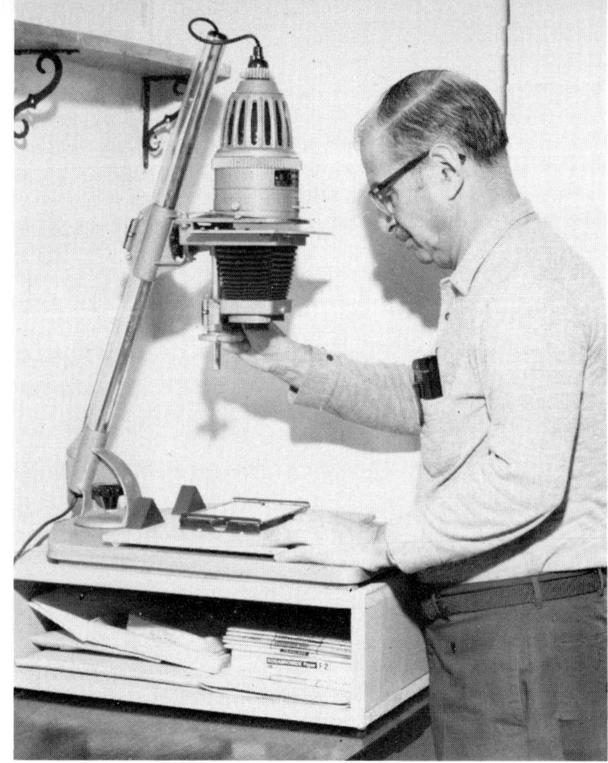

Figs. 4-4a and b. An ordinary kitchen table is too low to allow an adult to work at an enlarger in comfort. Experiment first with piles of books to determine a better height, and then make a simple box-stand as shown. This also provides an ideal storage place for envelopes of paper, easels, and other accessories, and when not in use can be stored, contents and all, in a closet.

Fig. 4-5. Interchangeable lenses, used in some enlargers, should be protected against dust. A wood or metal card file box is excellent for this purpose.

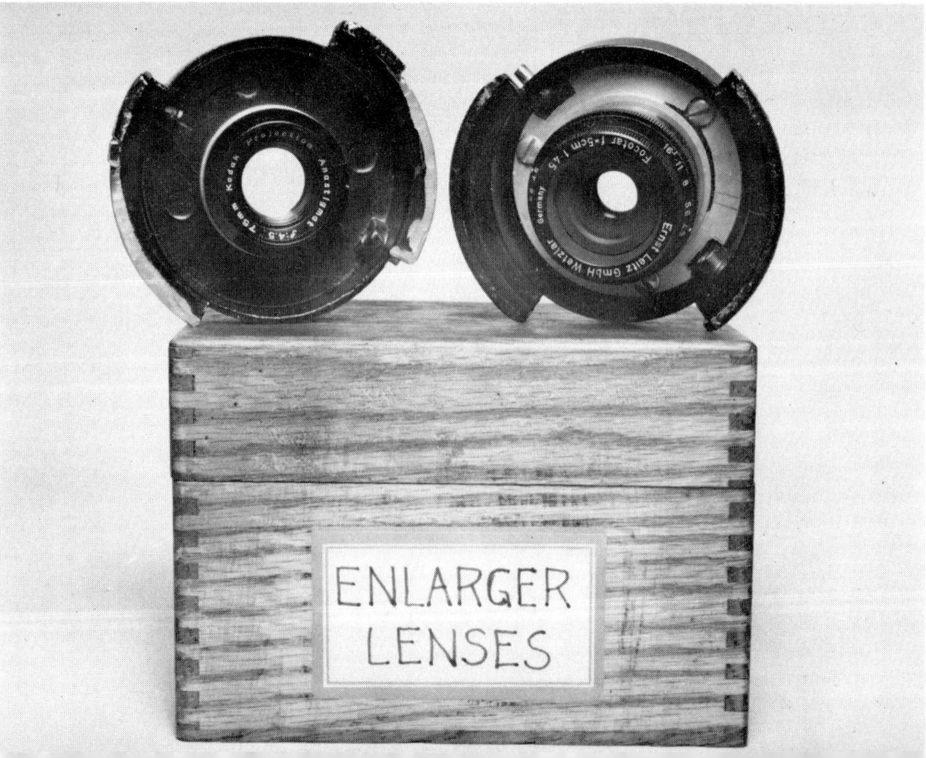

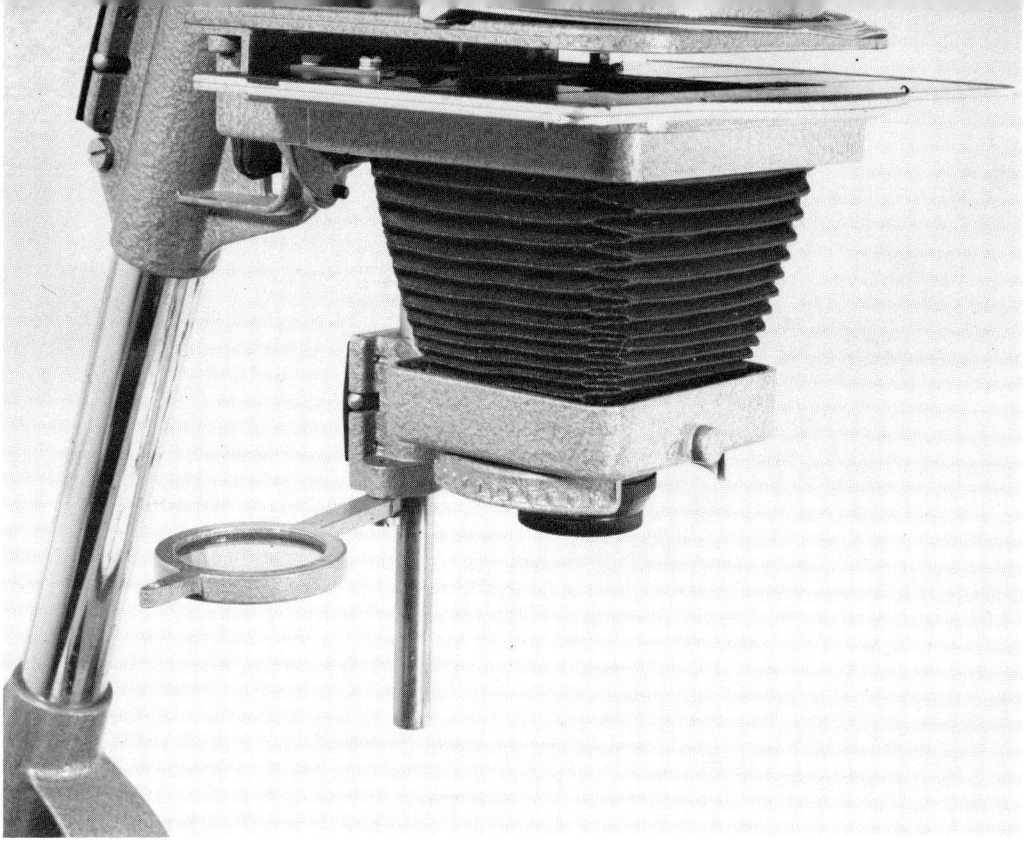

Figs. 4-6a and b. An essential element of an enlarger is a pivoted red filter. During focusing and actual exposure, this is kept away from the lens, to allow white light to pass. When a sheet of paper is positioned in the easel, the filter is swung under the lens. The red light that comes through does not affect the paper.

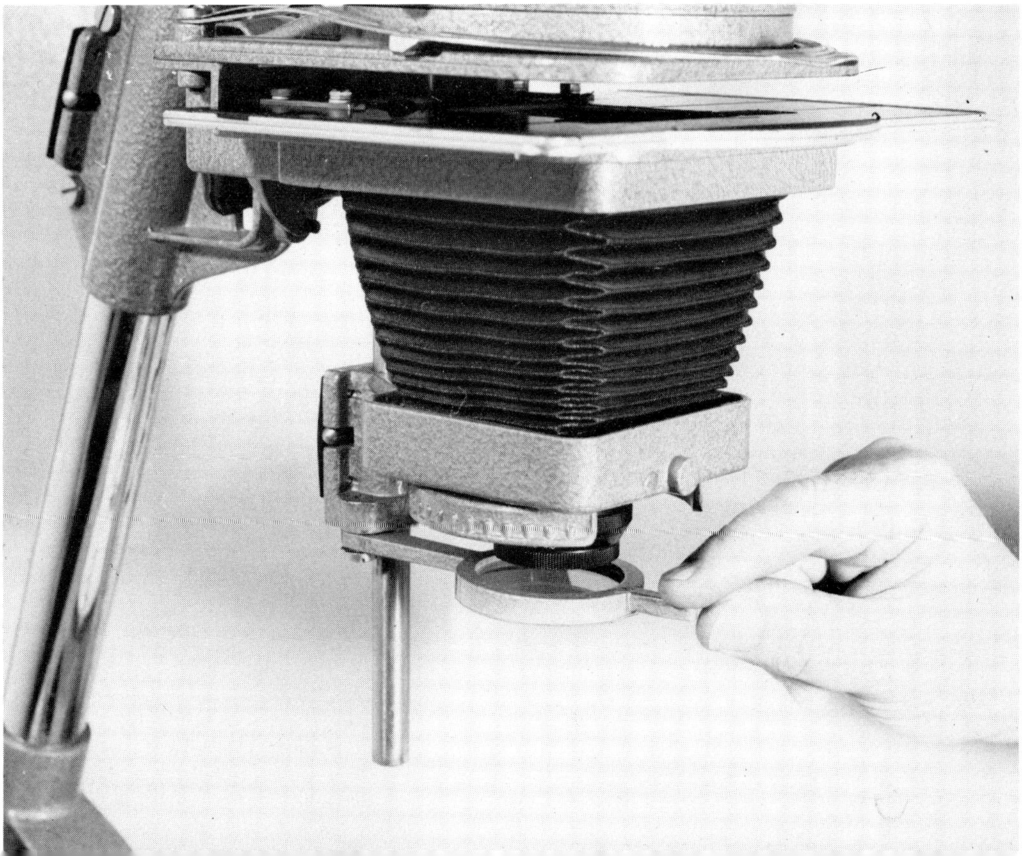

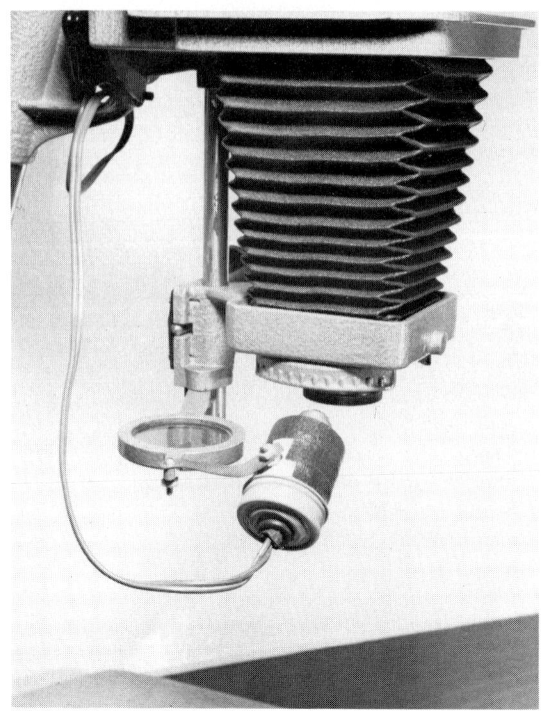

Fig. 4-7. A lens illuminator is of tremendous help in the darkened atmosphere of enlarging. It can be mounted easily and conveniently on the red filter by means of a strip of tin or aluminum cut from a juice can with scissors.

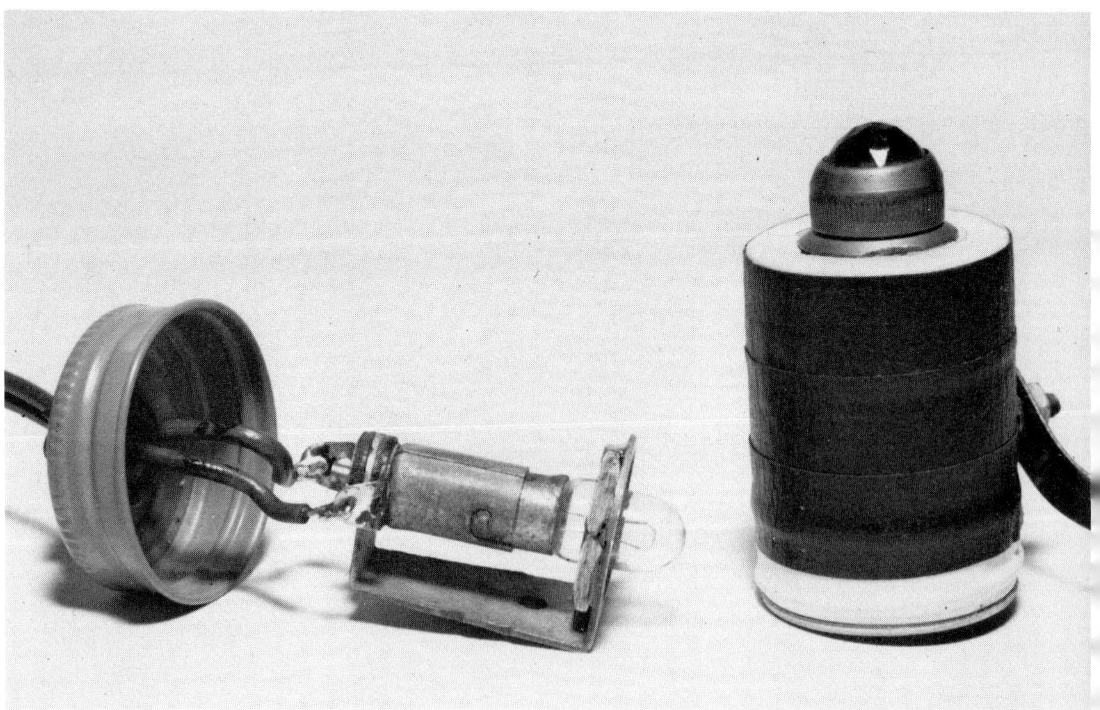

Fig. 4-8. The illuminator consists of a radio pilot light and a 35mm film can. The hole in the film can for the red cap can be easily cut in the soft aluminum with a knife.

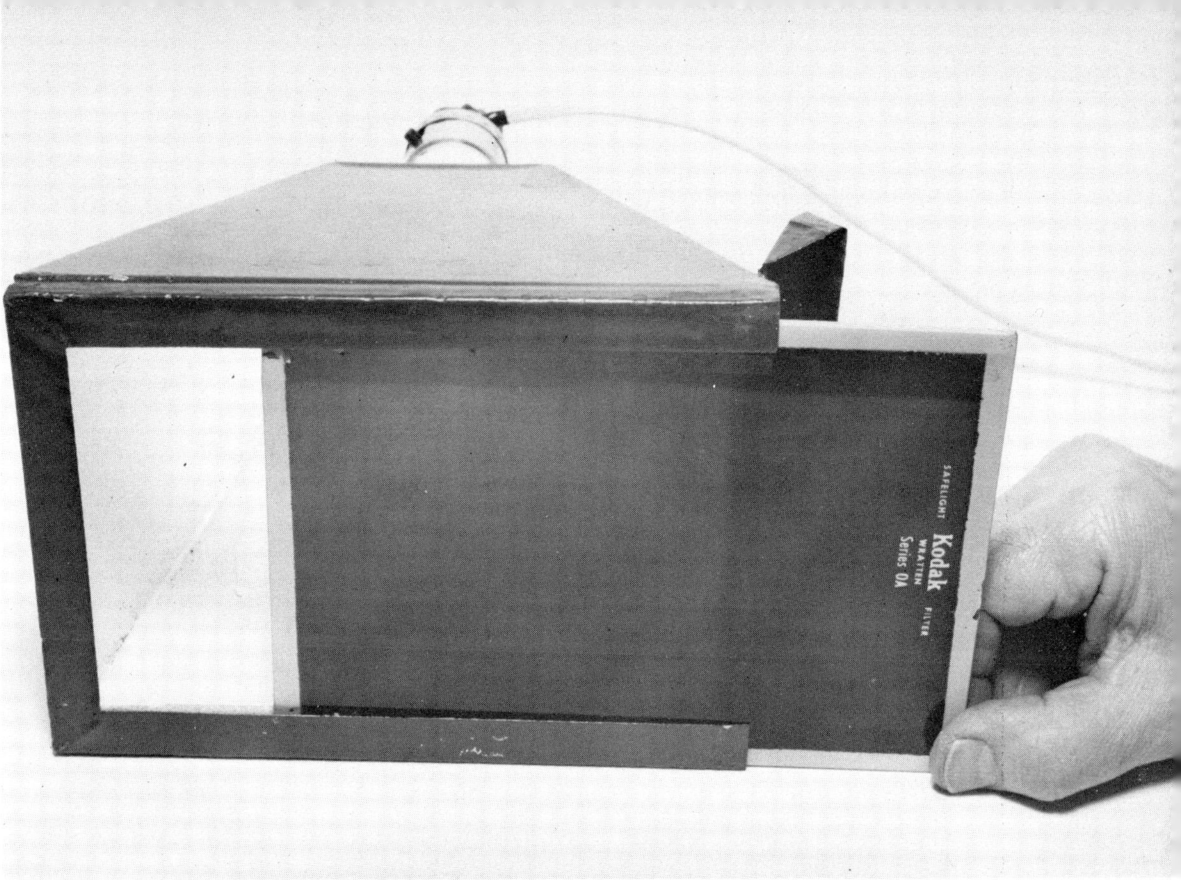

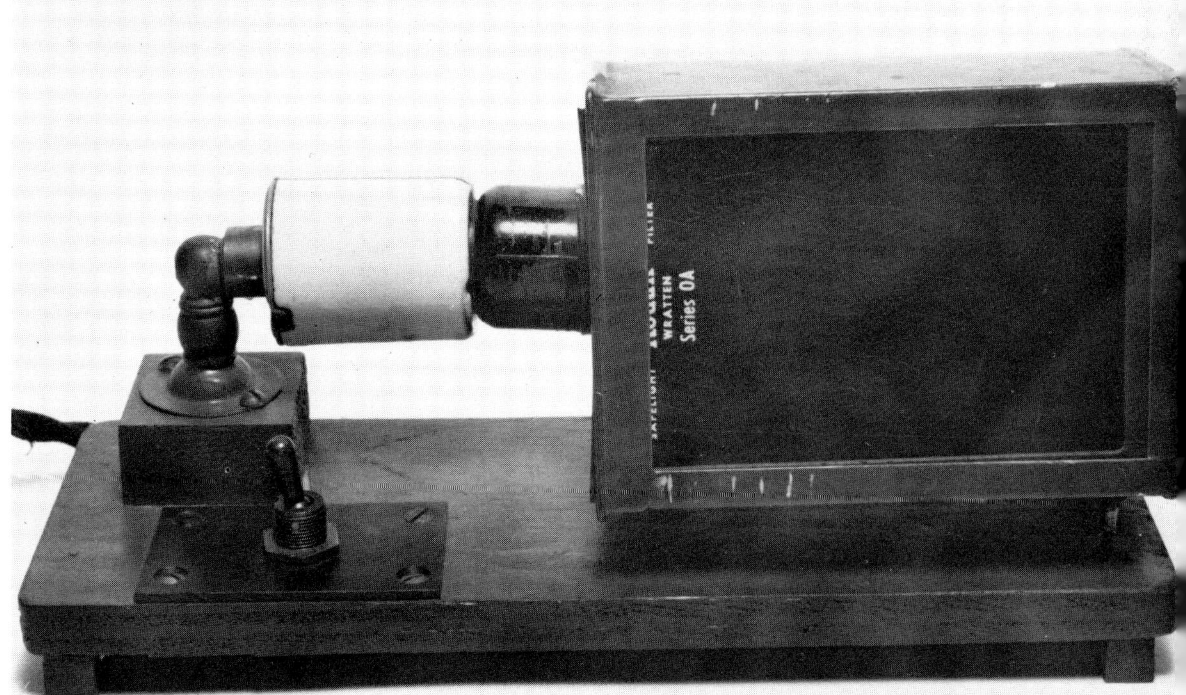

Figs. 4-9a and b. Photographic "safelights" are merely small metal or plastic boxes with removable glass filters. For enlarging work the filter is usually colored to let through only a dim yellowish light from the 15w lamps inside. This does not affect enlarging or contact paper.

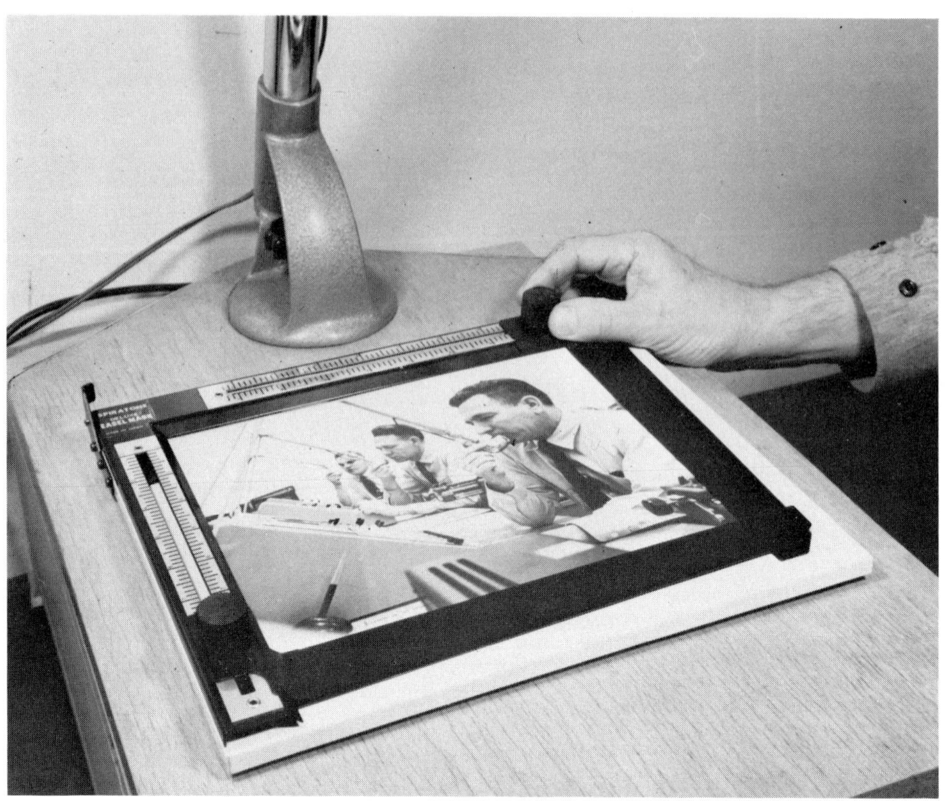

Figs. 4-10a and b. Easels are needed to hold paper flat during exposure. This Spiratone all metal model is typical of the adjustable type, accommodating sheets 8 × 10'' or smaller. Adjustment is made by means of two black masking bands that slide along measuring guides at the top and left edges of the frame.

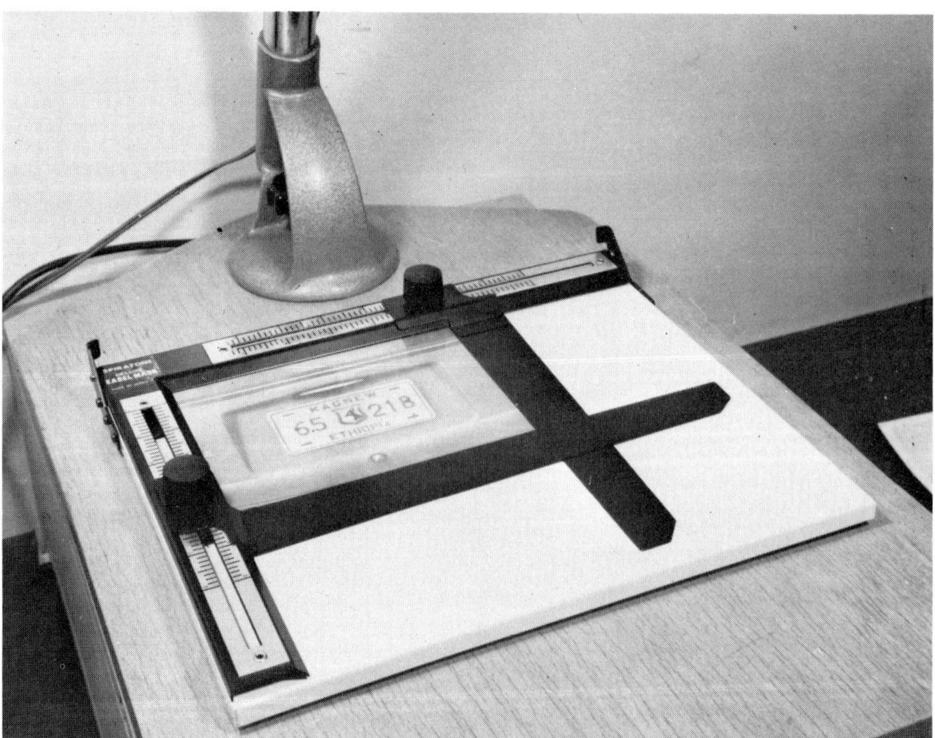

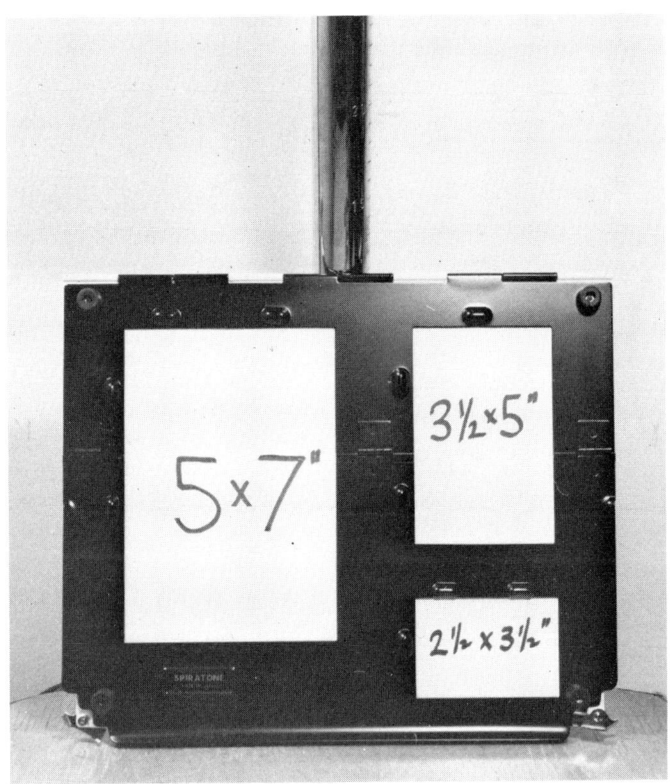

Figs. 4-11a and b. Consisting of two hinged metal plates, this ingenious Spiratone "4-in-1" easel takes four popular sizes of enlarging paper without adjustment; three on one side and full 8" × 10" on the other.

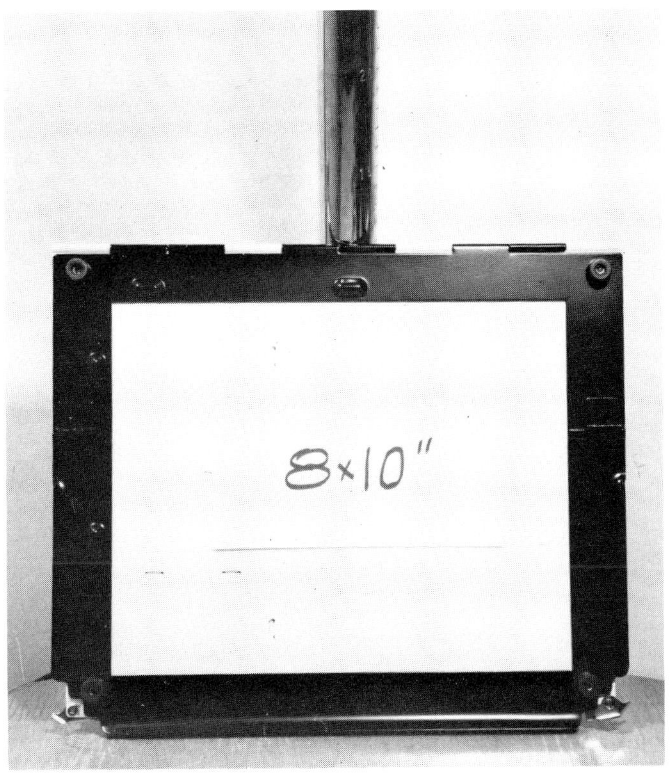

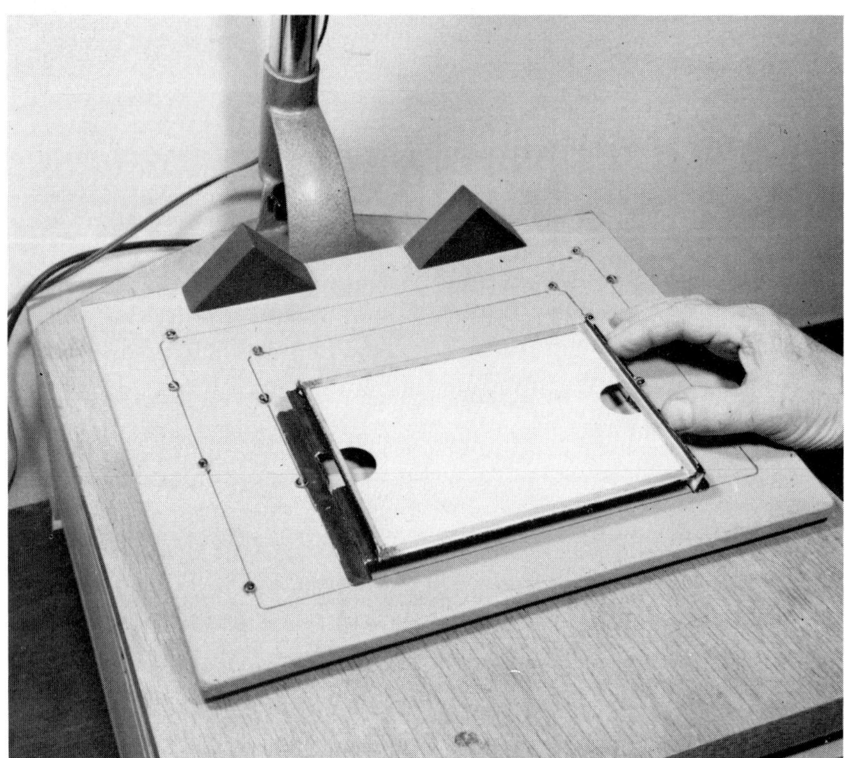

Figs. 4-12a and b. People who make most of their prints in a few standard sizes find the individual "Speed-Ez-Els" to be time savers. They are metal frames with fixed 1/4" margins and a smooth focusing surface. However, they are rather light, and should be secured to a weighted base like the one shown. The lower edges of the easel merely slide under small round-head wood screws.

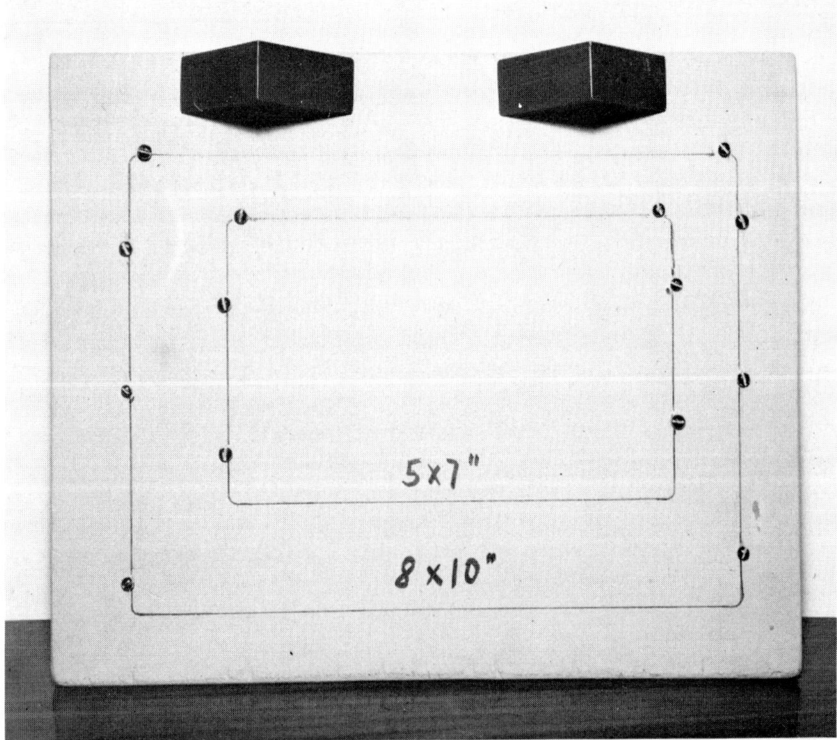

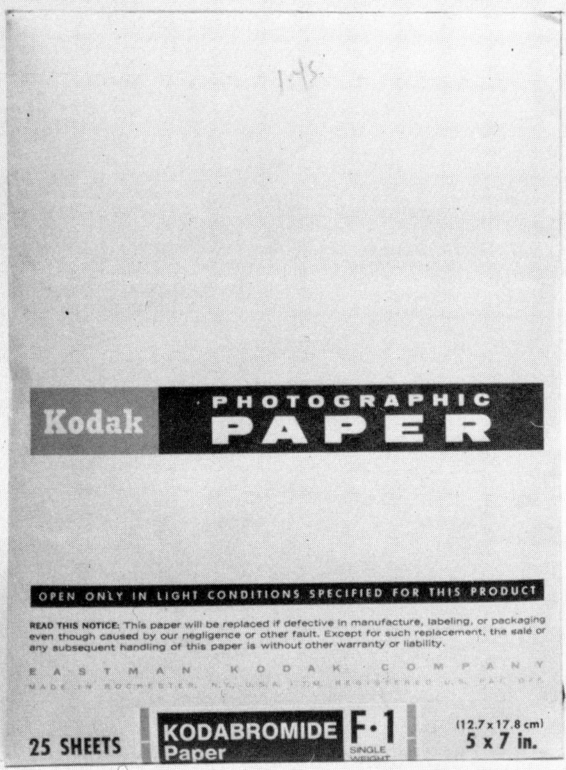
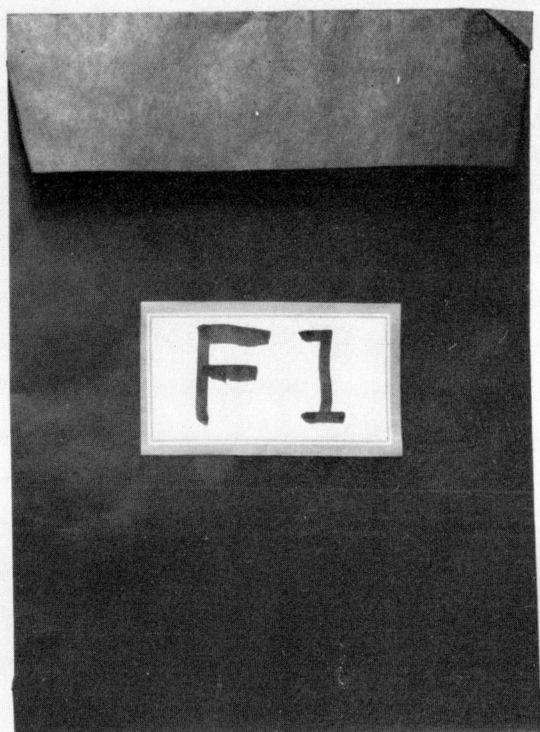

Fig. 4-13. Confusion and consternation are the result when black envelopes of enlarging paper are separated from the outer envelopes. A simple bit of insurance: Put a big label on each black container and mark the paper type and contrast number in big characters.

Figs. 4-14a and b. Cutting up test strips in advance of setting up for enlarging is a good idea. Working under safelight, cut them about 1" × 5", mark them on the back with a grease pencil, put them in similarly marked No. 6 envelopes, and put these into the main envelope.

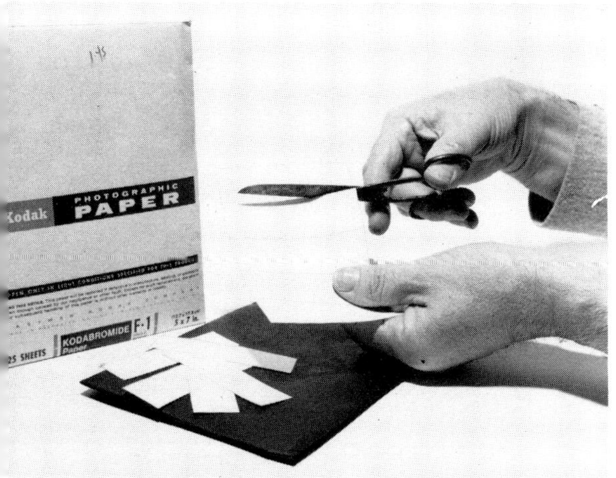
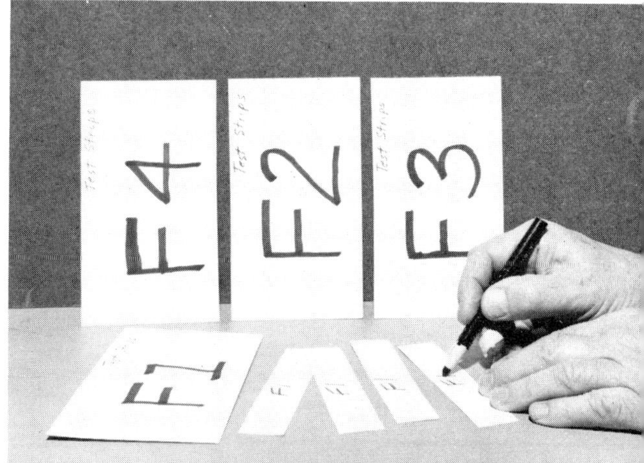

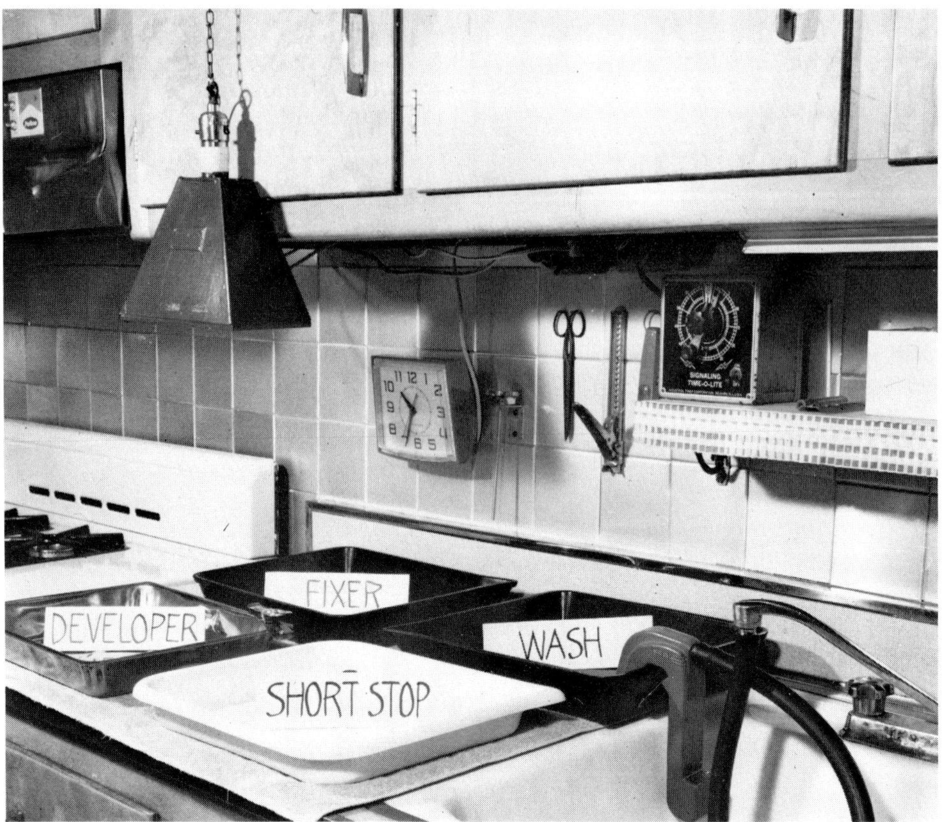

Fig. 4-15. This is the basic set-up for processing prints. All four trays fit neatly on a drainboard next to the kitchen sink. Note the safelight hanging from the towel bar, the clock on the wall behind the fixer tray, and the washing attachment on the last tray.

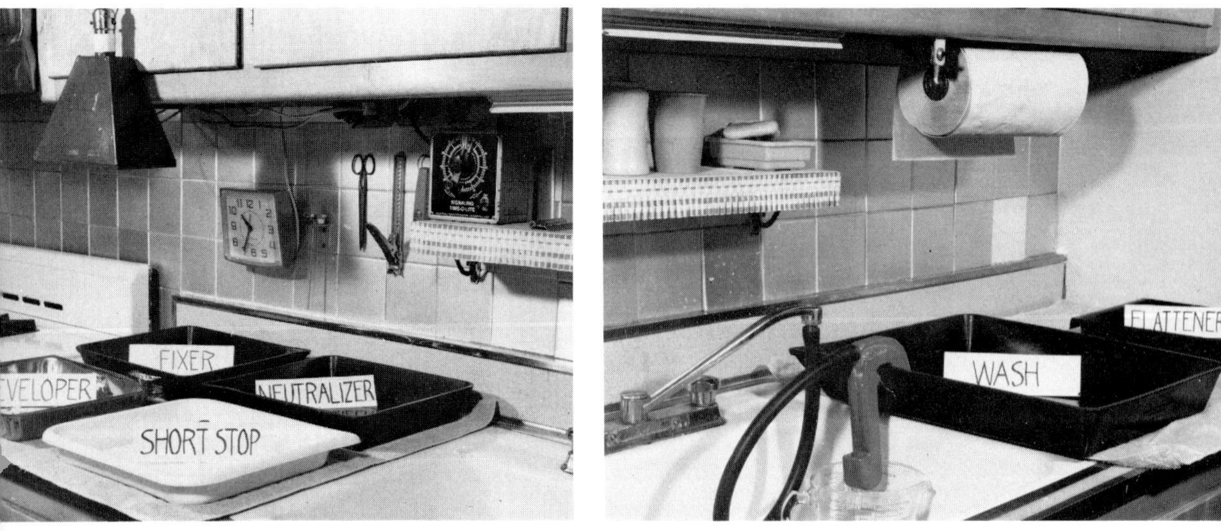

Figs. 4-16a and b. With both drainboards in use, this arrangement of six trays is better than the previous one because fixer neutralizer, flattening solution, and an 11" × 14" wash tray can be accommodated without crowding. Cup under overflow pipe of washing attachment is handy for rinsing print tongs.

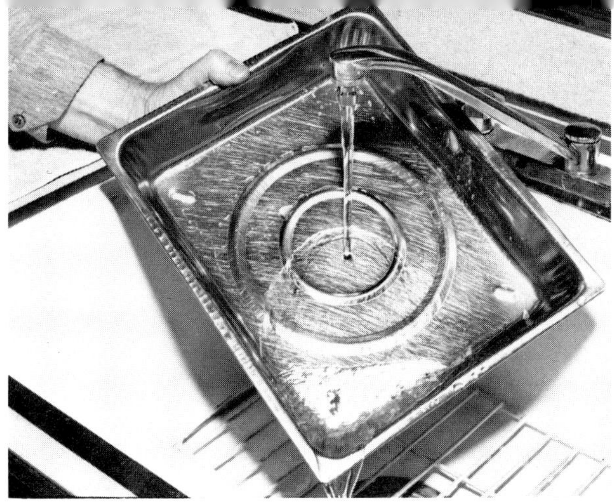

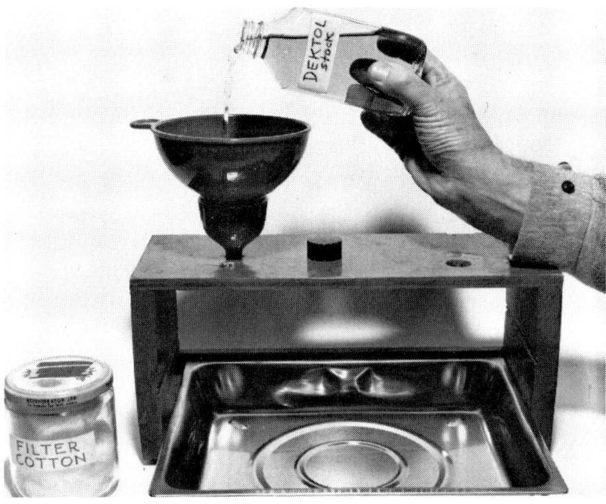

Fig. 4-17. Ready to get going? First step is to rinse all trays in preparation for filtering the various solutions into them.

Fig. 4-18. First filter an 8-ounce bottle of paper stock developer, using one funnel. While this is dribbling down, fill a graduate with water at about 68° F. or 70° F. Fill the empty bottle with water, pour this into the funnel, and repeat the step. You now have 24 ounces of working developer solution (1 part stock: 2 parts water) which is enough for an evening's work, and a clean empty bottle. Rinse the funnel.

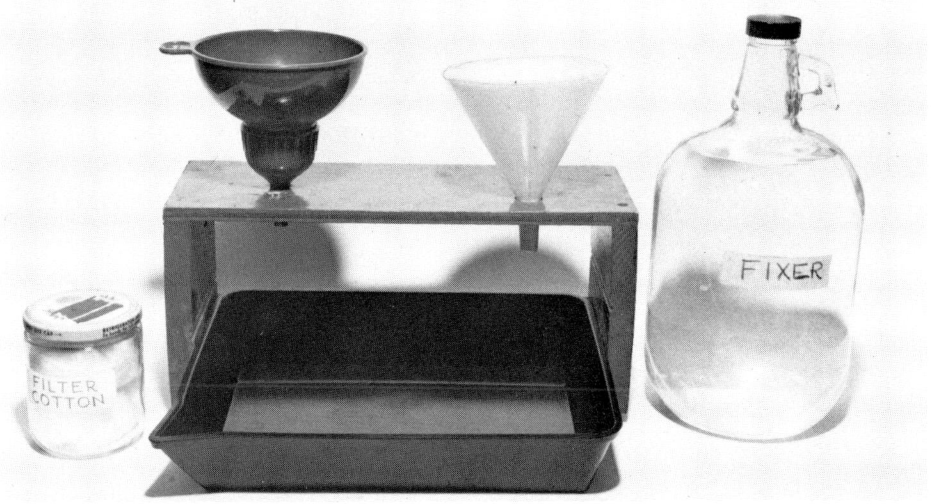

Fig. 4-19. Using two funnels to speed things up, filter about half a gallon each of fixer, fixer neutralizer, and print flattener; and with one funnel, a quart of short stop. Of course, rinse the funnels thoroughly between jobs.

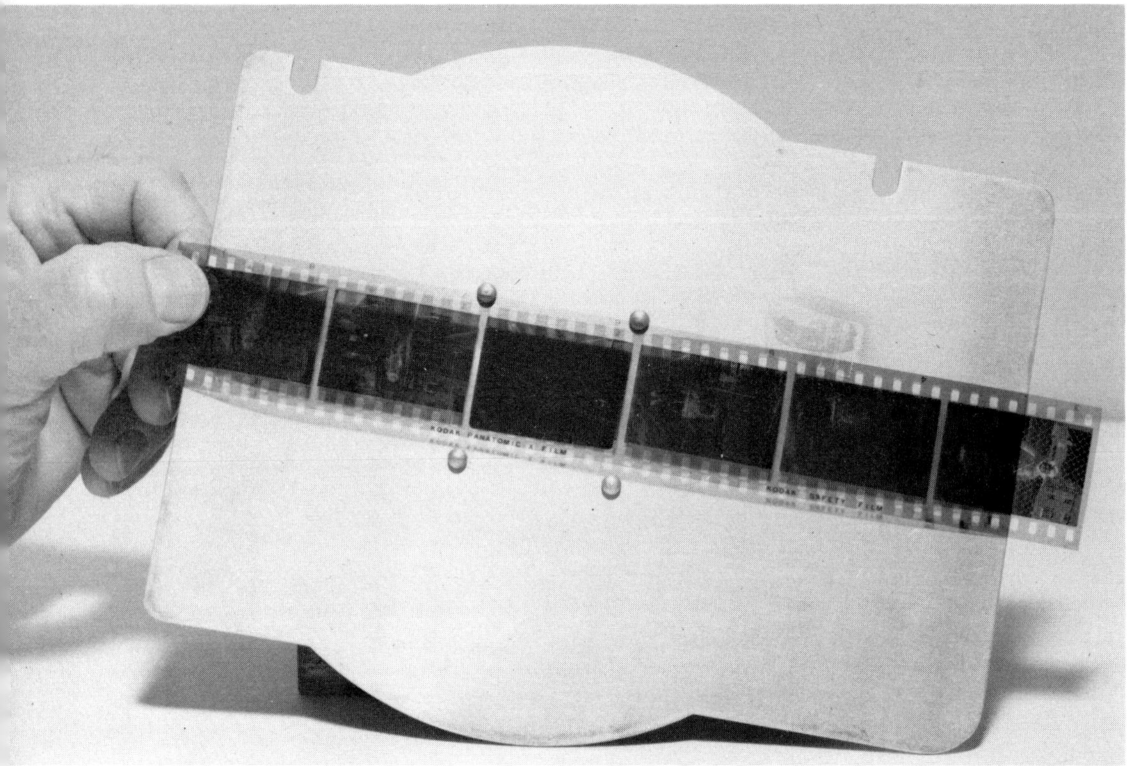

Figs. 4-20a and b. Negative holders generally consist of two mating halves, with the film placed between them like the filling of a sandwich. Position the film so that the dull side is down, facing the lens, when the holder is inserted in the enlarger.

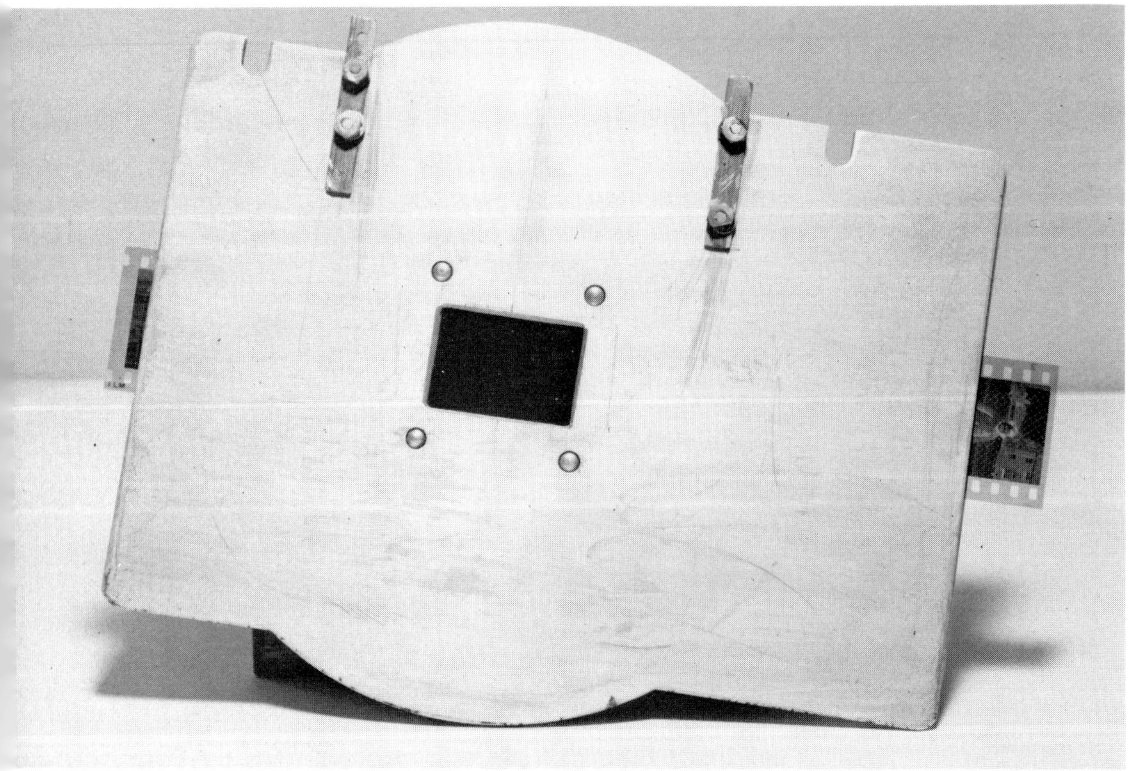

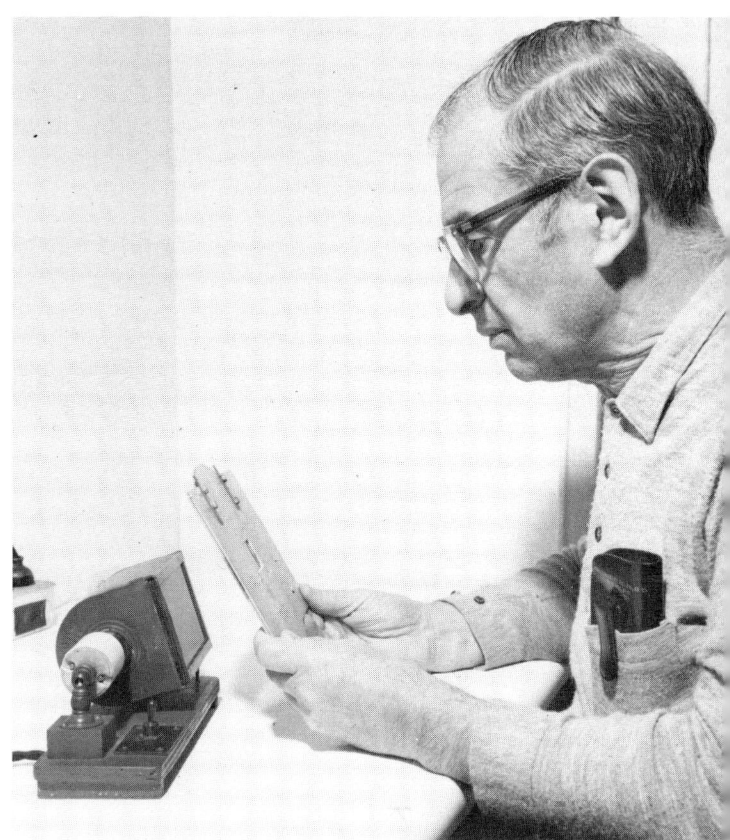

Fig. 4-21. Hold the holder against a small safelight and make sure that the selected frame fills the opening.

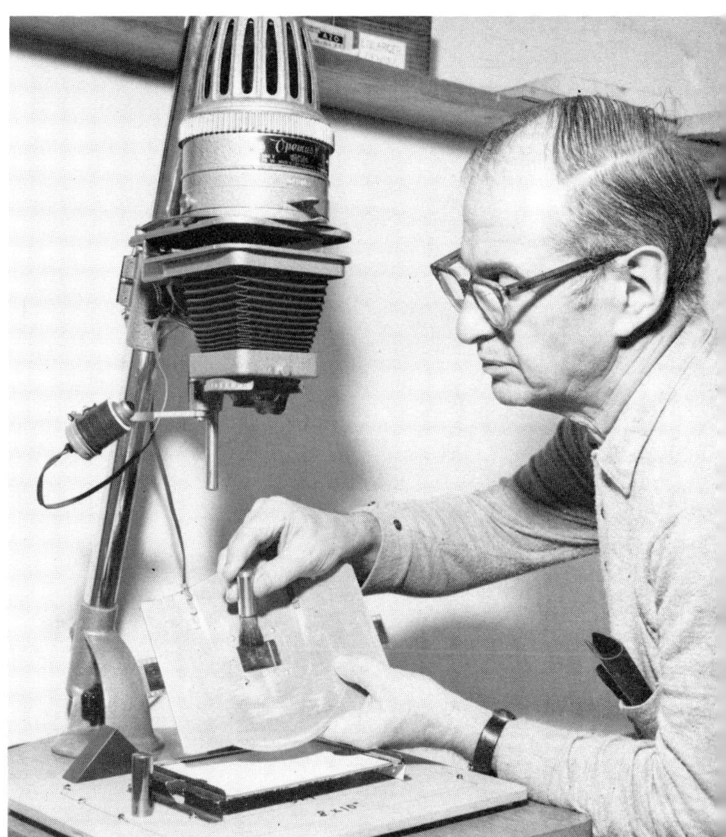

Fig. 4-22. Check the film for dust, and if necessary flick it clean with a soft brush. One type of cleaner combines a brush with a soft rubber squeeze ball that squirts air across the film surface.

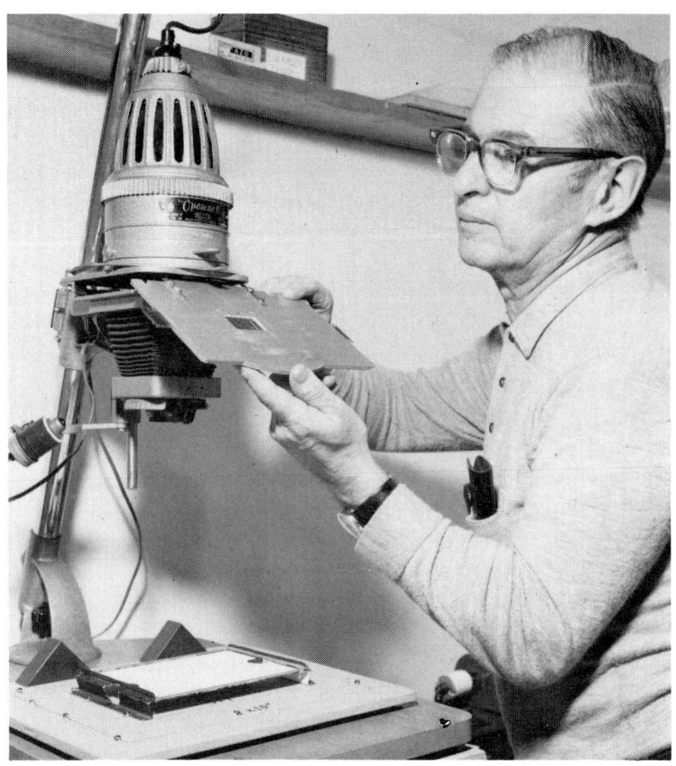

Fig. 4-23. Slip the holder carefully into the head of the enlarger.

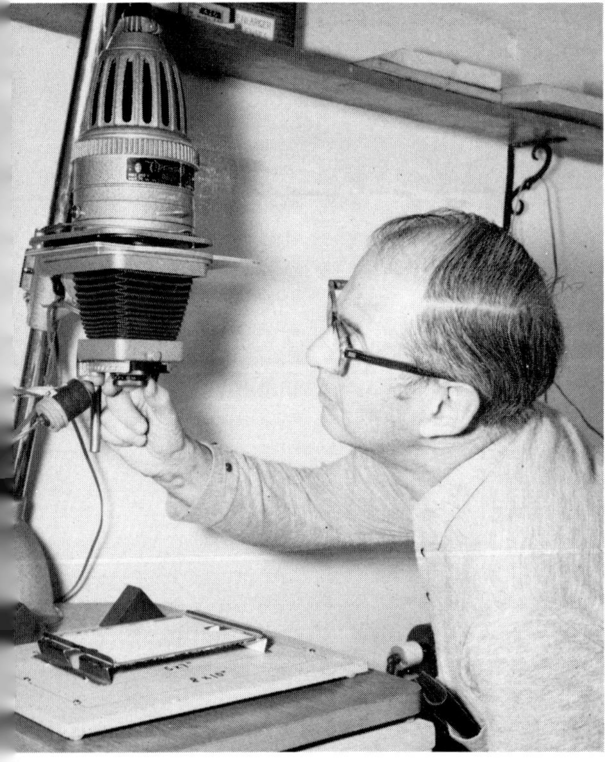

Fig. 4-24. Swing the illuminator close to the lens so that you can see the markings clearly, and open the diaphragm to its maximum setting. With most enlarger lenses this is $f/4.5$.

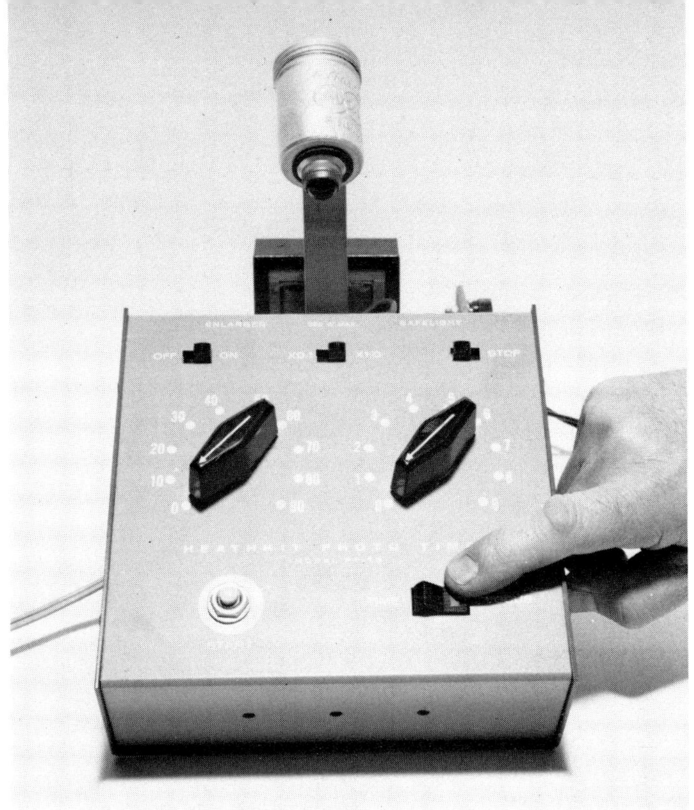

Fig. 4-25. Turn the enlarger on by hitting the "focus" button on the timer.

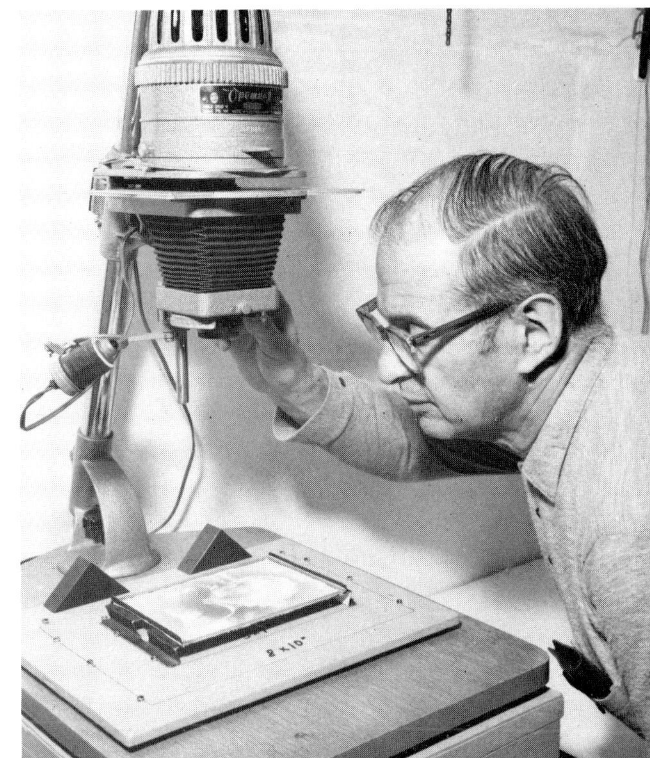

Fig. 4-26. Move the enlarger head up or down, at the same time making approximate focusing adjustments, until the projected image fills the easel. Then focus slowly for the sharpest picture. Turn the enlarger off.

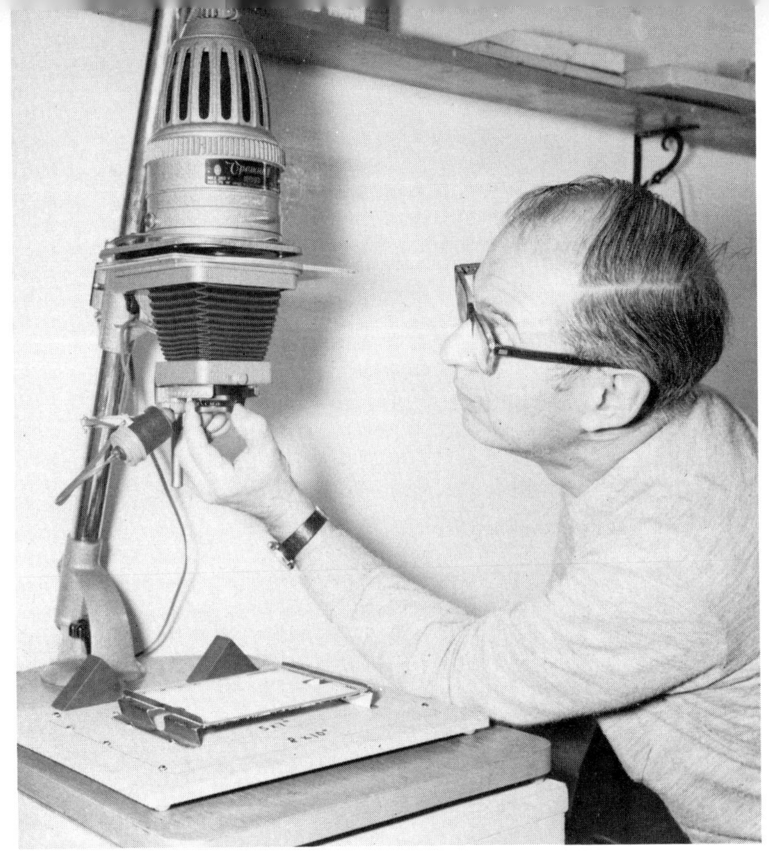

Fig. 4-27. Turn the enlarger on again. Set the lens diaphragm to *f*/8. Keep your finger away from the glass!

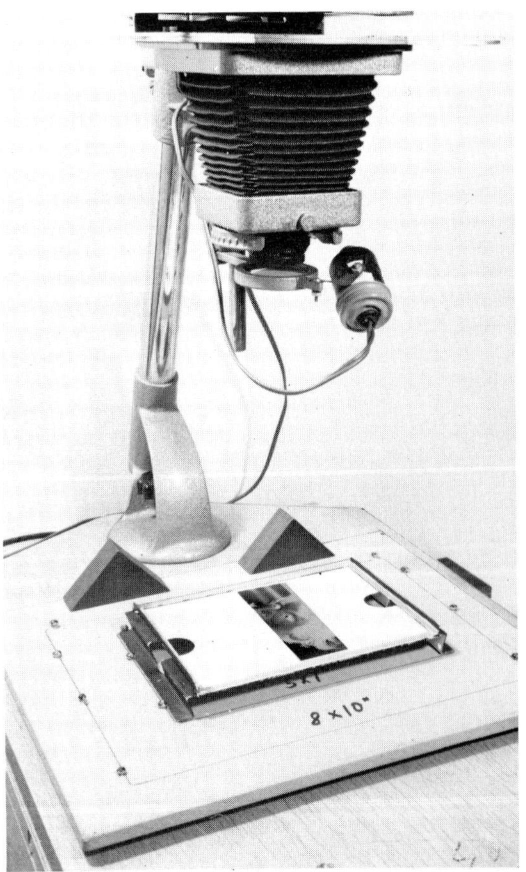

Fig. 4-28. Swing the red filter under the lens. Position a test strip so that it shows the central point of interest in the picture.

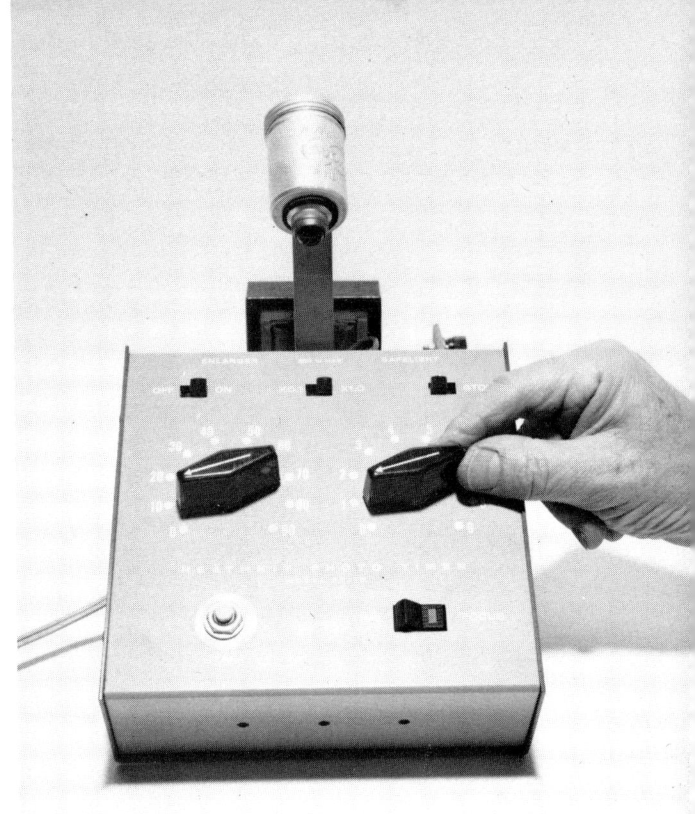

Fig. 4-29. Set the timer for an exposure of 10 seconds.

Fig. 4-30. Move the time-focus switch of the timer to "time." This will automatically shut off the enlarger after 10 seconds.

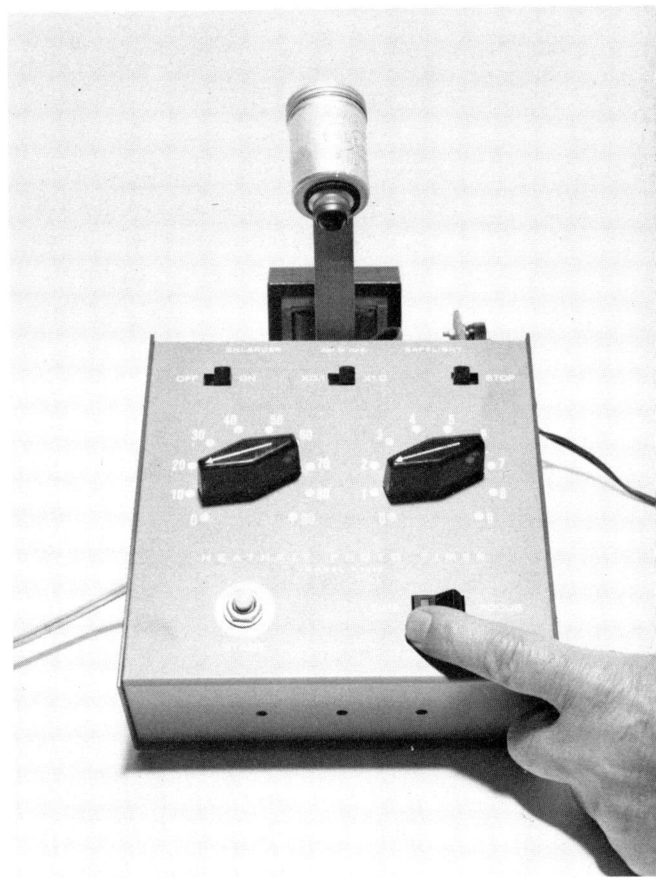

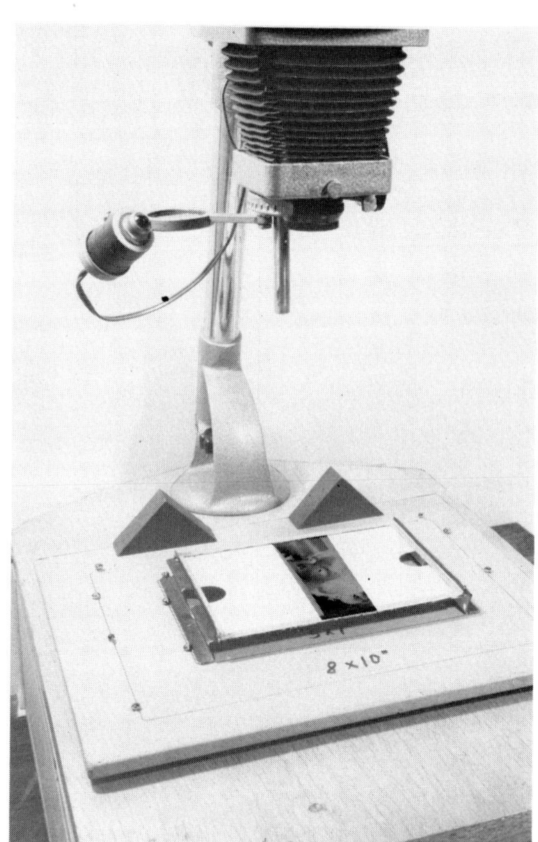

Fig. 4-31. Swing the red filter away from the lens.

Fig. 4-32. Touch the start button of the timer. The enlarger will come on for 10 seconds and then turn off automatically.

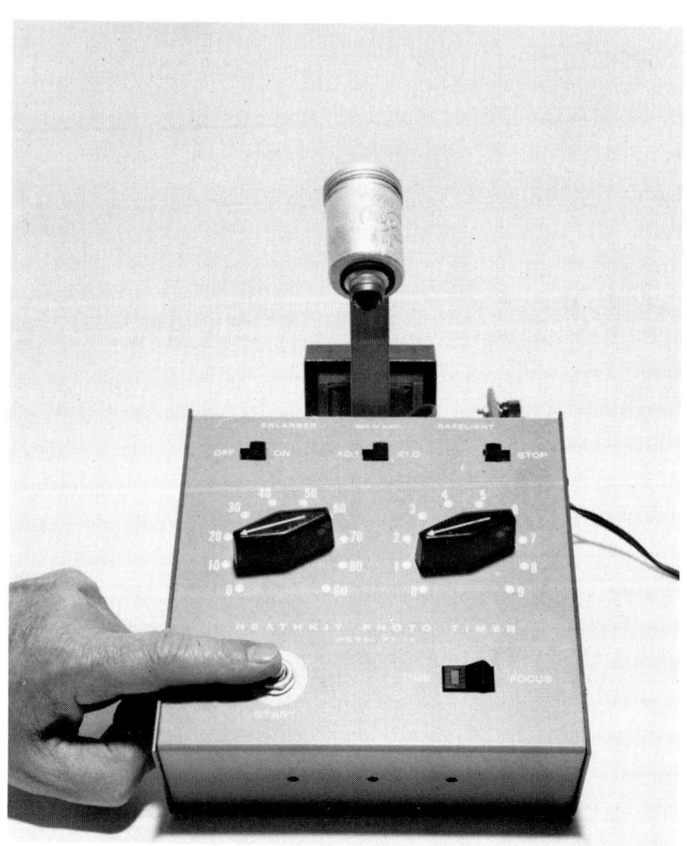

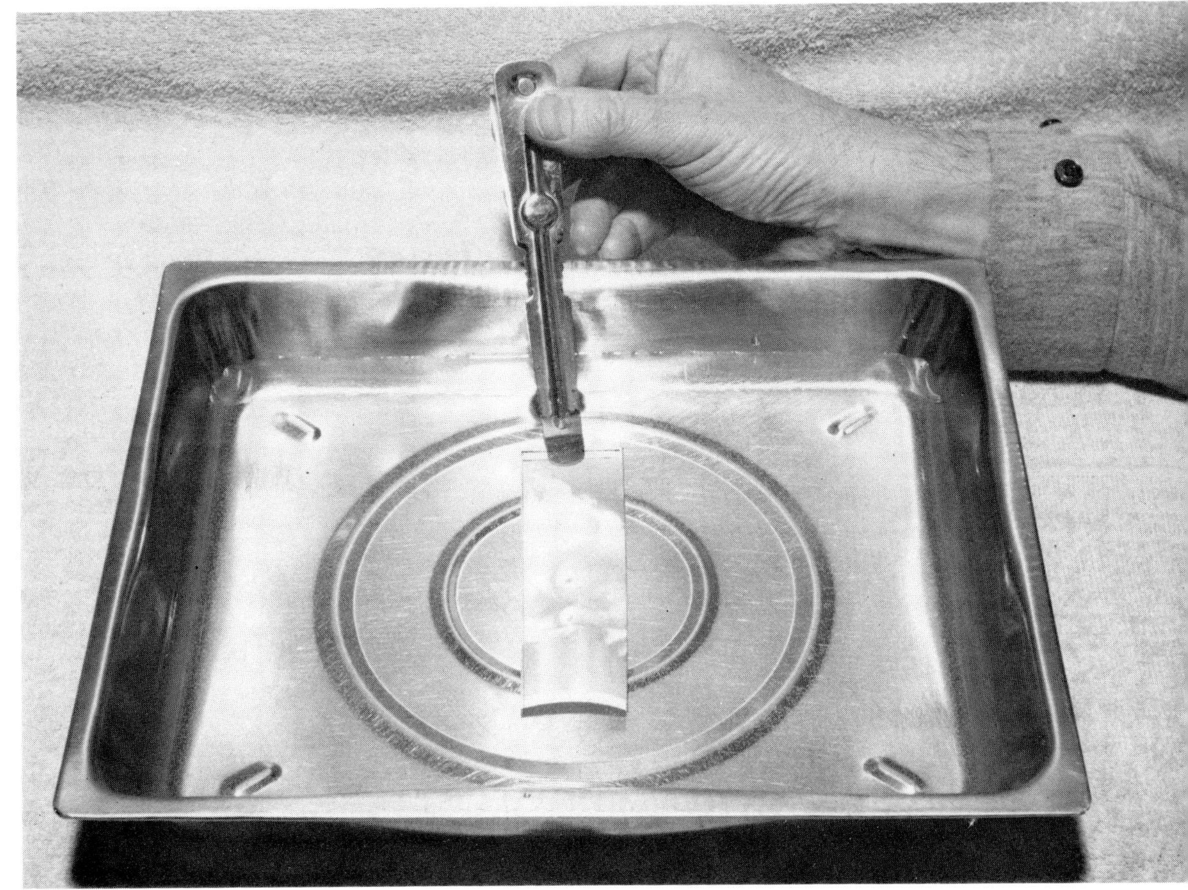

Fig. 4-33. Grab one end of the test strip with the tongs, put it in the developer, and note the position of the sweep-second hand of the electric clock. Move the strip gently through the solution and check the immersion time as prescribed in the text.

Figs. 4-34a-h. The prints of a typical baby picture reproduced on the following pages were all made with a fixed enlarger lens opening of f/8 but at different timer settings from 1 to 8 seconds, and with uniform processing to 90 seconds. a, b, and c are clearly underexposed; d is better, but still a bit on the light side; both e and f are good; g and h are obviously overexposed.

Under the relatively weak light of a yellow filter, black-and-white prints tend to appear a little darker than they really are. To compensate for this illusion, let them develop a few seconds more than seems necessary, and then drop them into the stop bath.

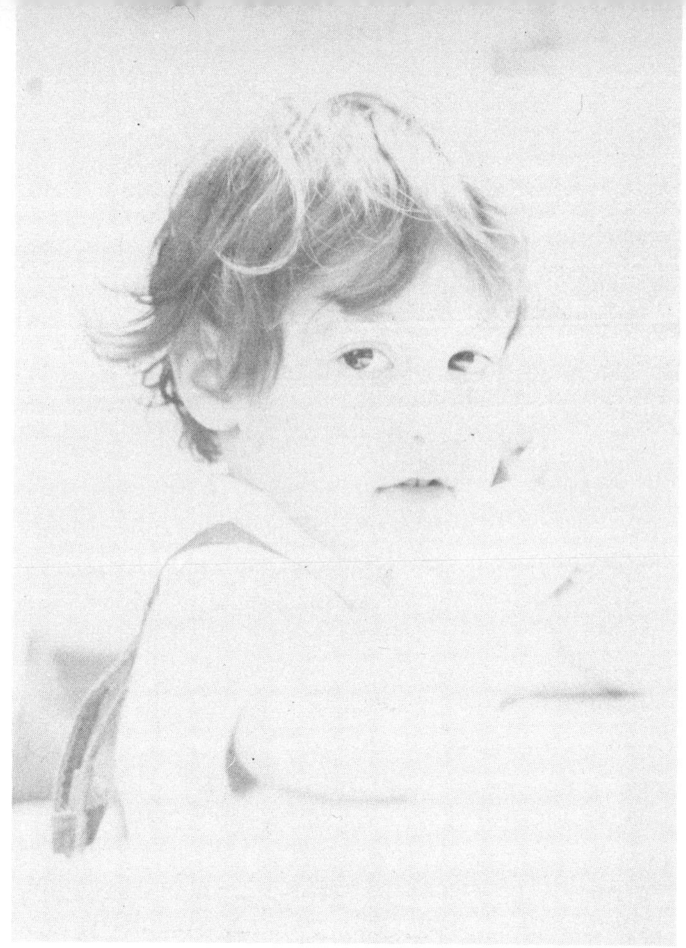

1 second

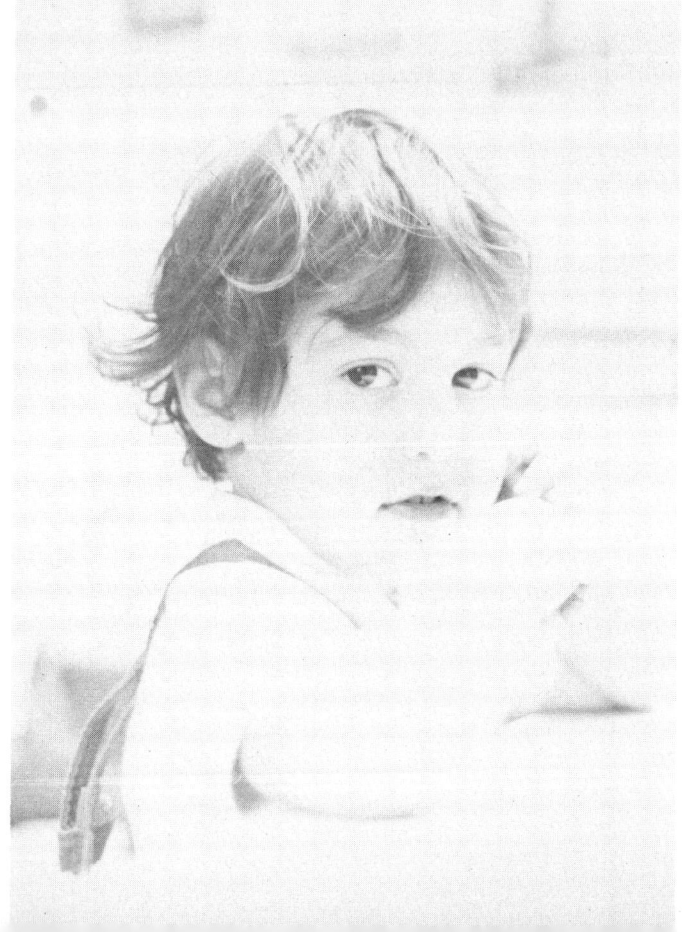

2 seconds

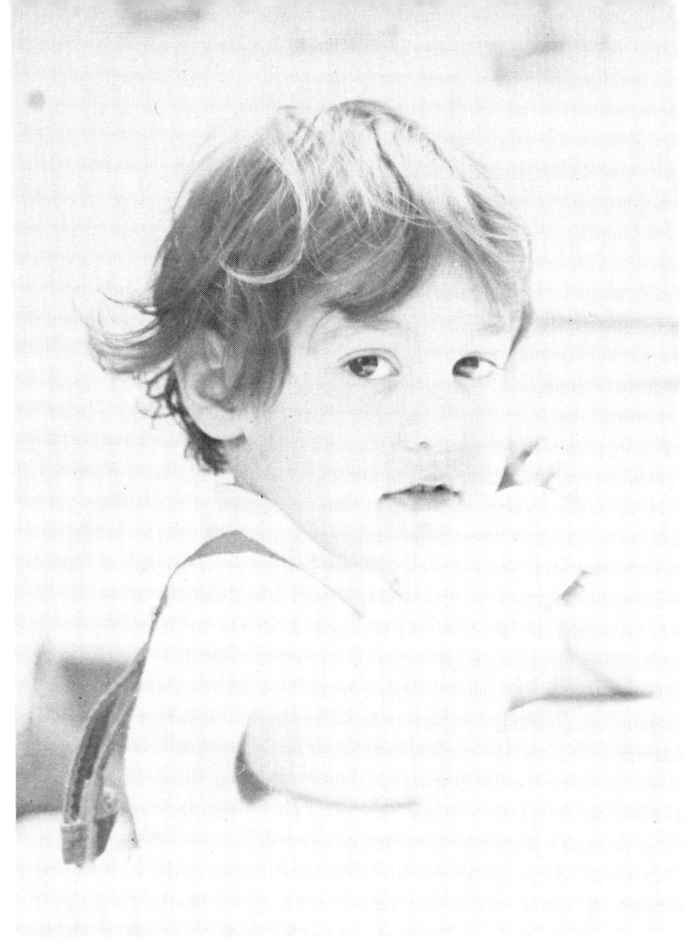

3 seconds

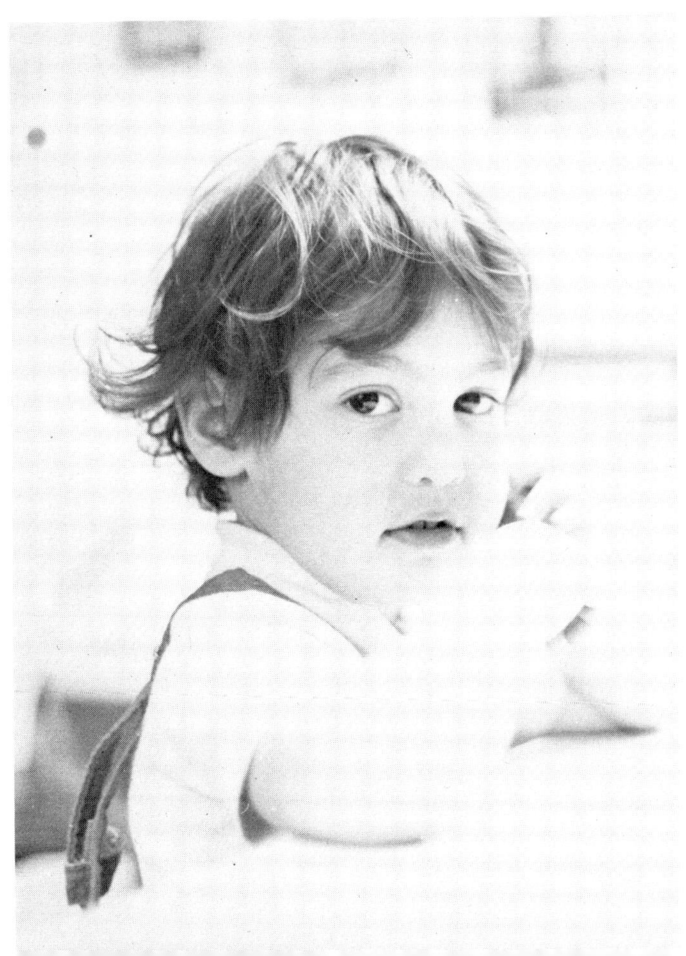

4 seconds

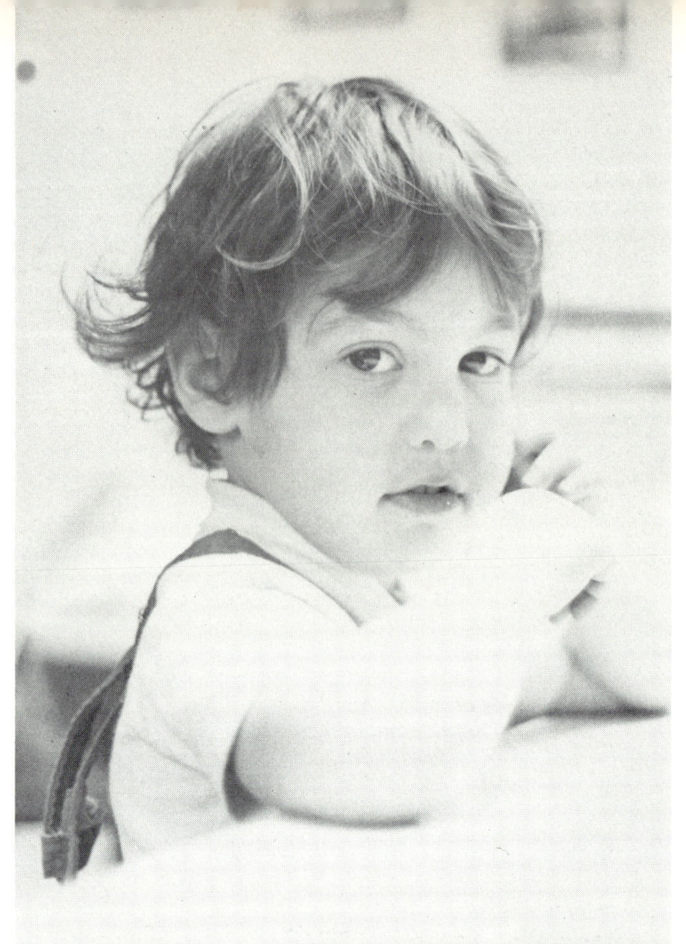

5 seconds

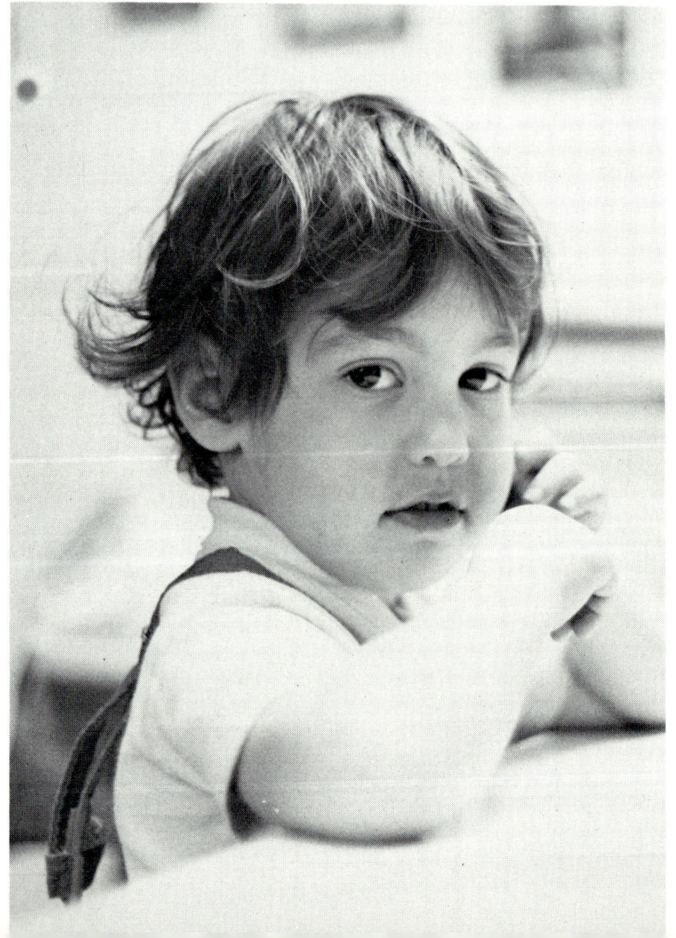

6 seconds

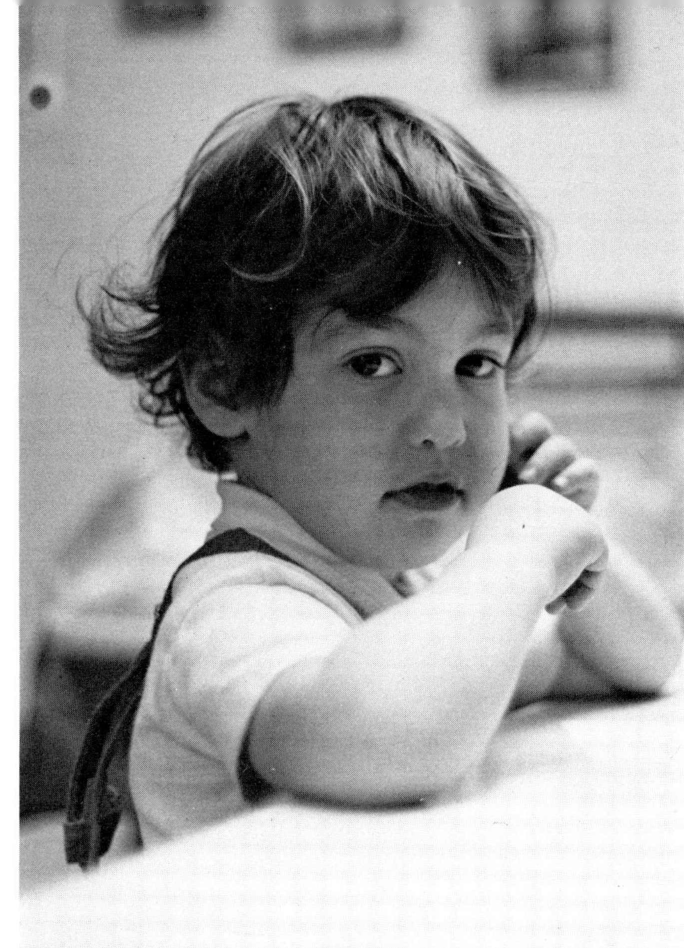

7 seconds

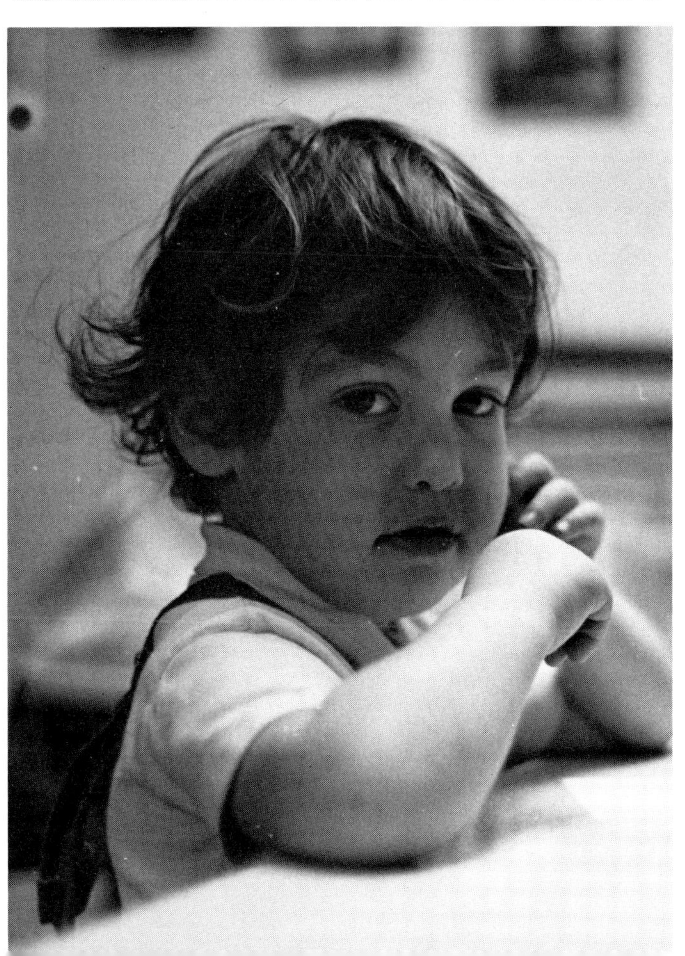

8 seconds

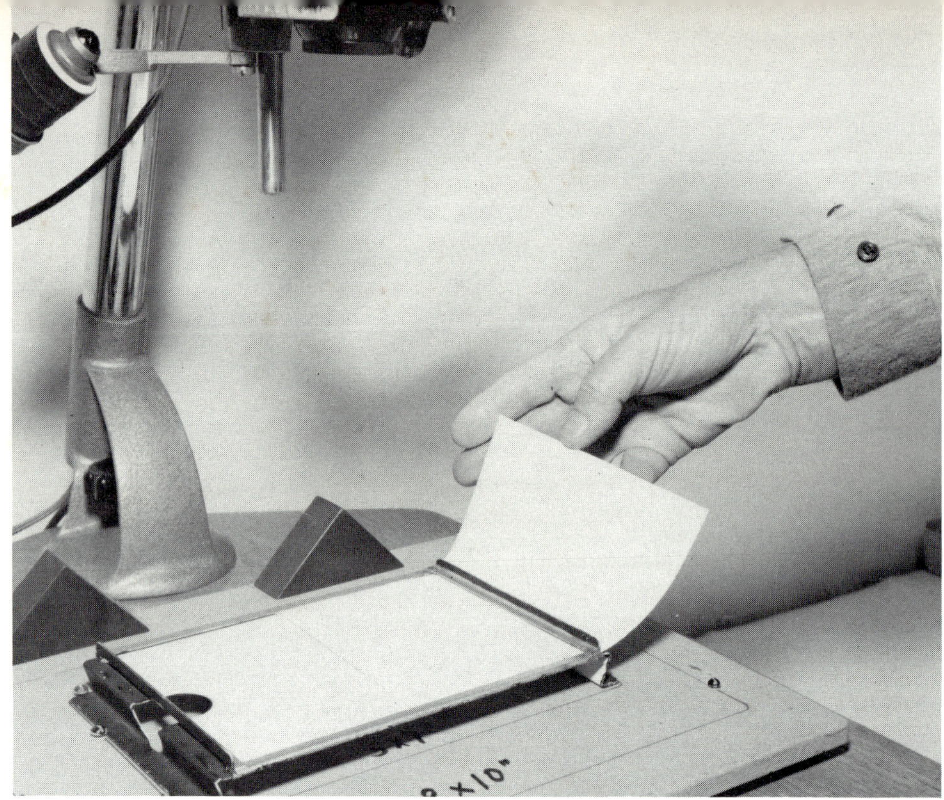

Fig. 4-35. After arriving at a suitable exposure time by means of test strips, switch to full sheets and try for a real print. A good starting size is 5'' × 7''. Here a piece of paper is going into a Speed-Ez-El. Note how fingers touch only the edges.

Fig. 4-36. Holding the exposed paper by one corner, push it into the developer with one quick movement.

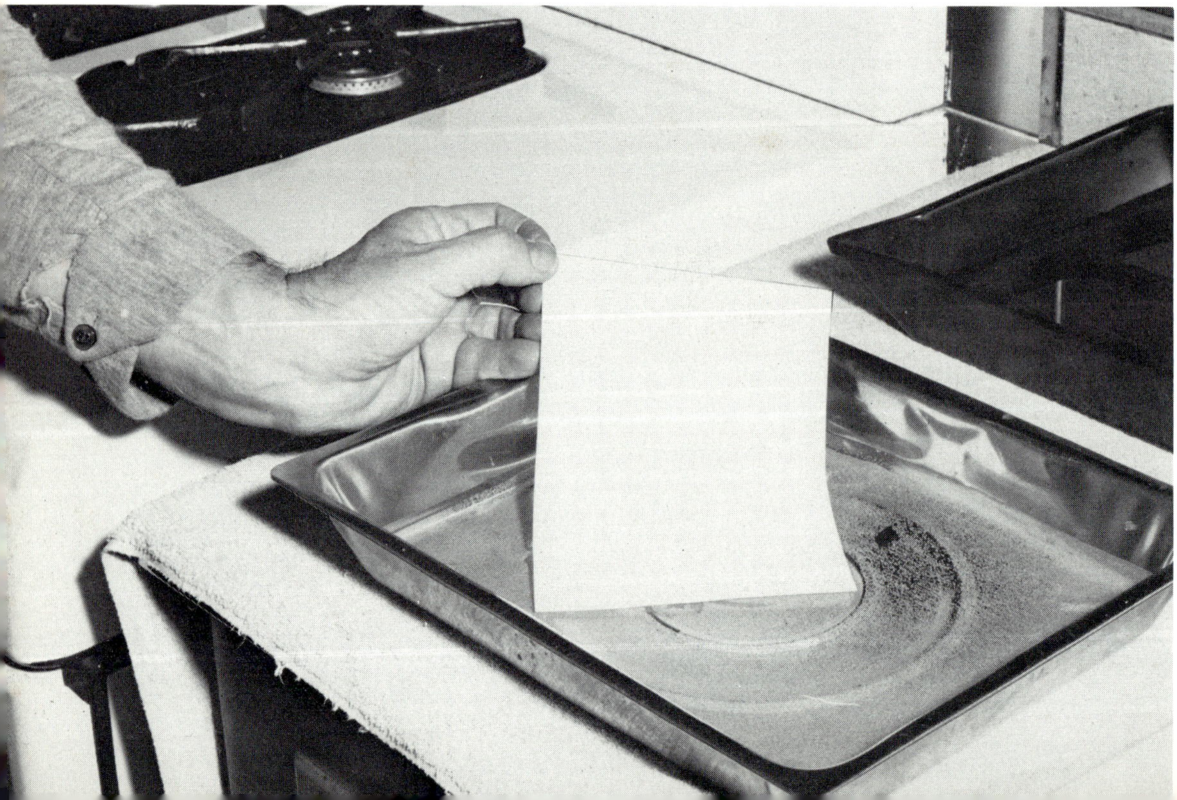

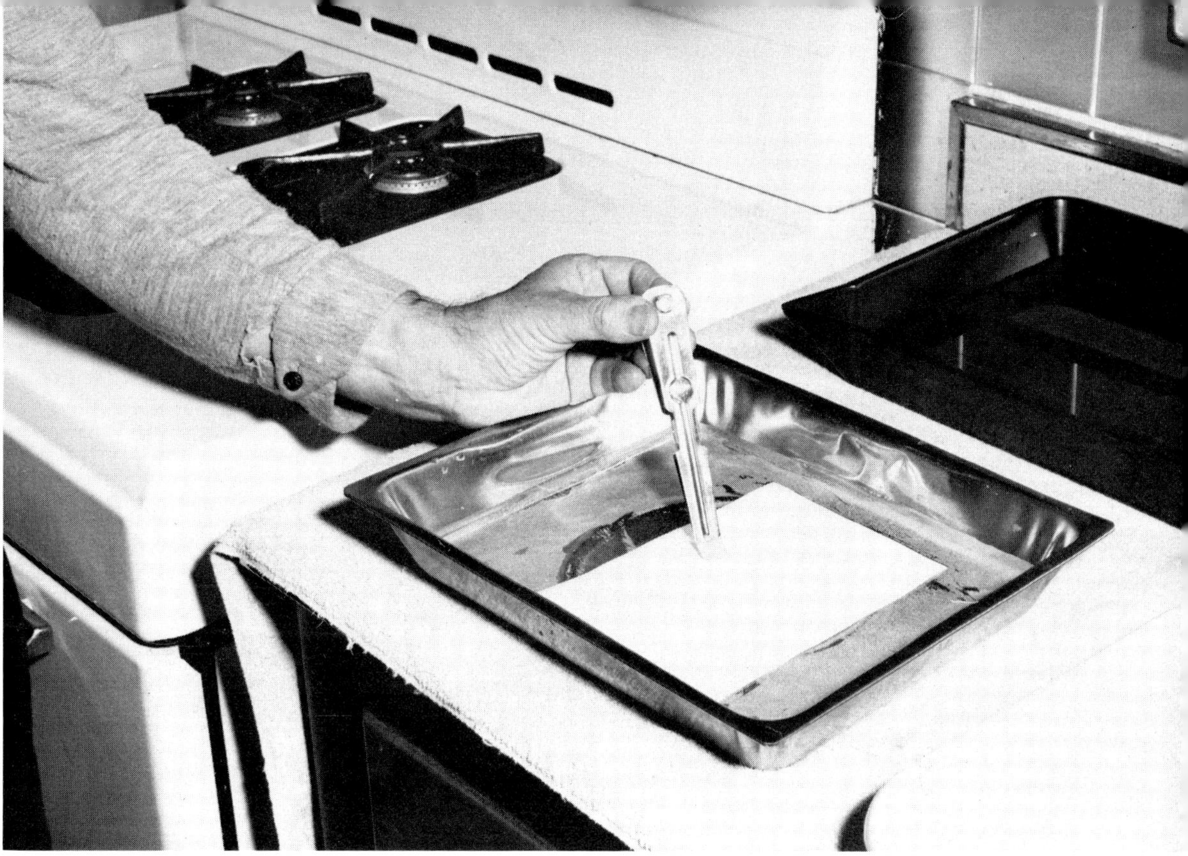

Fig. 4-37. With the tongs, press the print down gently to make sure that the entire surface is submerged.

Fig. 4-38. Raise one end of the tray and rock it slowly so that the developer sloshes back and forth across the paper. This insures uniform development.

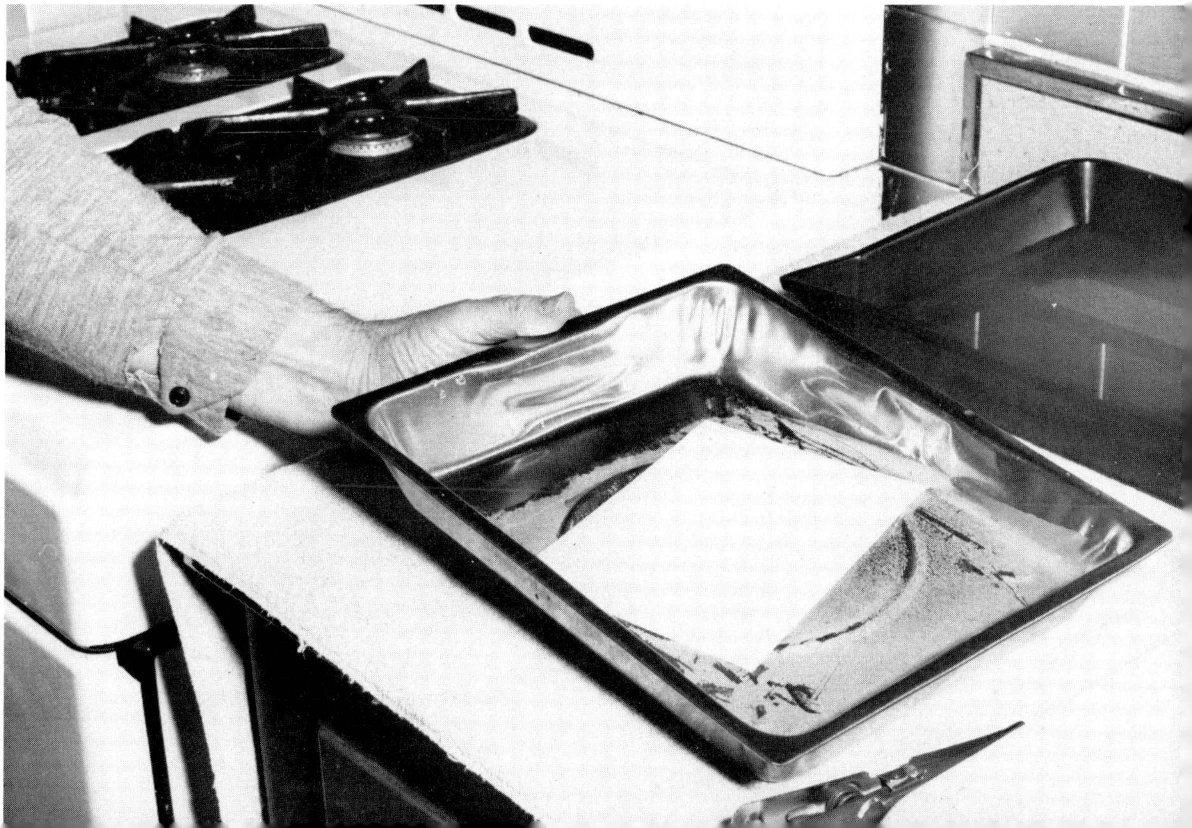

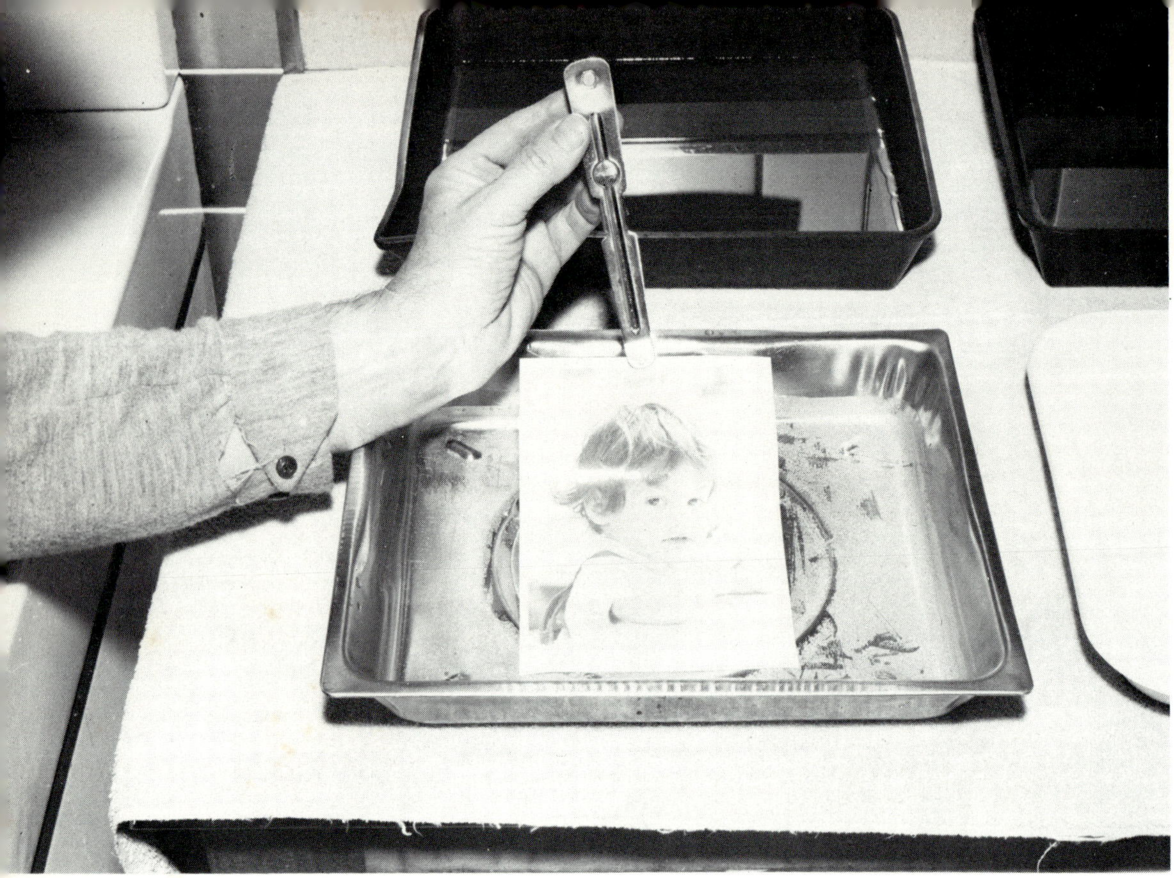

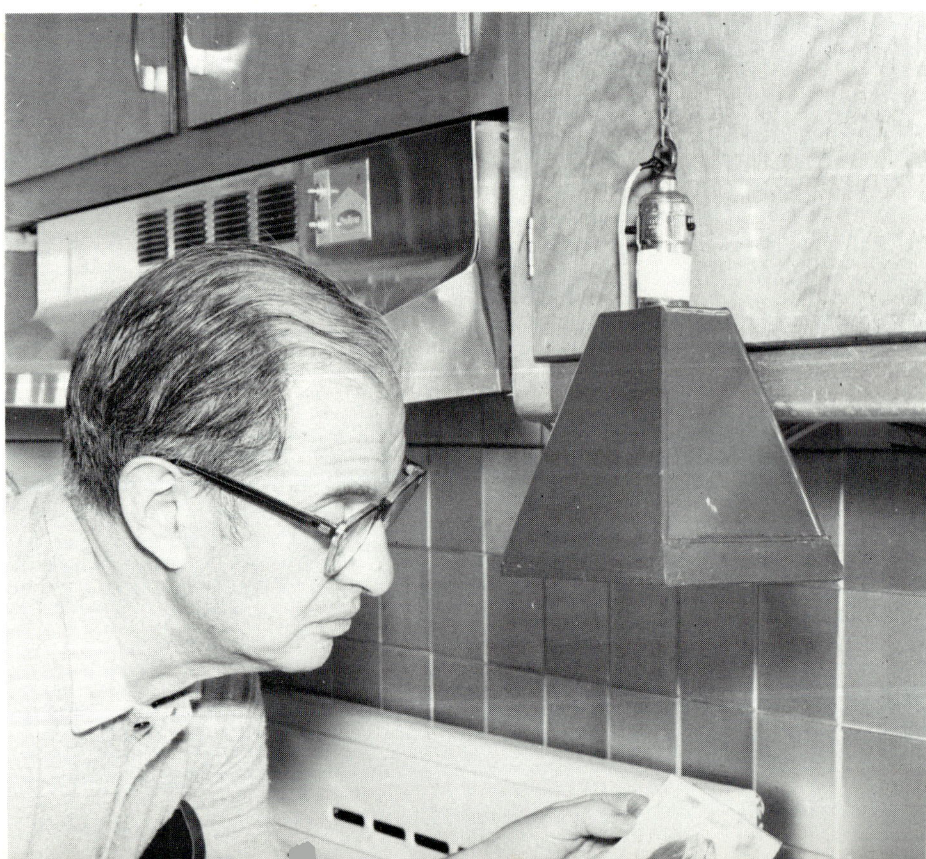

Fig. 4-39. Success! A discernable image is appearing on the paper as if by magic.

Fig. 4-40. Give the print a few more seconds. For a closer look, hold it over the tray and under the safelight. It looks good, but it's not dark enough. Back to the tray.

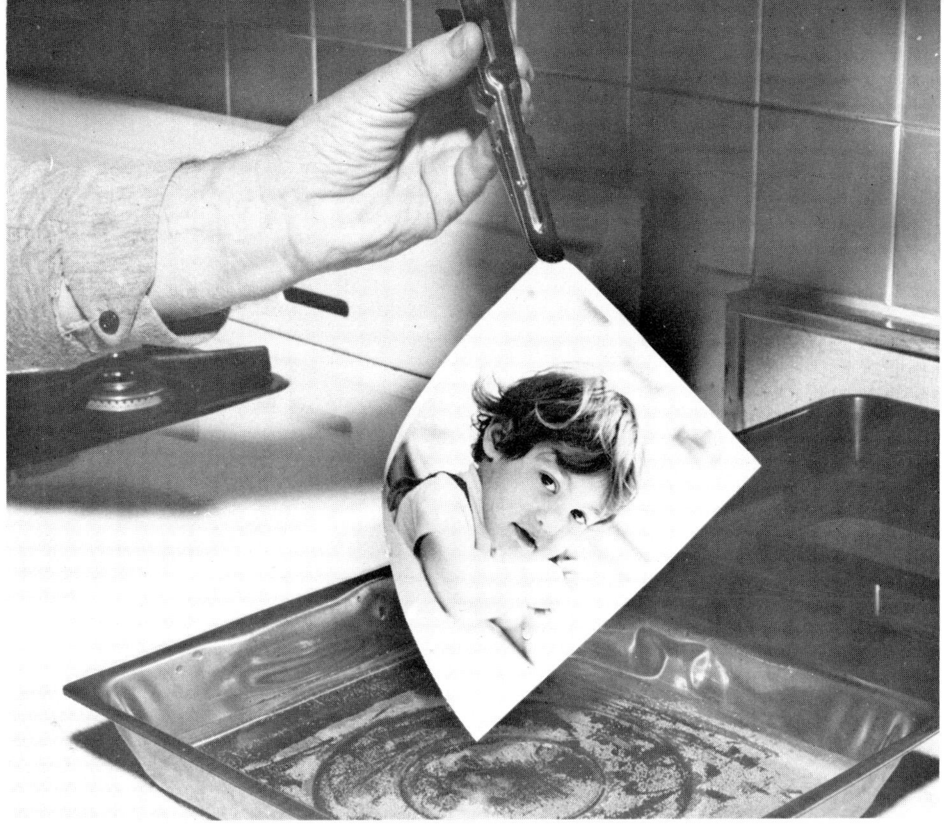

Fig. 4-41. Another extra few seconds in the developer and this beautiful print is the result. Let it drain a bit.

Fig. 4-42. Then transfer it to the short stop. A minute or two here is enough. While it's in this tray you can start another print, but to avoid confusion the whole developing process is shown in this picture sequence with only this one print. Rinse the tongs.

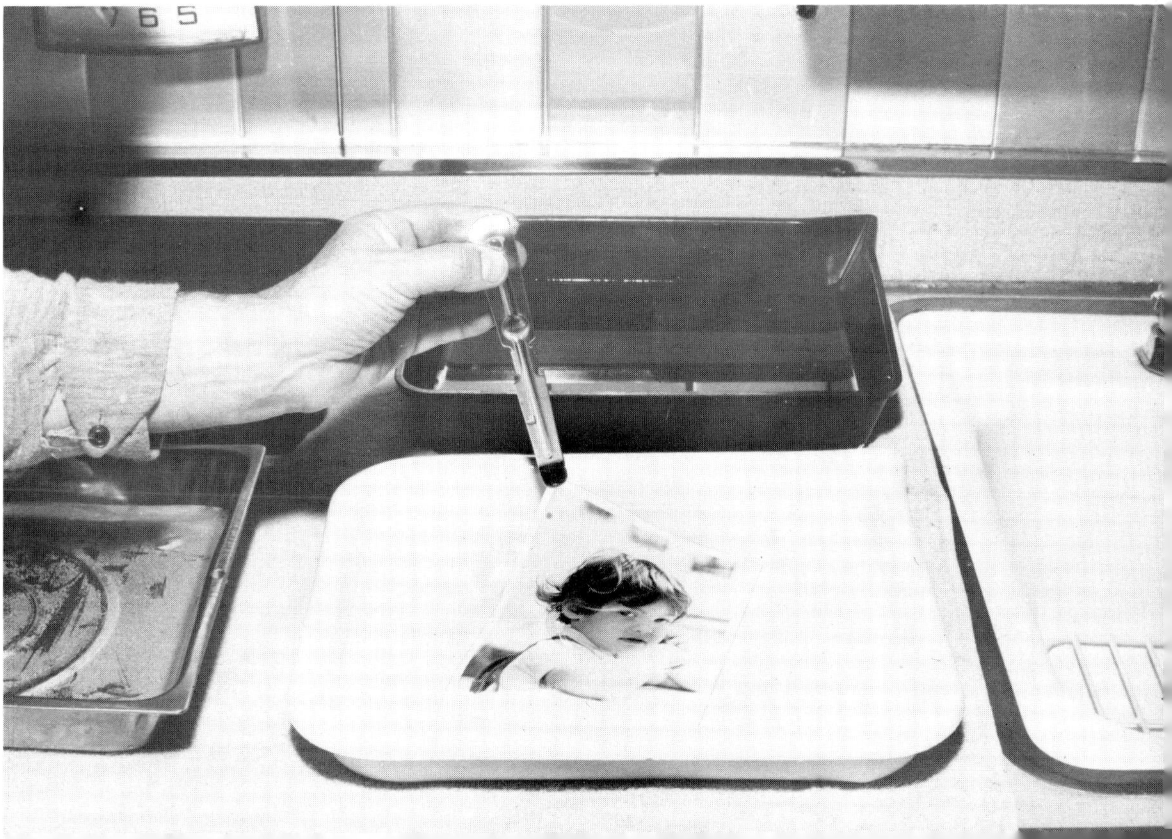

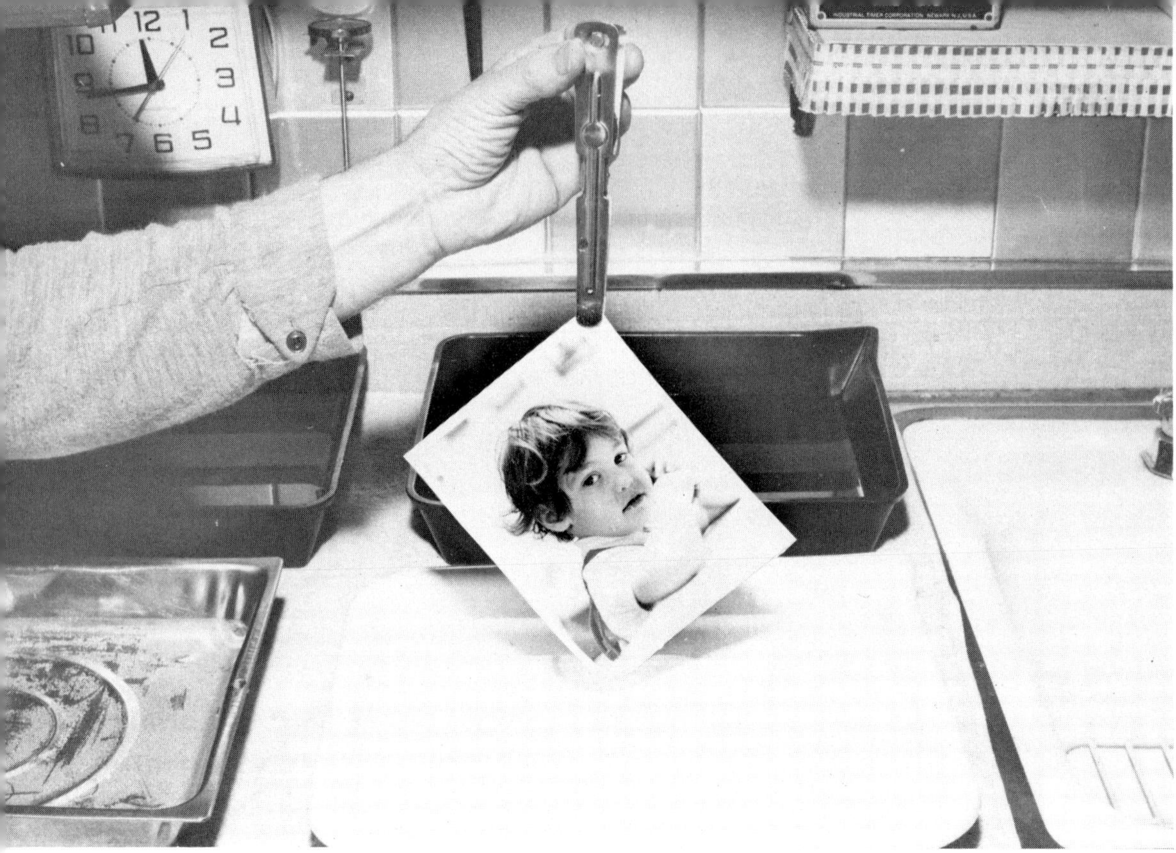

Fig. 4-43. Again using the tongs to keep your fingers from getting wet, drain the print well over the short-stop tray.

Fig. 4-44. Avoiding the developer tray on the way, drop the print into the fixer bath, where it must remain between 10 and 15 minutes. Rinse the tongs.

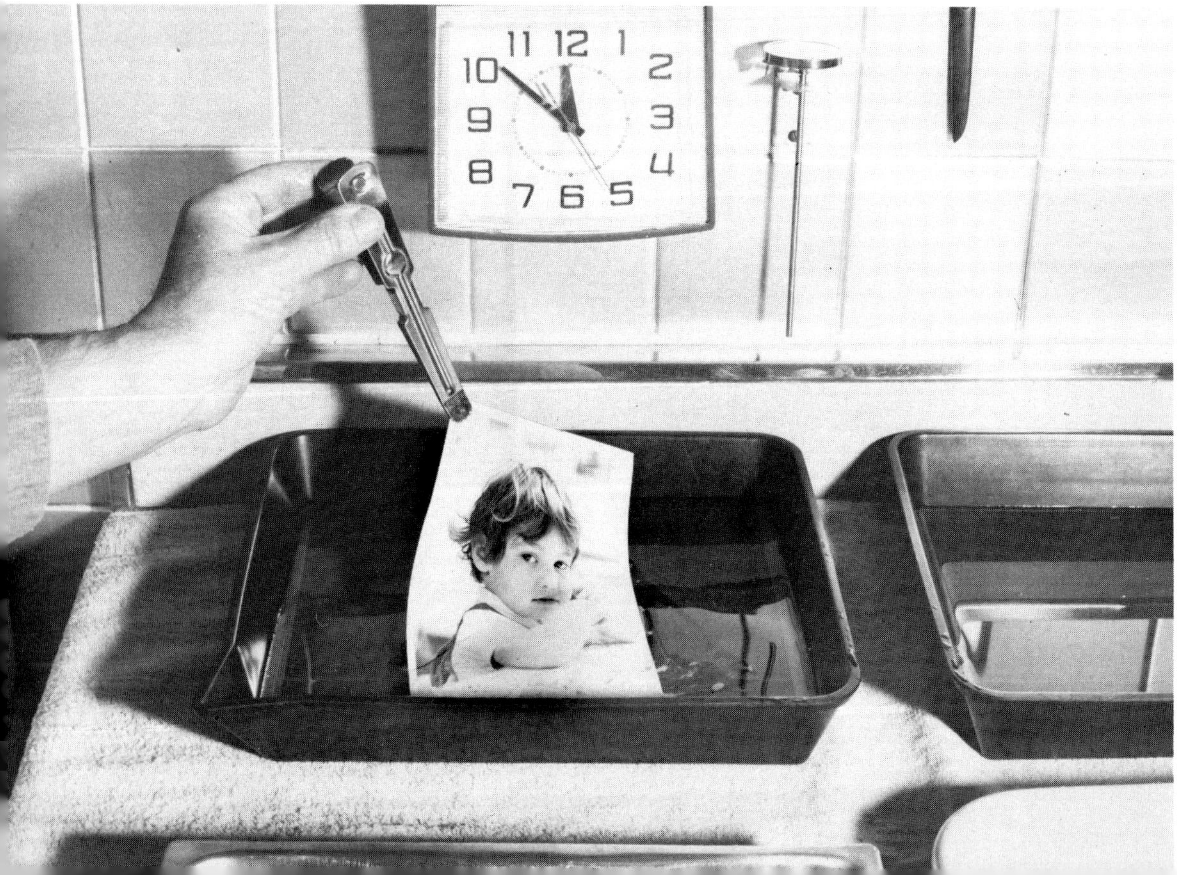

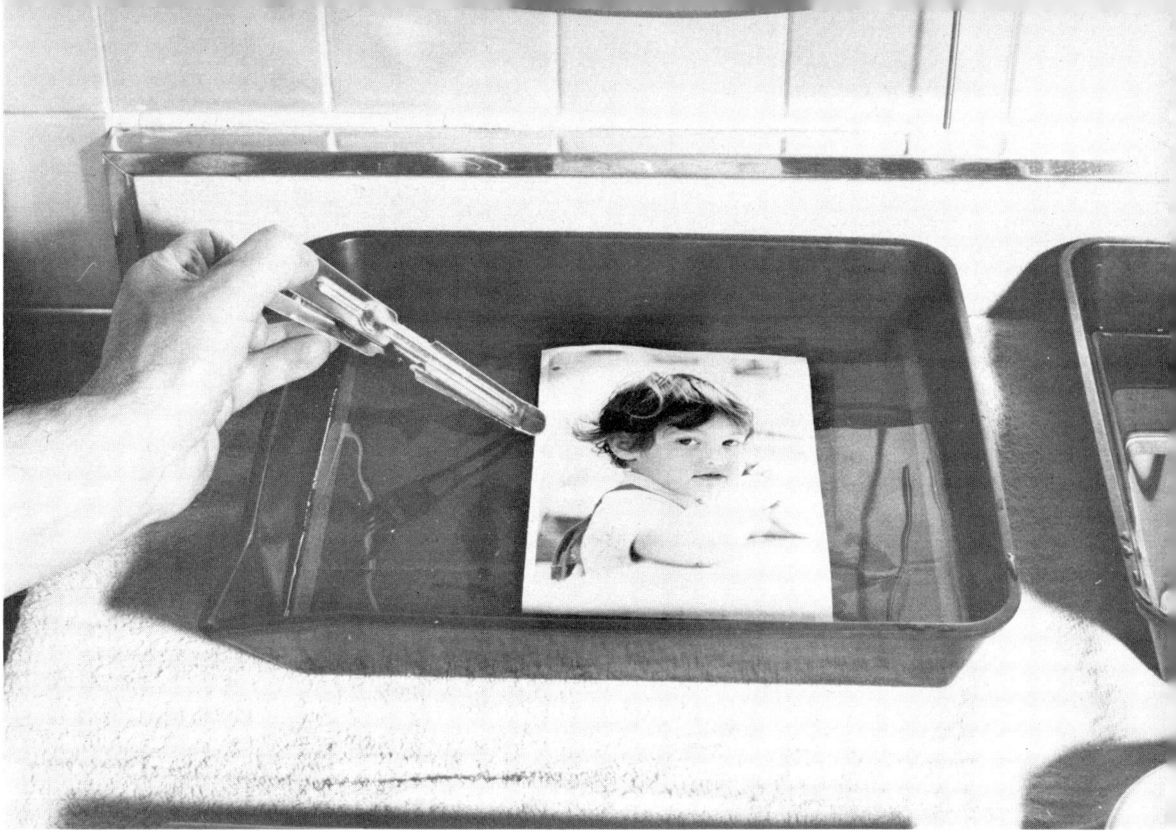

Fig. 4-45. To insure thorough fixing, move prints in the fixer every couple of minutes. Rinse the tongs.

Fig. 4-46. What's going on here? Is that milk being poured into the black print washing tray? Yes, but only to test how fast the flowing water is clearing the tray. The water faucet (all cold) should be turned up high enough to clear the tray in about five minutes; it will then be just right for washing prints. If you have a light-colored plastic tray, use a few drops of ink to check the effectiveness of the washing attachment.

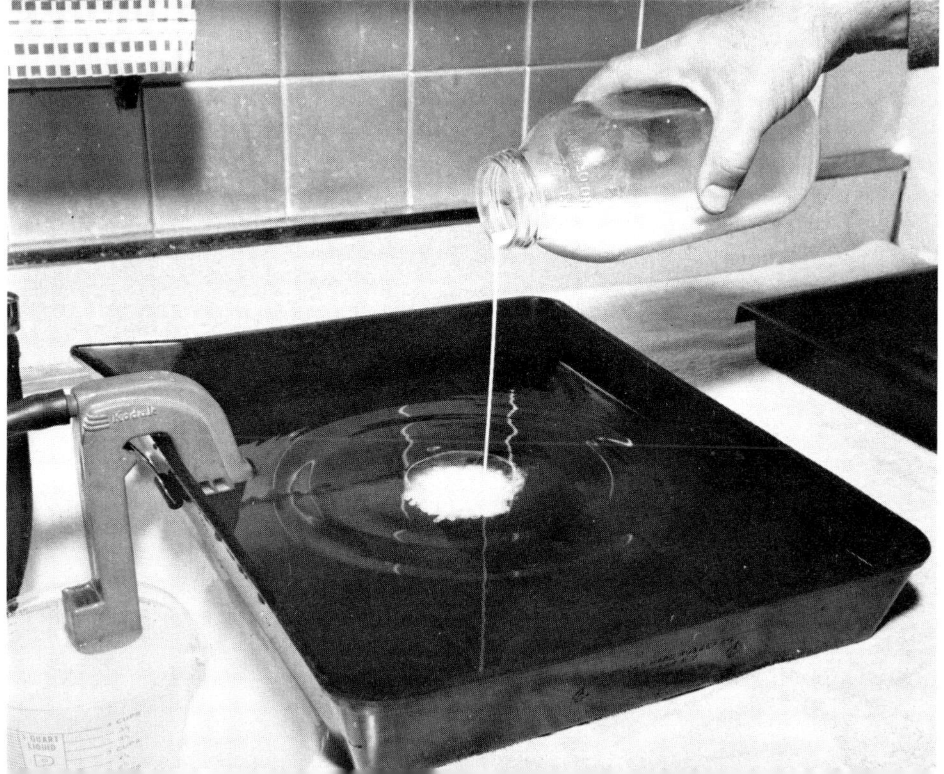

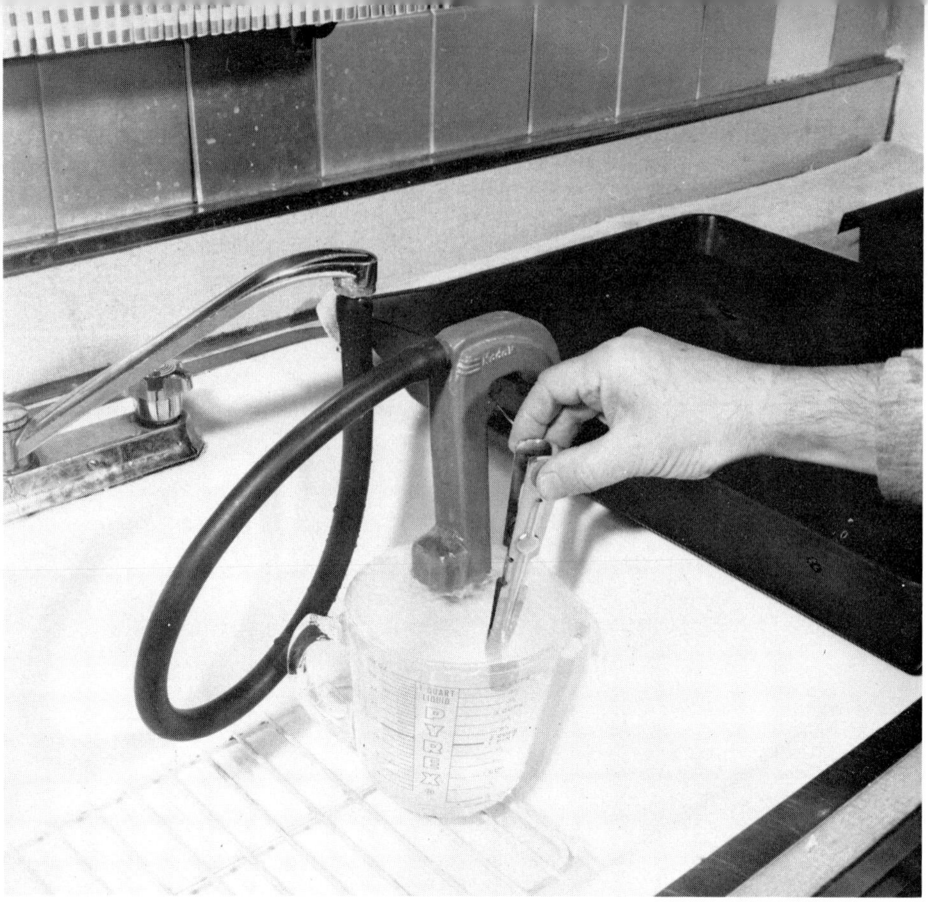

Fig. 4-47. A good habit to develop in the darkroom: keep the print tongs clean.

Fig. 4-48. After its prescribed time in the fixer, remove the print with tongs and let it drain well.

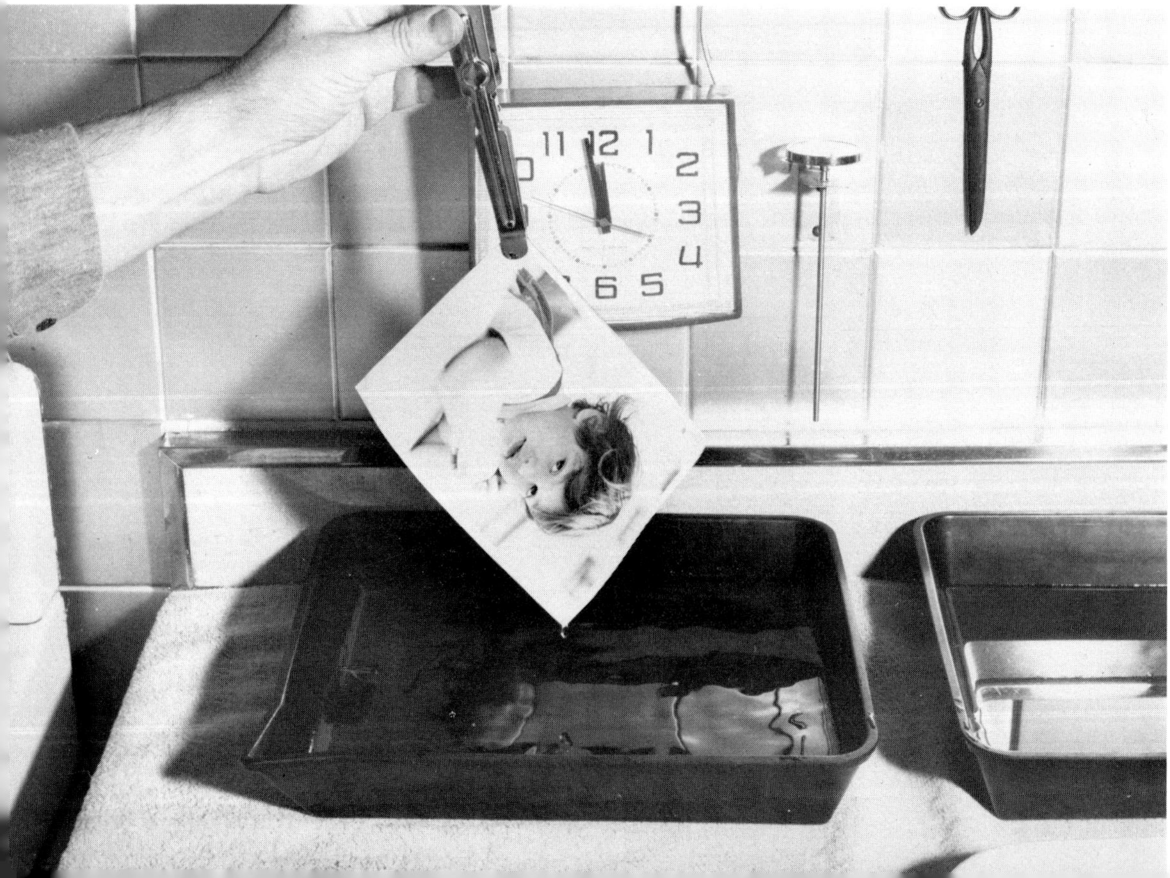

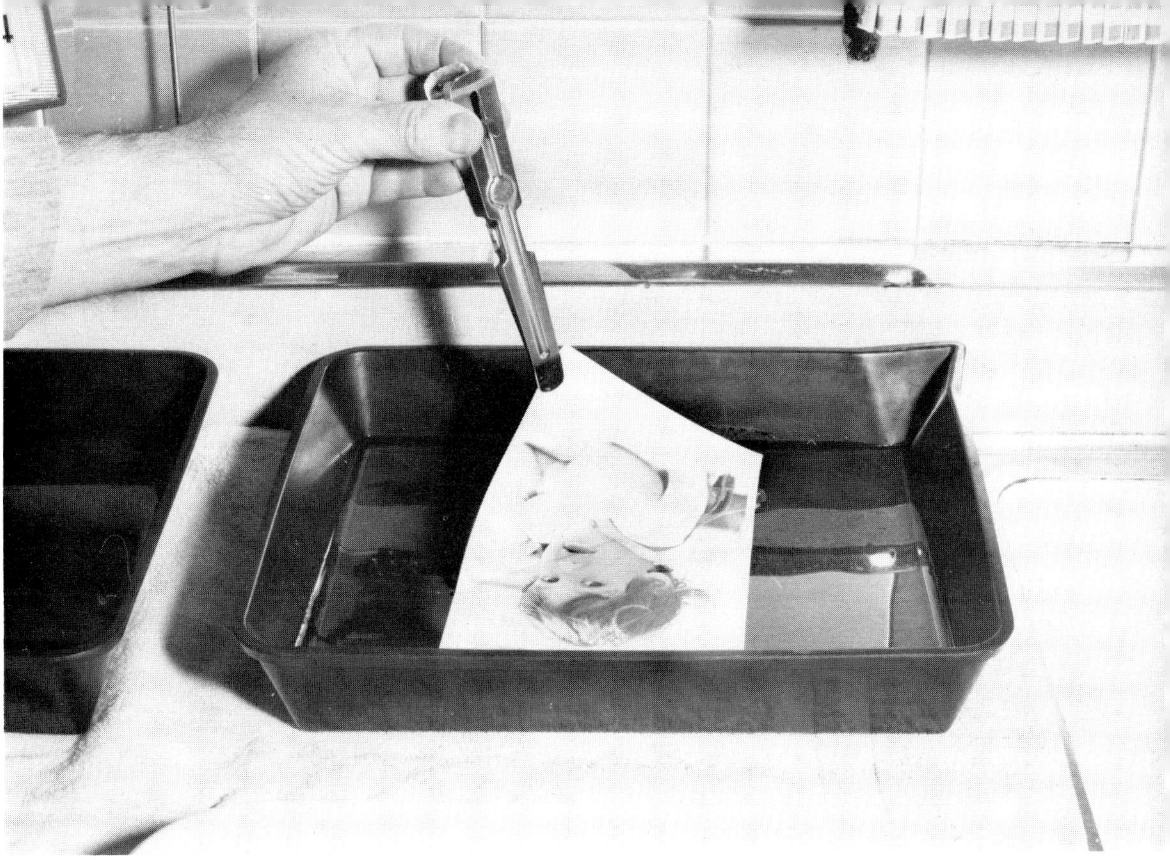

Fig. 4-49. Drop it into the fixer-neutralizer bath, where it will remain for about five minutes.

Fig. 4-50. Remove the print from the fixer-neutralizer and place it into the washer. Five minutes in the gurgling water is usually enough to remove any remains of fixer and neutralizer.

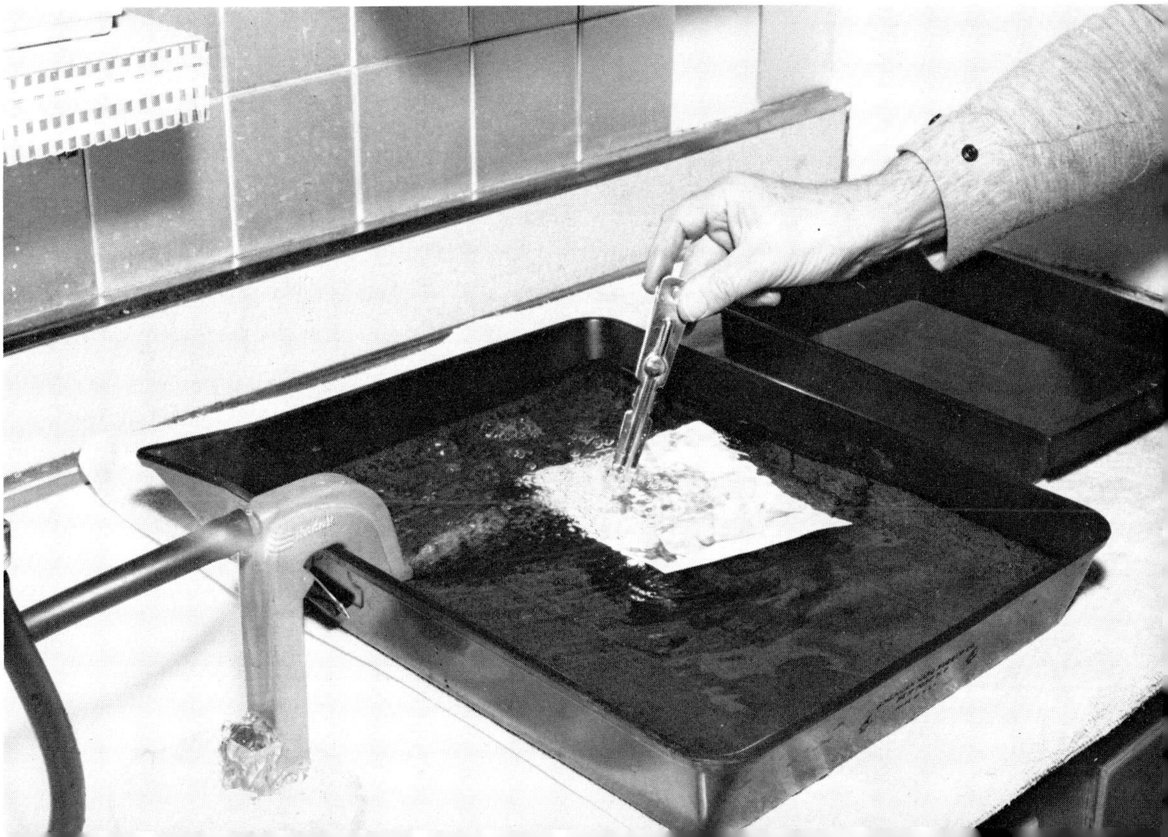

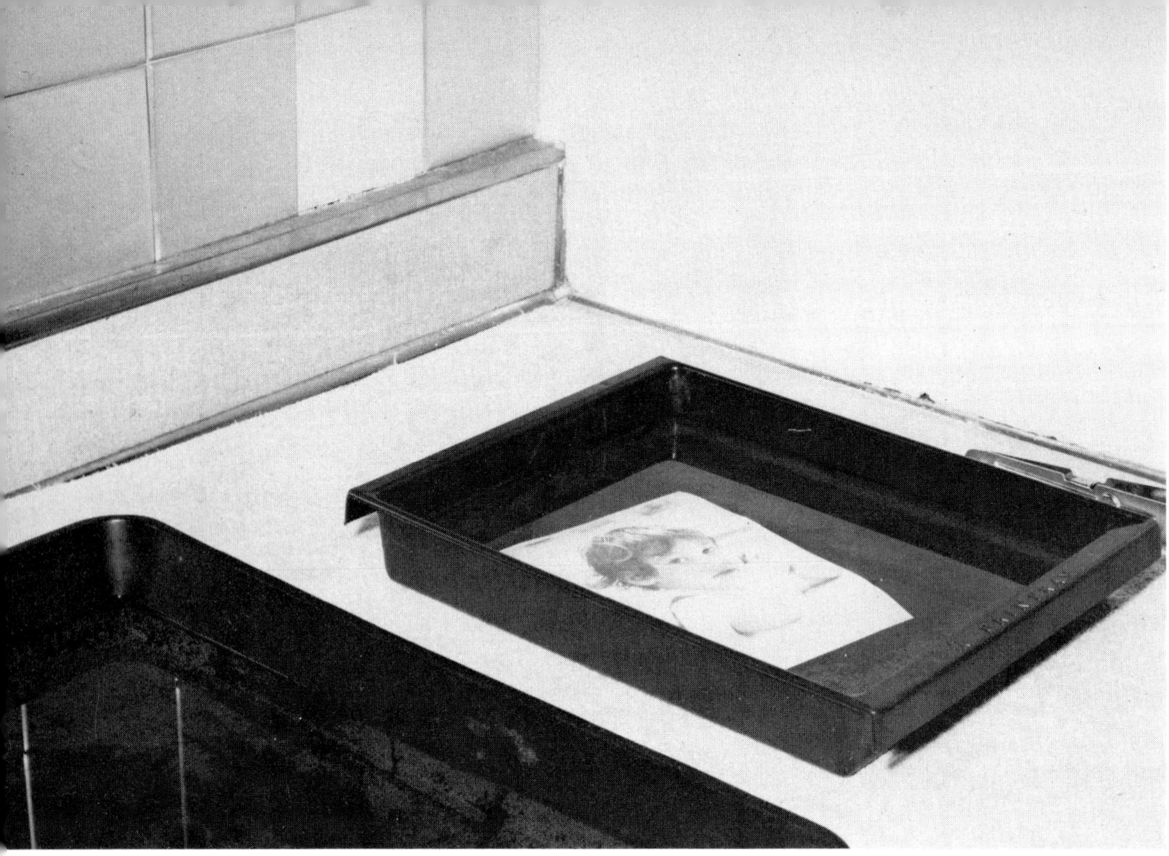

Fig. 4-51. From the washer the print goes to the print-flattener, to soak for another five-minute spell.

Fig. 4-52. While the print is in its last tray, prepare a table for the drying step by covering it with newspapers. These are intended to soak up any excess moisture.

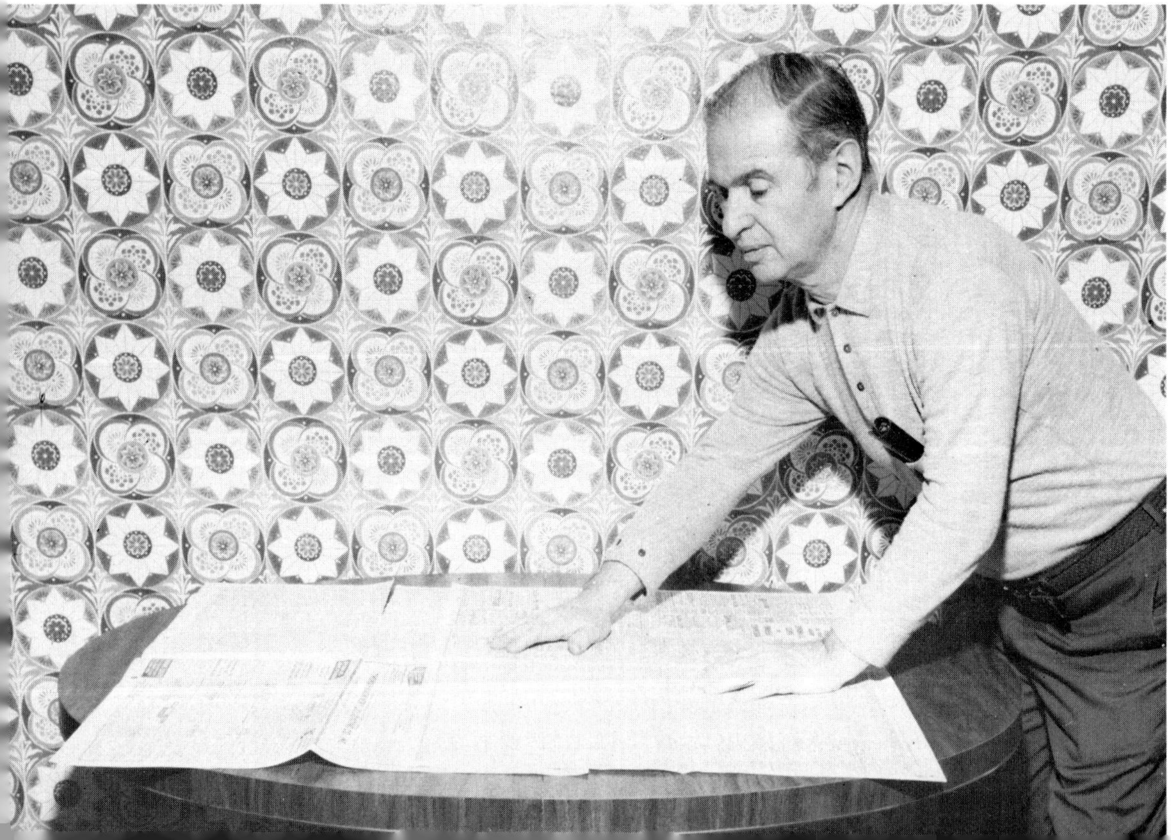

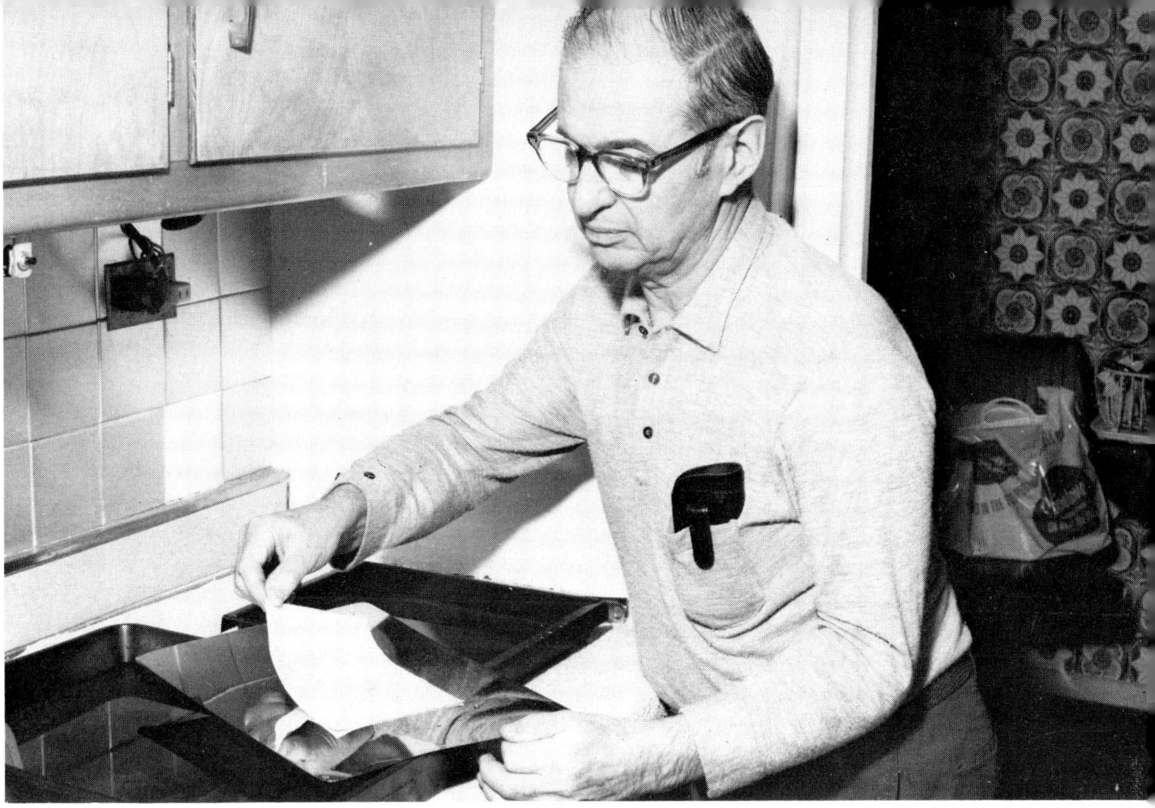

Fig. 4-53. For a high gloss finish, remove the wet print face down from the flattening solution onto a shiny ''ferrotype'' plate, which is actually made of chrome-plated steel, stainless steel or plastic. (In the early days of photography the plates were made of sheet iron; hence ''ferro'' in the name.)

Fig. 4-54. Put a photographic blotter over the print and with a print roller squeeze it into smooth contact with the polished surface. Against the wall is a 12'' × 17'' ''ferrotype'' plate. This is a convenient size, as it takes two 8'' × 10'' prints or four 5'' × 7'' prints.

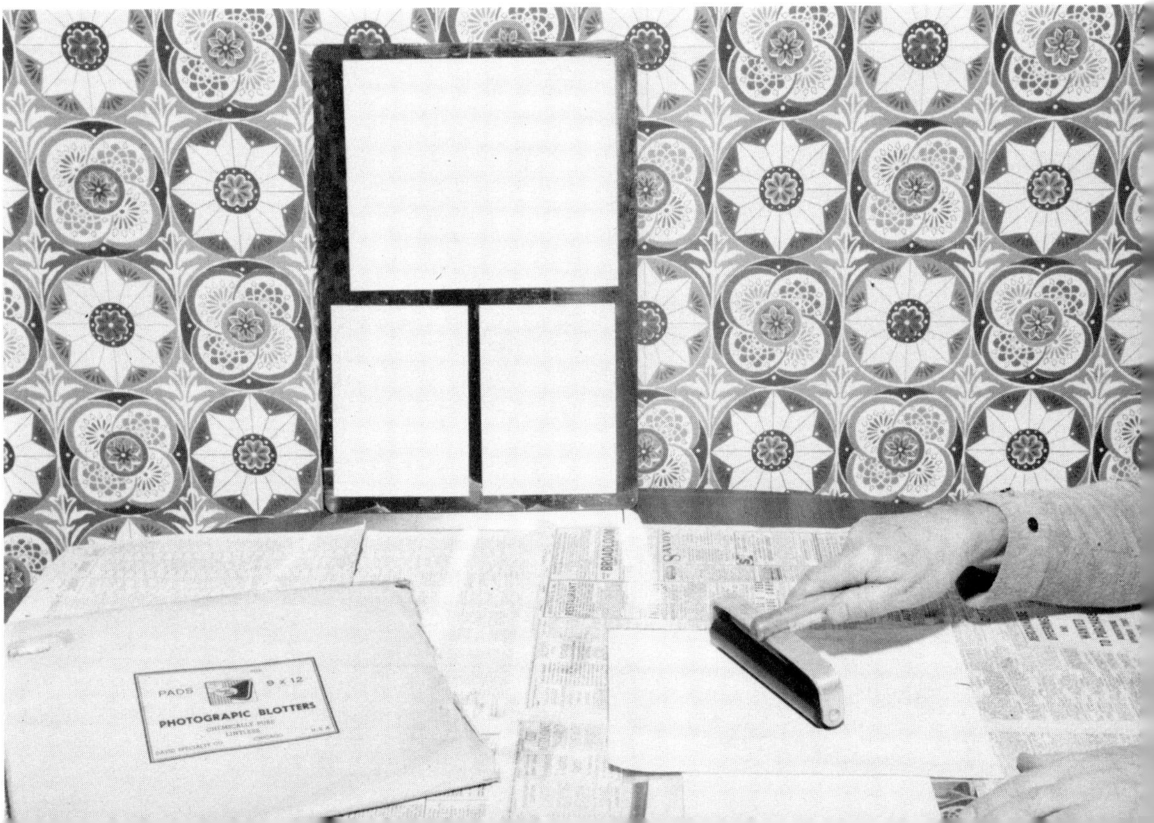

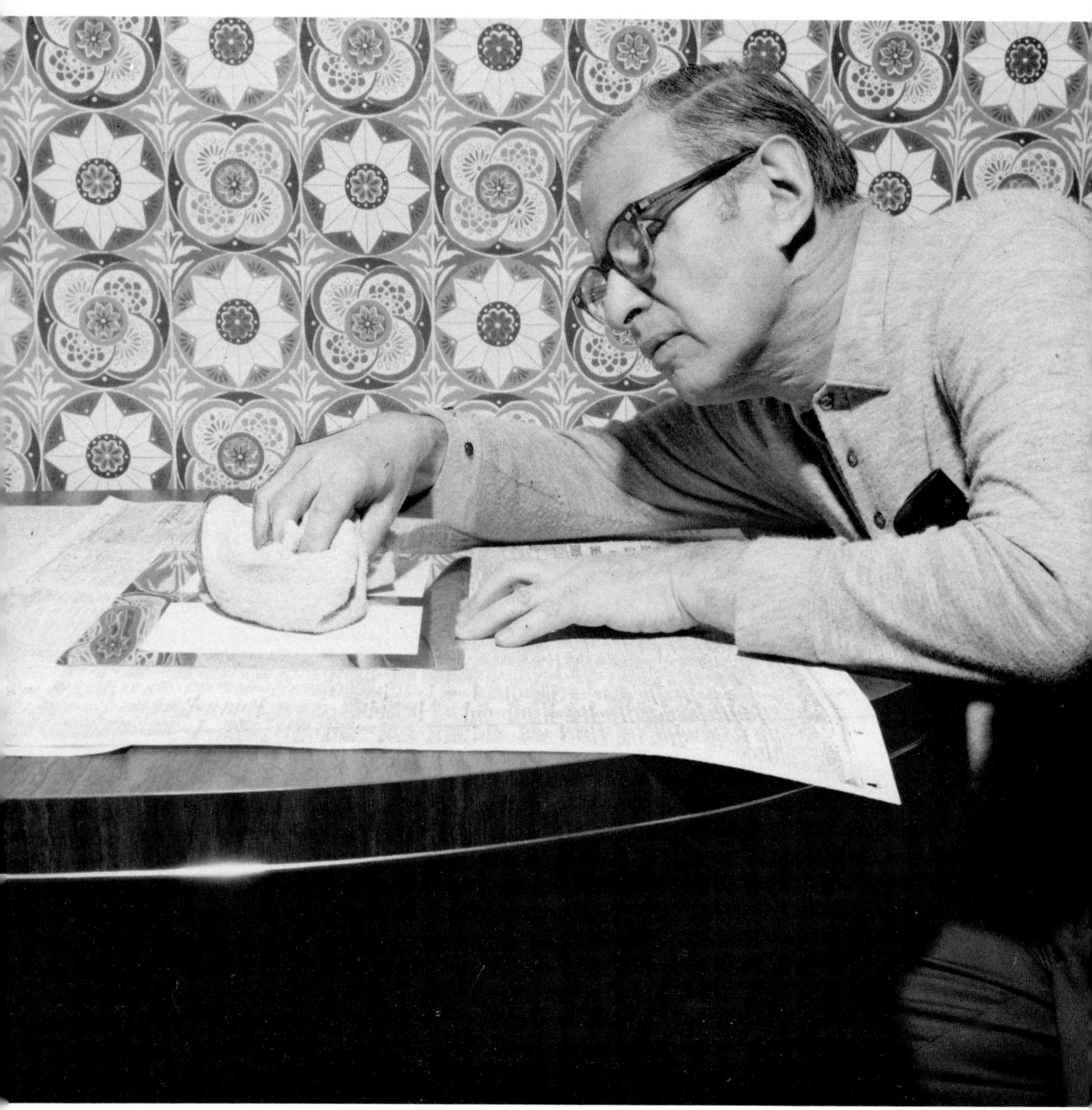

Fig. 4-55. Squint along the surface and look for possible air bubbles. Smooth them out gently with a wadded towel.

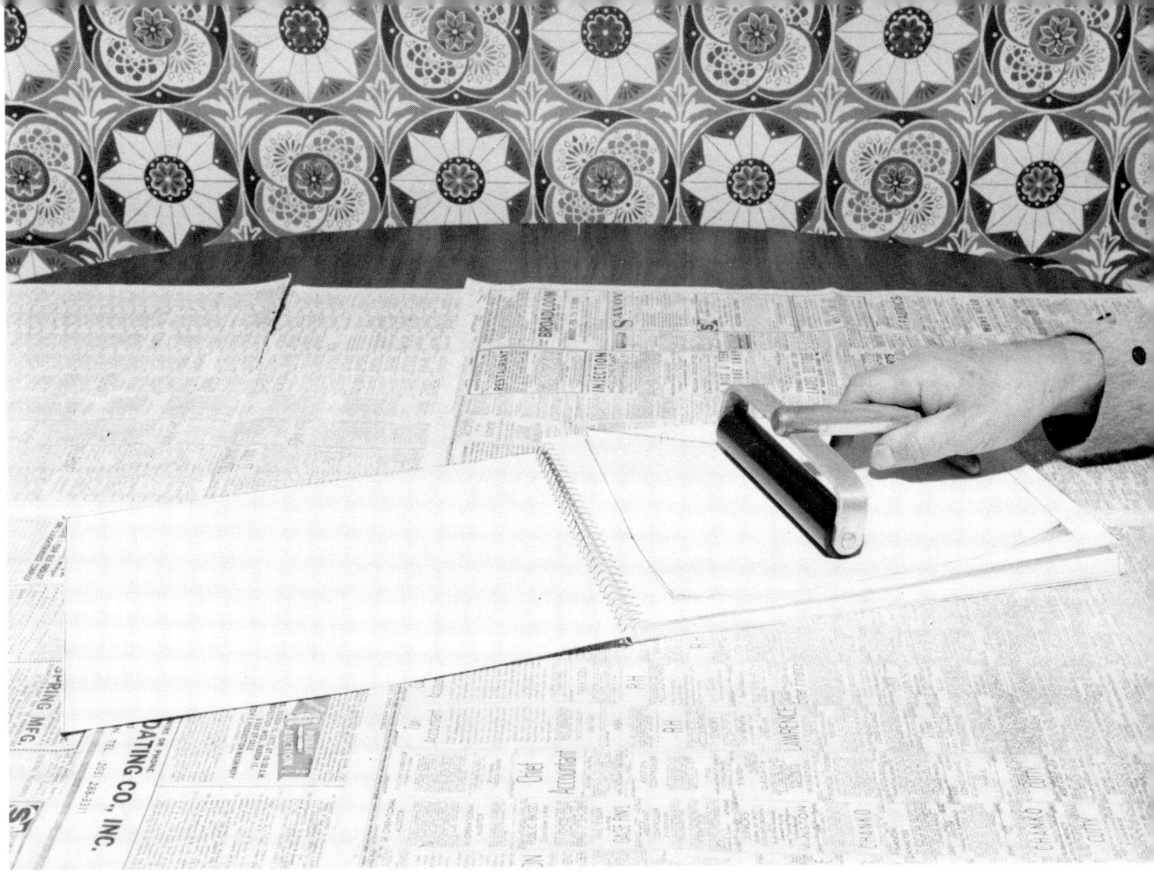

Figs. 4-56a and b. For prints of semi-matte finish, use a blotter book. This has the blotters interleaved with sheets of waxed paper, all in a spiral binding. First roll out the wet print face down on a blotter, turn to a dry page, and place the print face up against a waxed sheet.

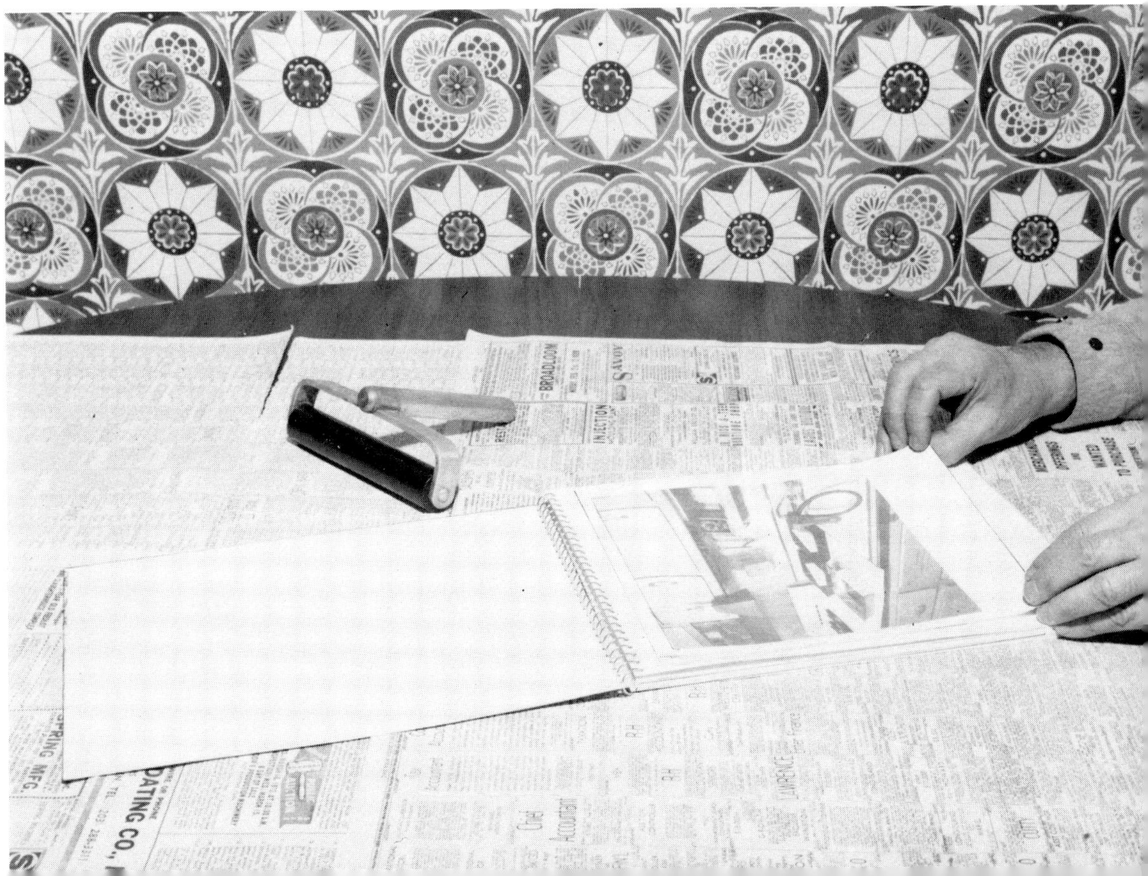

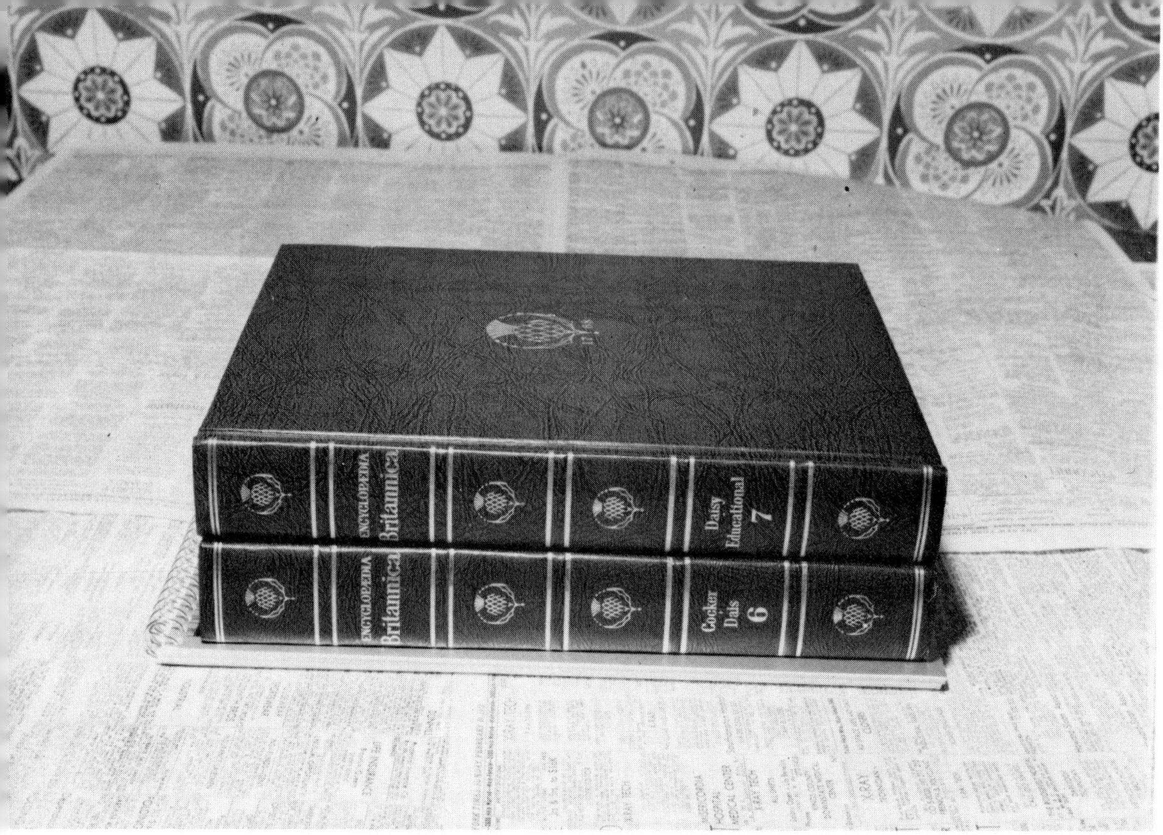

Fig. 4-57. Weight the blotter book down with a couple of heavy books and let it sit overnight to dry.

Fig. 4-58. Print developer can't be saved, but all the other solutions can be poured back into their bottles for further use. Rinse all vessels and put them away to dry.

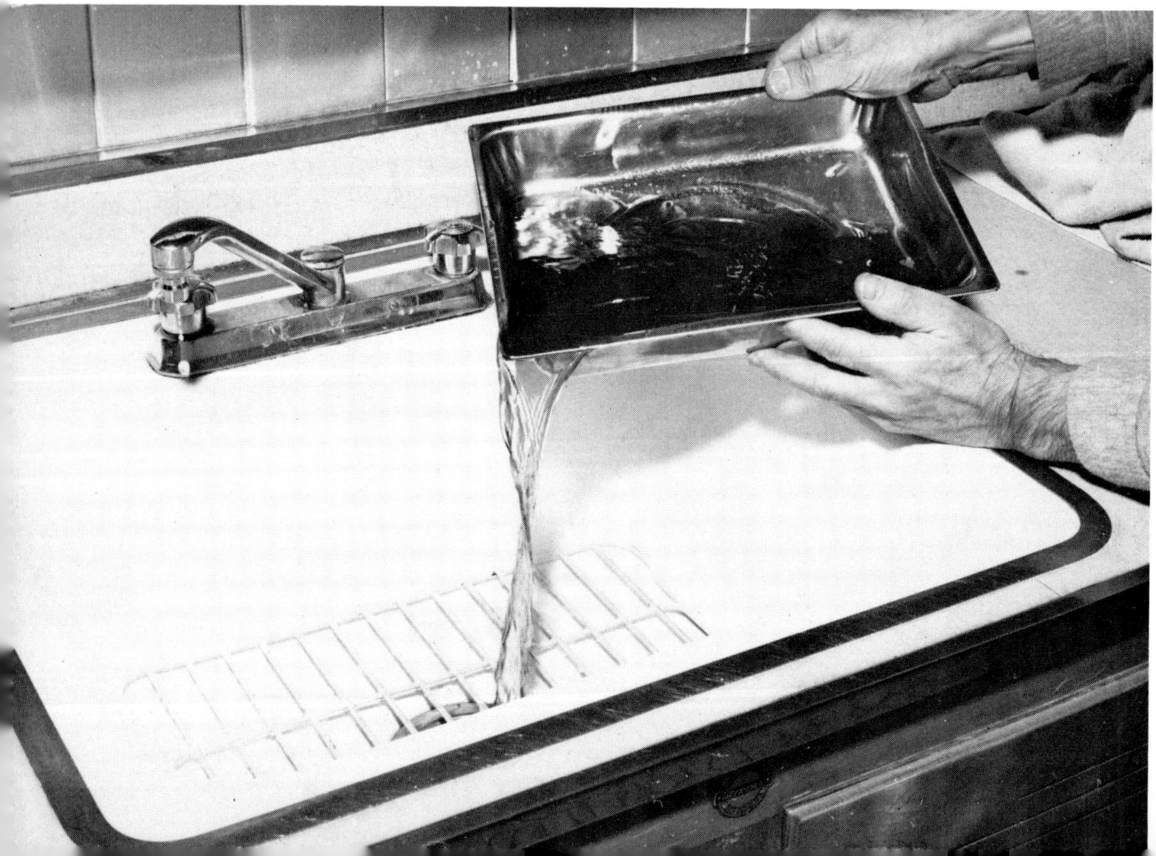

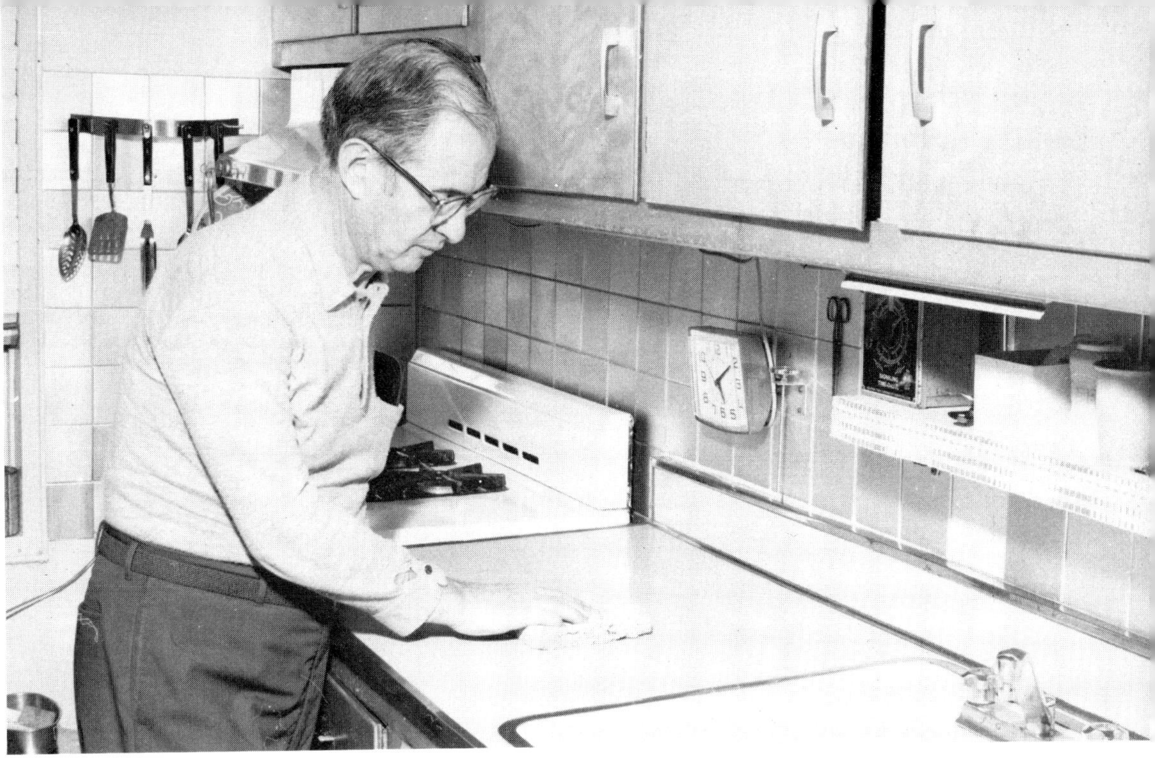

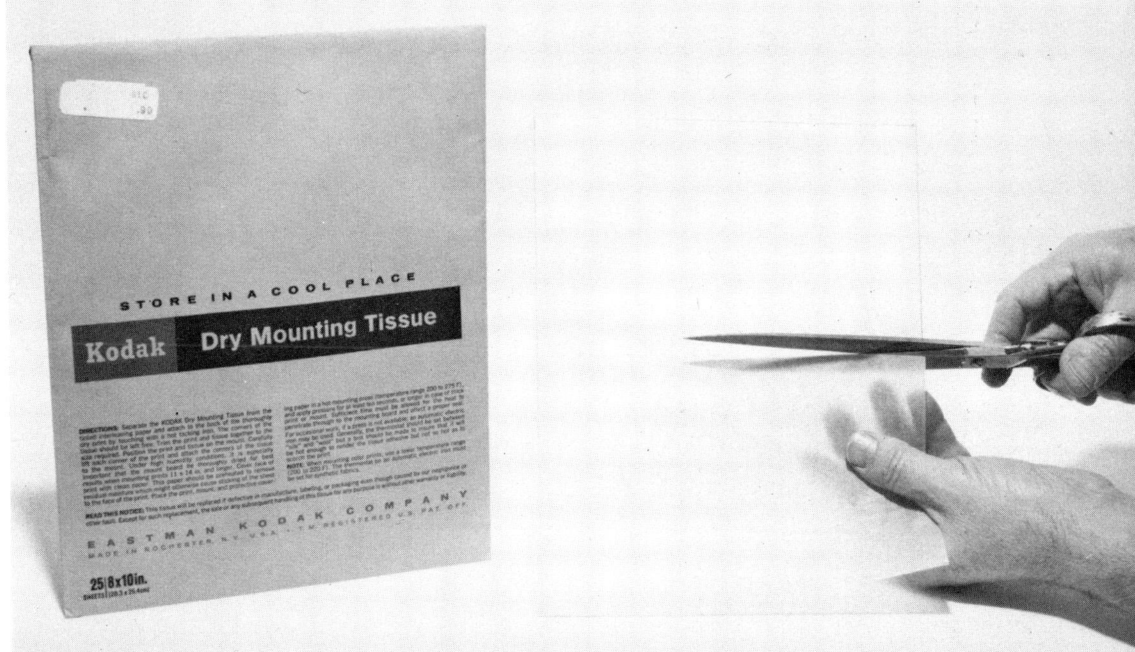

Fig. 4-59. The towels that were spread on the drainboards will soak up spillovers from the trays, but the surface should be rinsed off anyway as the last operation of the evening. Otherwise, a few white spots will show in the morning. Fortunately, all the processing chemicals dissolve readily in plain water.

Fig. 4-60. After you've had a little experience with enlarging, you might well decide that some prints are worth framing or at least mounting. Mounting is worthwhile, because it is protection for the pictures and by itself it is a form of framing. **Do not use rubber cement or common glues;** they will attack the print and cause it to fade. By far the best adhesive is "dry mounting tissue," a flexible, translucent, thermo-setting plastic that can be processed with an ordinary pressing iron. Experiment first with a small spare print. To start, cut a piece of tissue slightly larger than the picture.

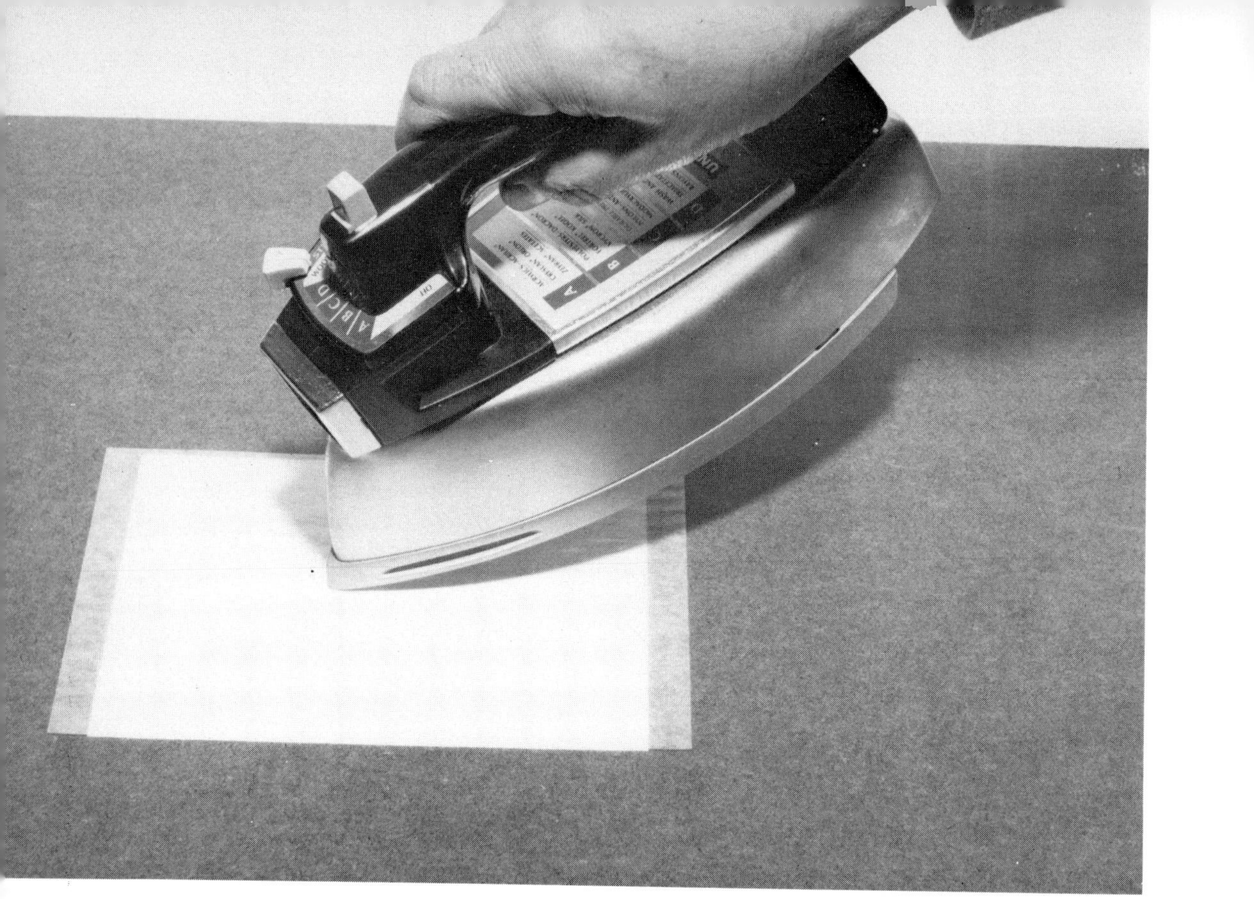

Fig. 4-61. With the iron set for low heat, "tack" the tissue to the back of the print in several places with a light touch of the tip of iron.

Fig. 4-62. Turn the print over and trim it and the tissue on all four edges.

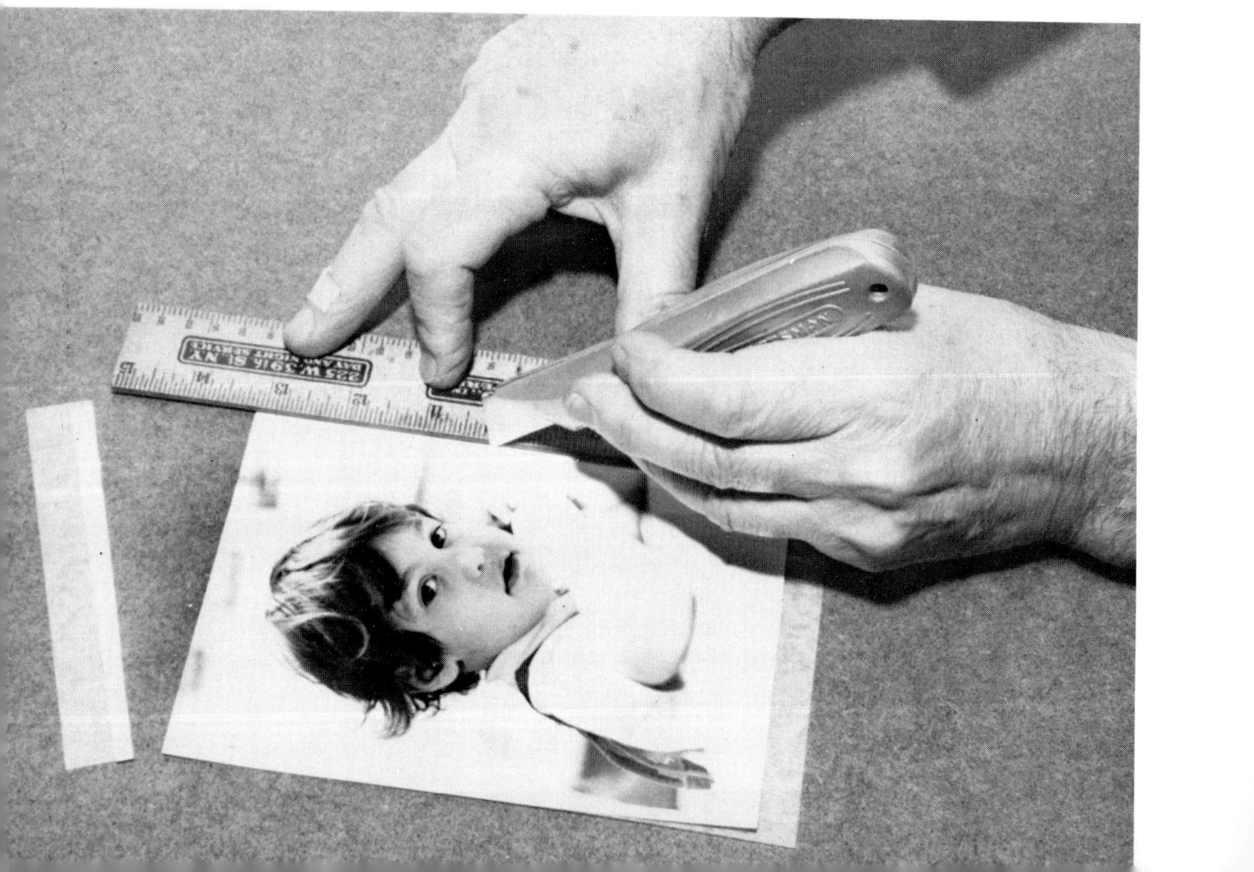

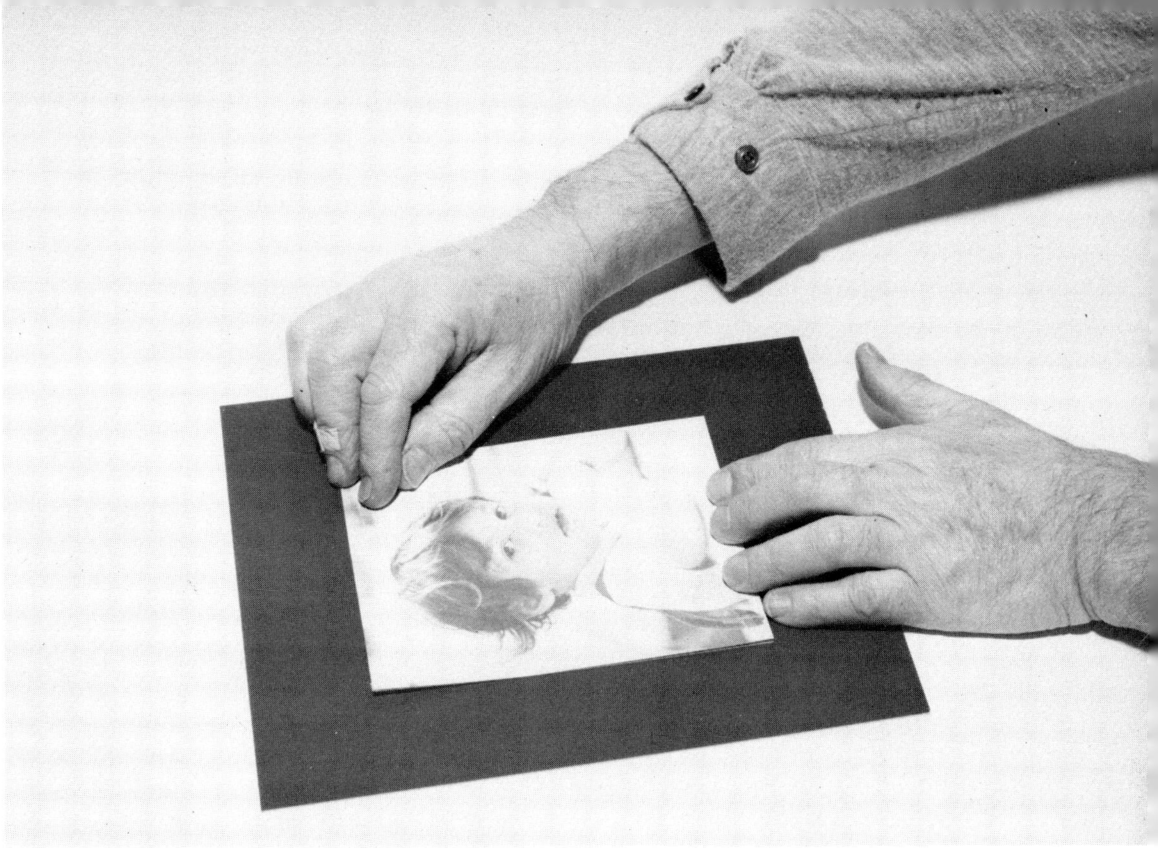

Fig. 4-63. Standard mounting boards have one white and one black side. Position the print as you like it.

Fig. 4-64. Holding the print down with one hand, lift the edges slightly and tack the tissue to the board in a couple places. This will keep the print in place.

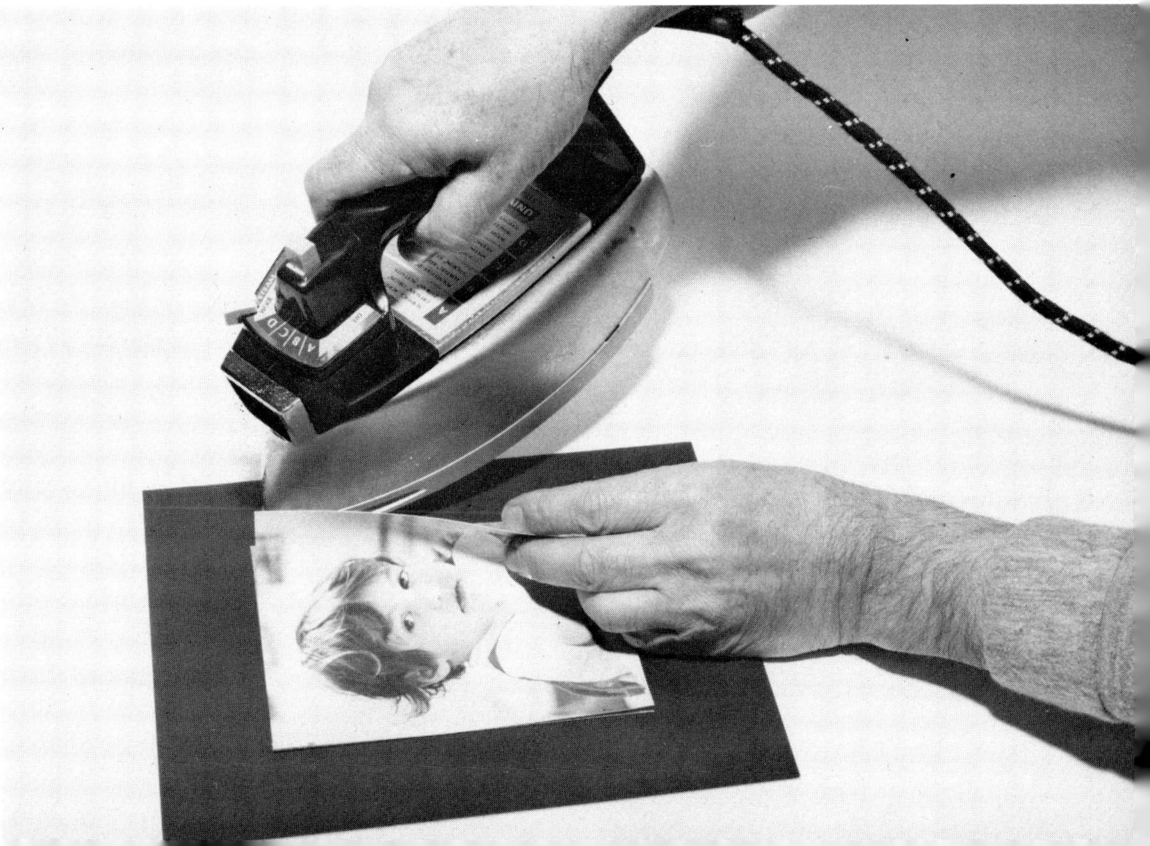

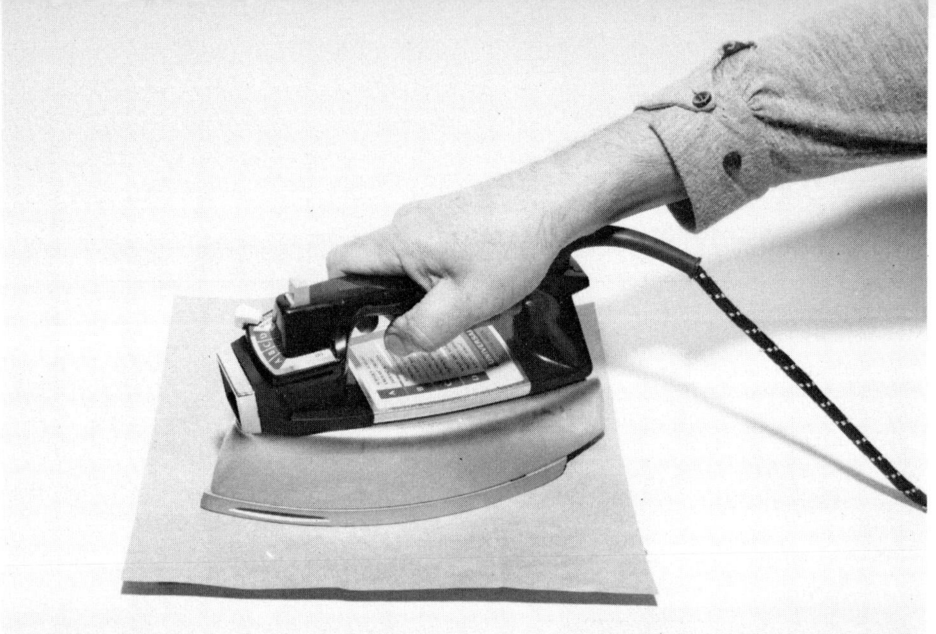

Fig. 4-65. Cut a clean piece out of a grocery bag or heavy wrapping paper, place it over the print, and start ironing. Press down only lightly. It's the heat that does the trick. The weight of the iron is needed only to keep the print flat until the tissue binds. Lift the iron frequently and examine the print closely for adhesion. Of course, excessive heat will scorch any paper, but this is not likely to occur if you are careful.

Fig. 4-66. A mounted picture often takes on a new appearance, and a small one looks bigger than it really is. Witness this 5'' × 7'' print on an 8'' × 10'' board.

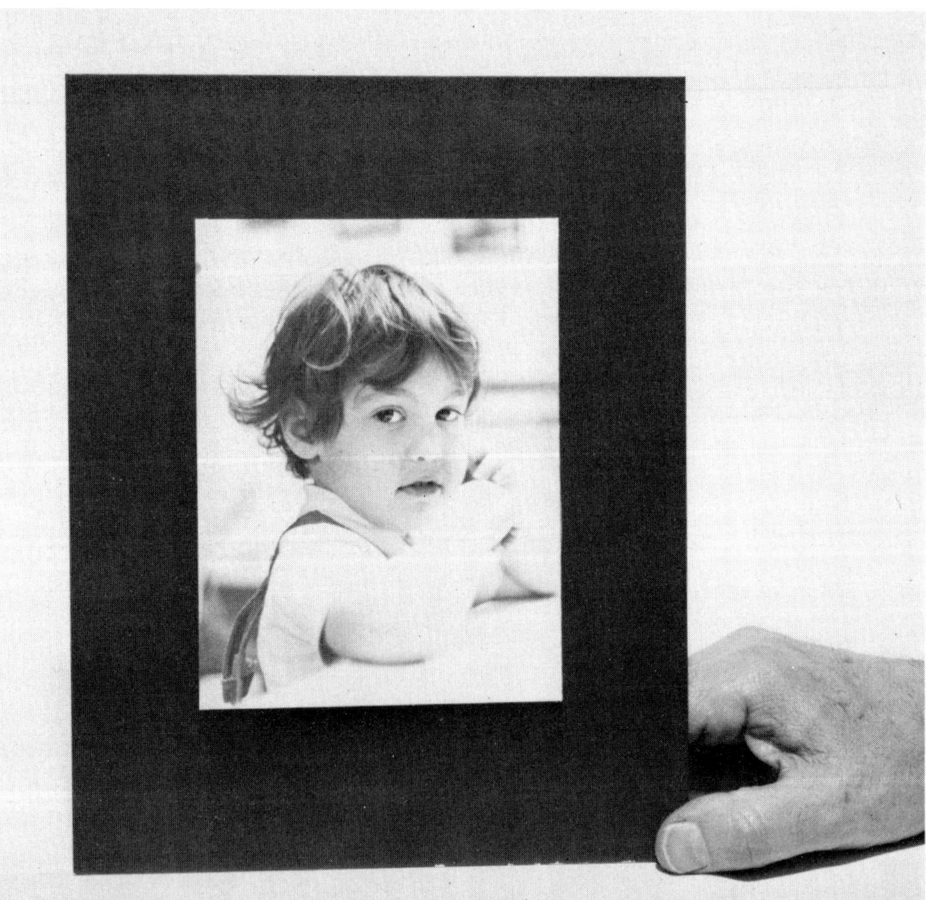

5
COLOR PROCESSING

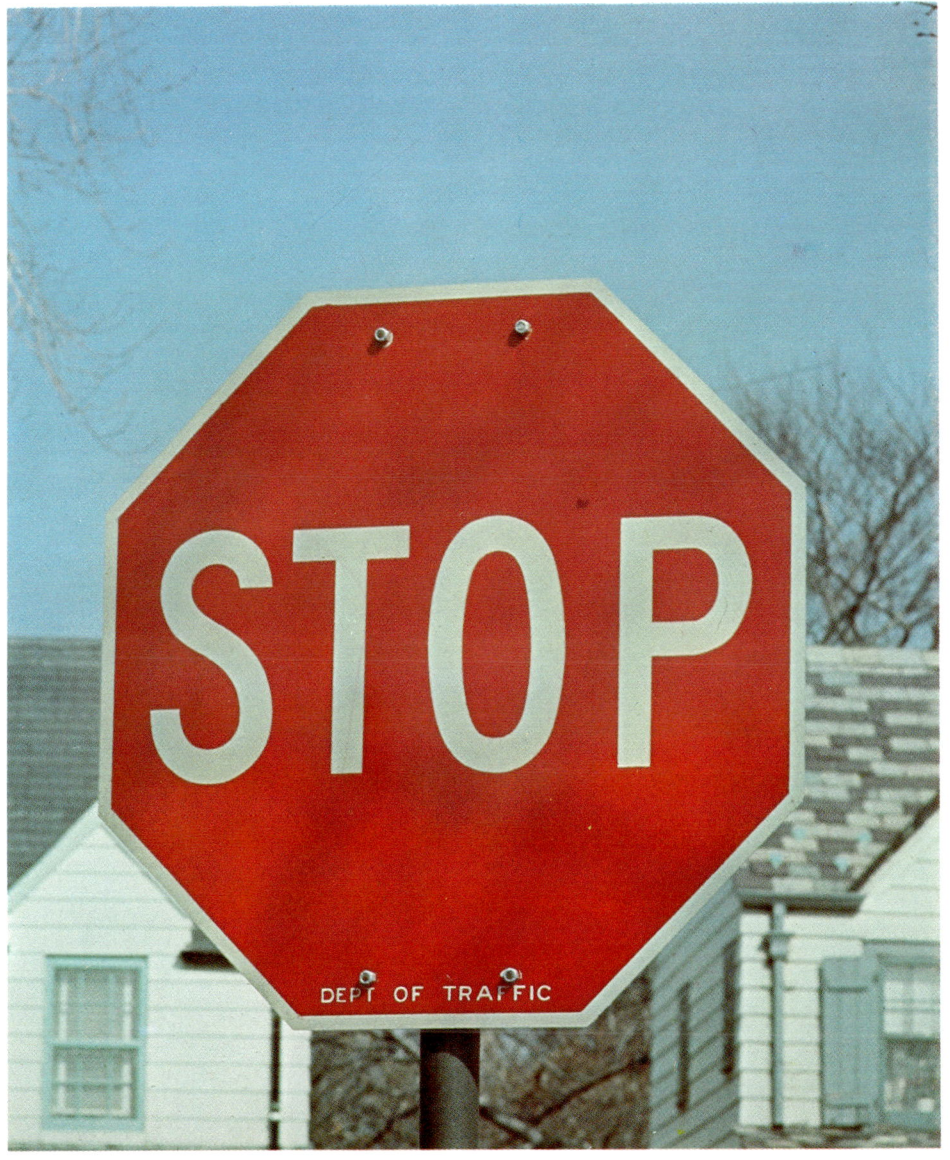

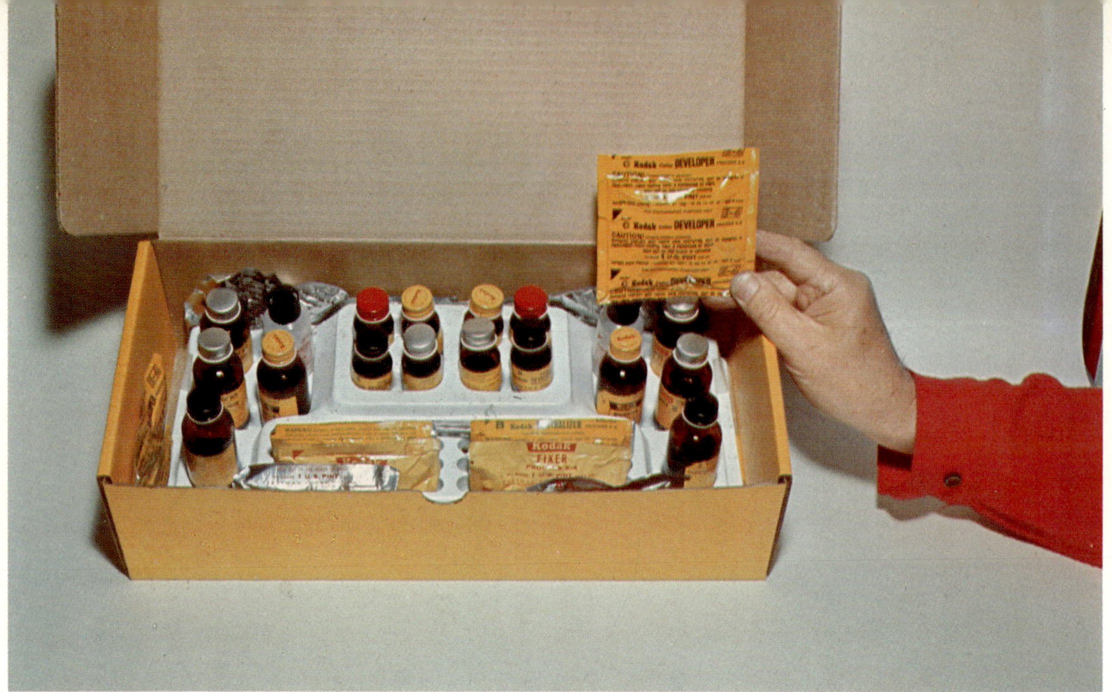

The Kodak Process E-4 color kit is actually two kits in one, with enough chemicals to make two 9-bottle sets of solutions, one pint to a bottle. The small bottles of stock solutions are held in a plastic mold, while the dry powders are in loose foil packets. This handy kit will produce fine color results like these pages.
You'll be rightly pleased and proud when you hang your first home-processed color slides up to dry.

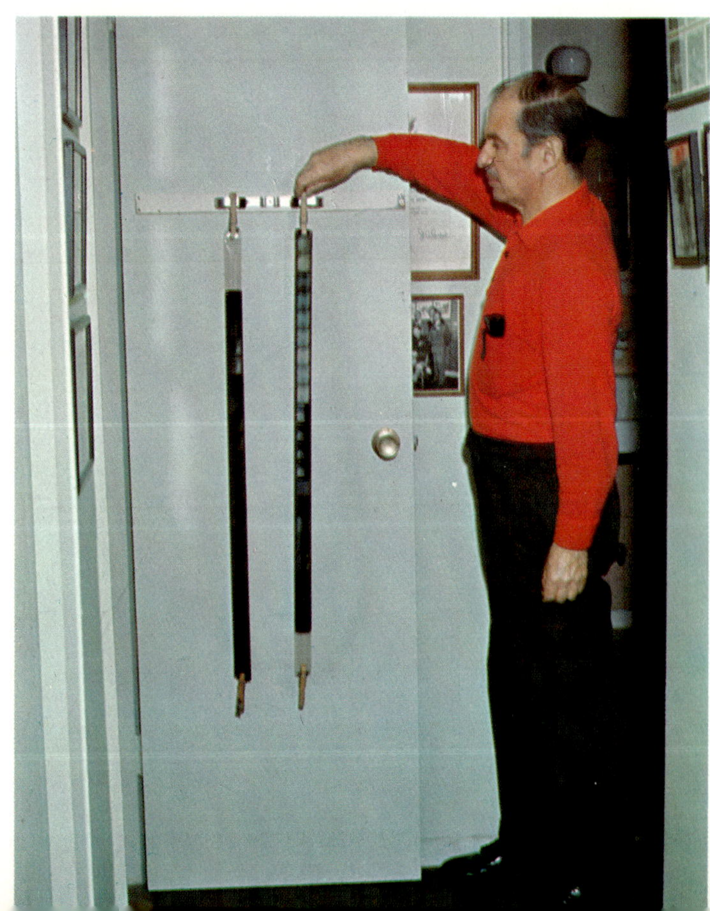

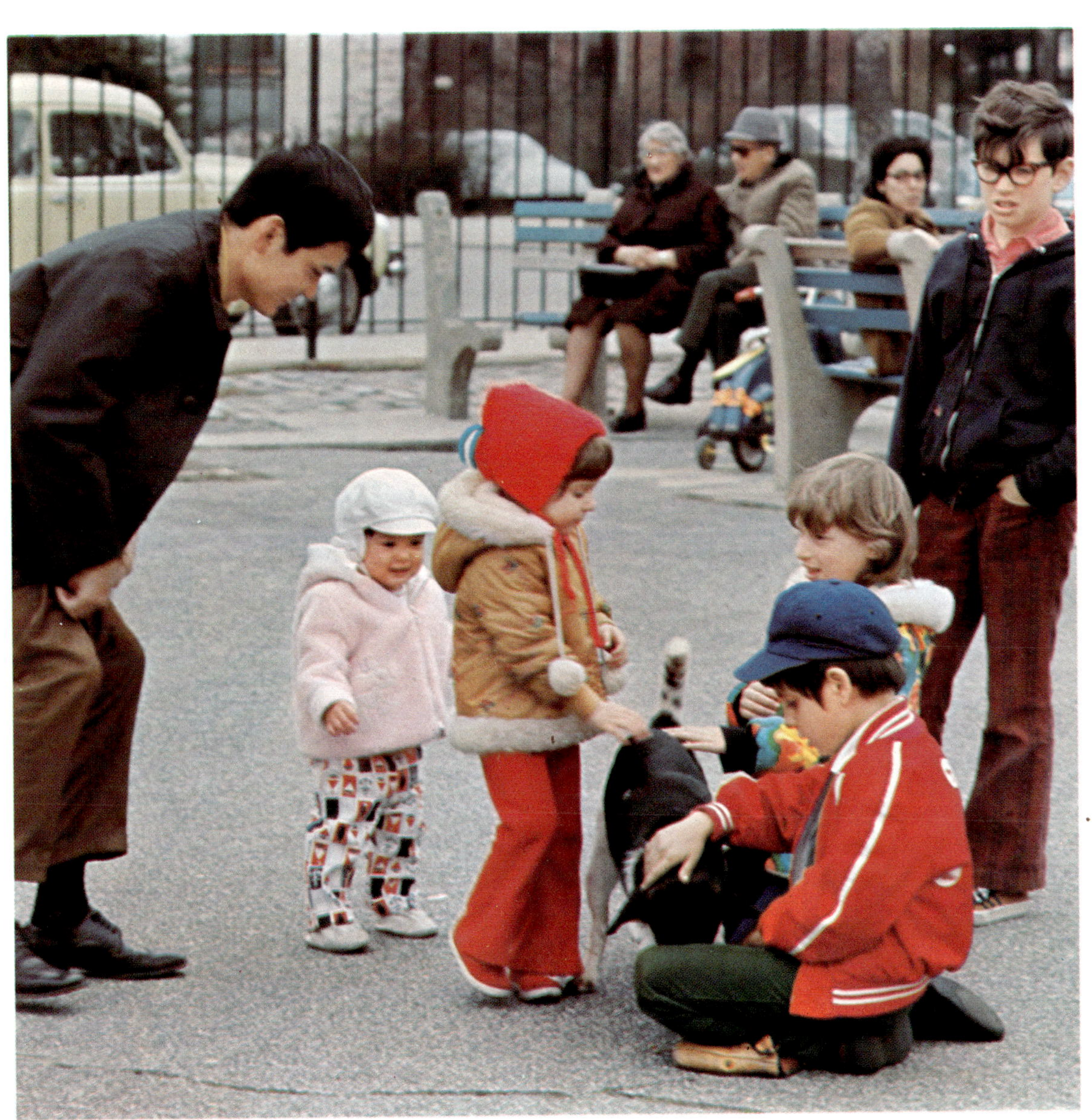

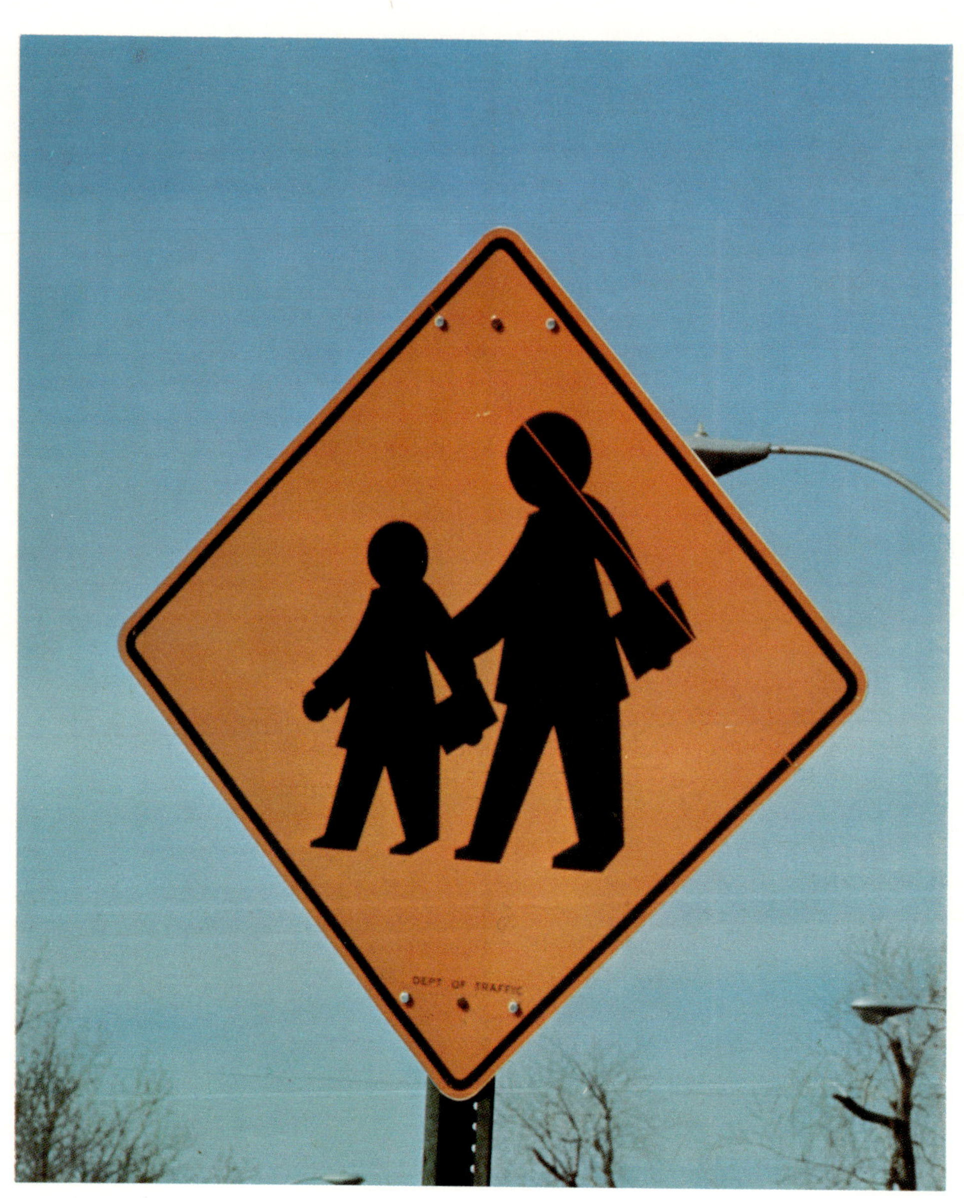

DEPT OF TRAFFIC

COLOR PROCESSING

It's easier than you thought.

A THIRTEEN STEP COLOR KIT

Do-it-yourself processing of Ektachrome-X and High Speed Ektachrome transparencies is just as practical and gratifying as conventional processing of black-and-white film. It's even more so, because in as little as 90 minutes after you have loaded the exposed color film into your regular developing tank and have poured in the first solution, you can be putting finished slides into your projector and blowing them up to full screen size in glorious color. What a thrill!

Perhaps you have shied away from slide processing because you have heard or read that temperature control of the chemicals is critical and that the solutions themselves are toxic. This is true up to a point, but don't let it discourage you. If you bought a good thermometer for your black-and-white work, as previously recommended, you will find it entirely suitable for color. If you wear a pair of household rubber gloves, your hands will be well protected against all the color chemicals. The actual processing, like that of black-and-white, consists entirely of pouring solutions into and out of bottles and the tank. It requires no technical skill of any kind; only close attention to instructions.

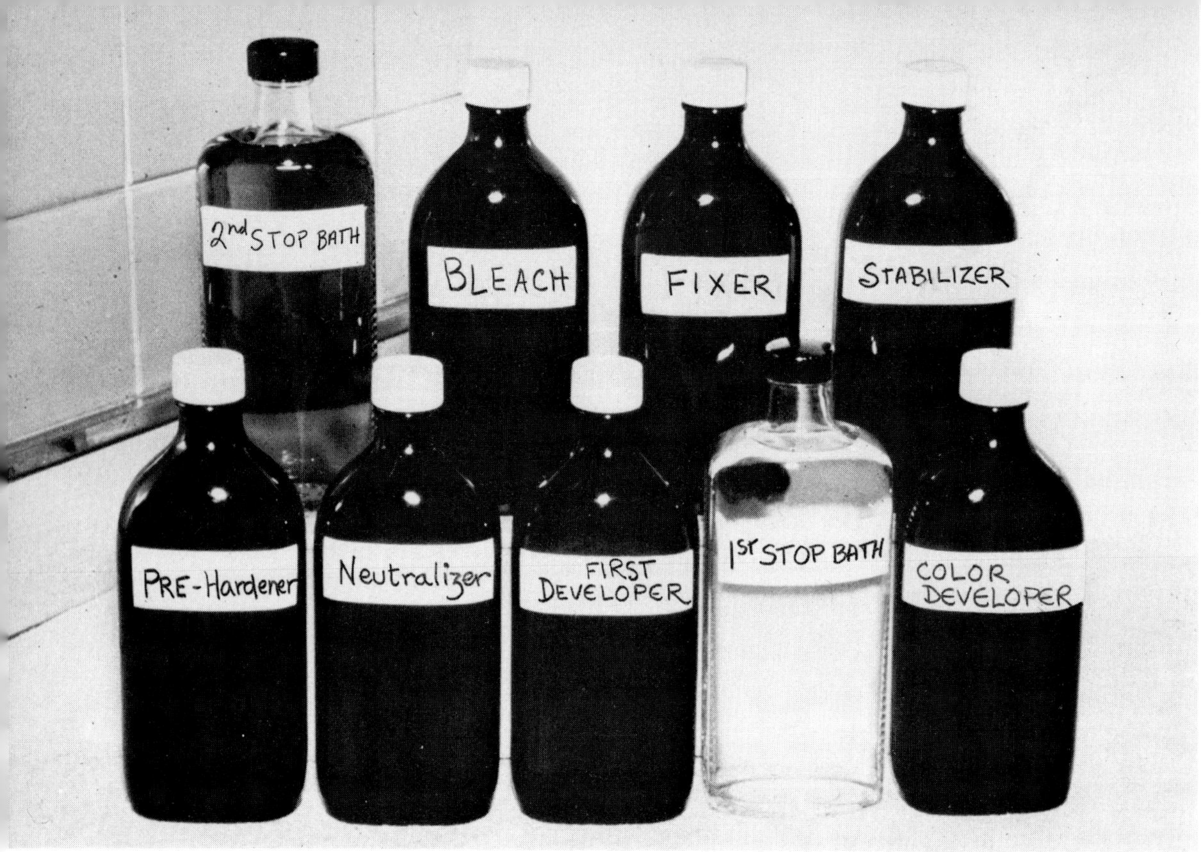

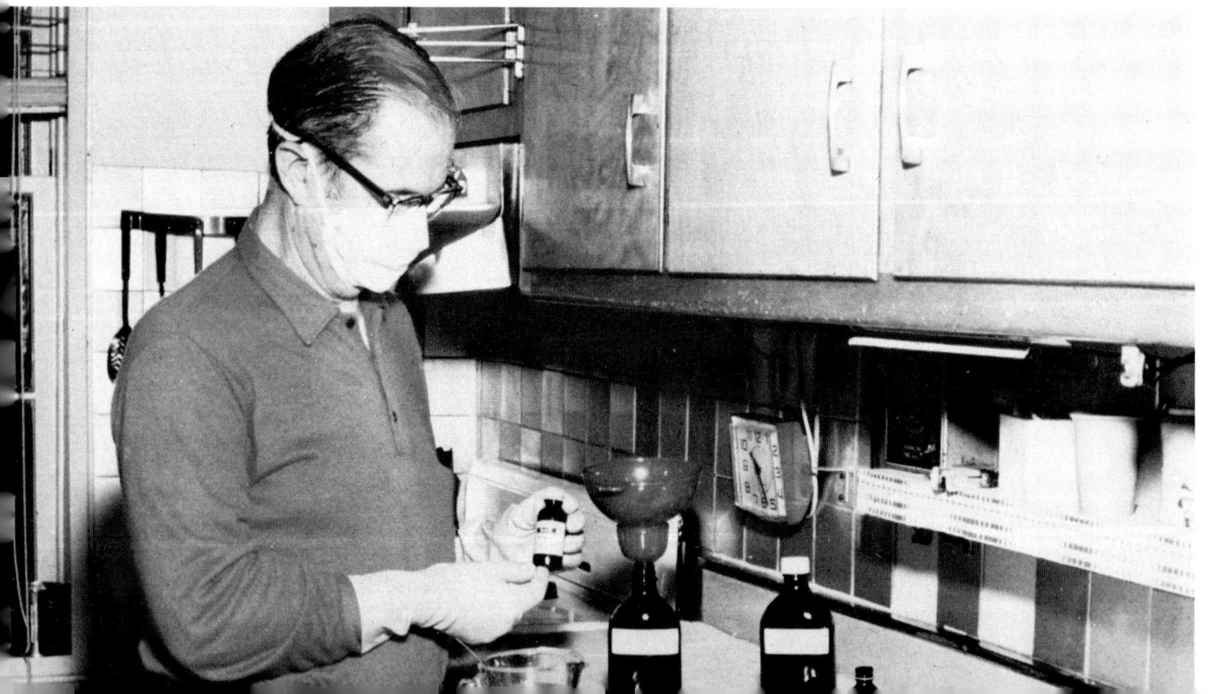

Fig. 5-1. The line-up of nine bottles needed for processing Ektachrome is impressive, but only one is used at a time. For labels, use waterproof adhesive tape and write on them with a grease pencil.

Fig. 5-2. To protect your arms, hands, and face when you mix the various color chemicals, it is absolutely necessary to wear a long sleeve shirt and rubber gloves, and a simple cotton face mask of the kind used by parents when handling infants. The mask can be discarded for the developing process, as all the chemicals are now in diluted liquid form, but the gloves should be retained because there is bound to be some dripping from the bottles.

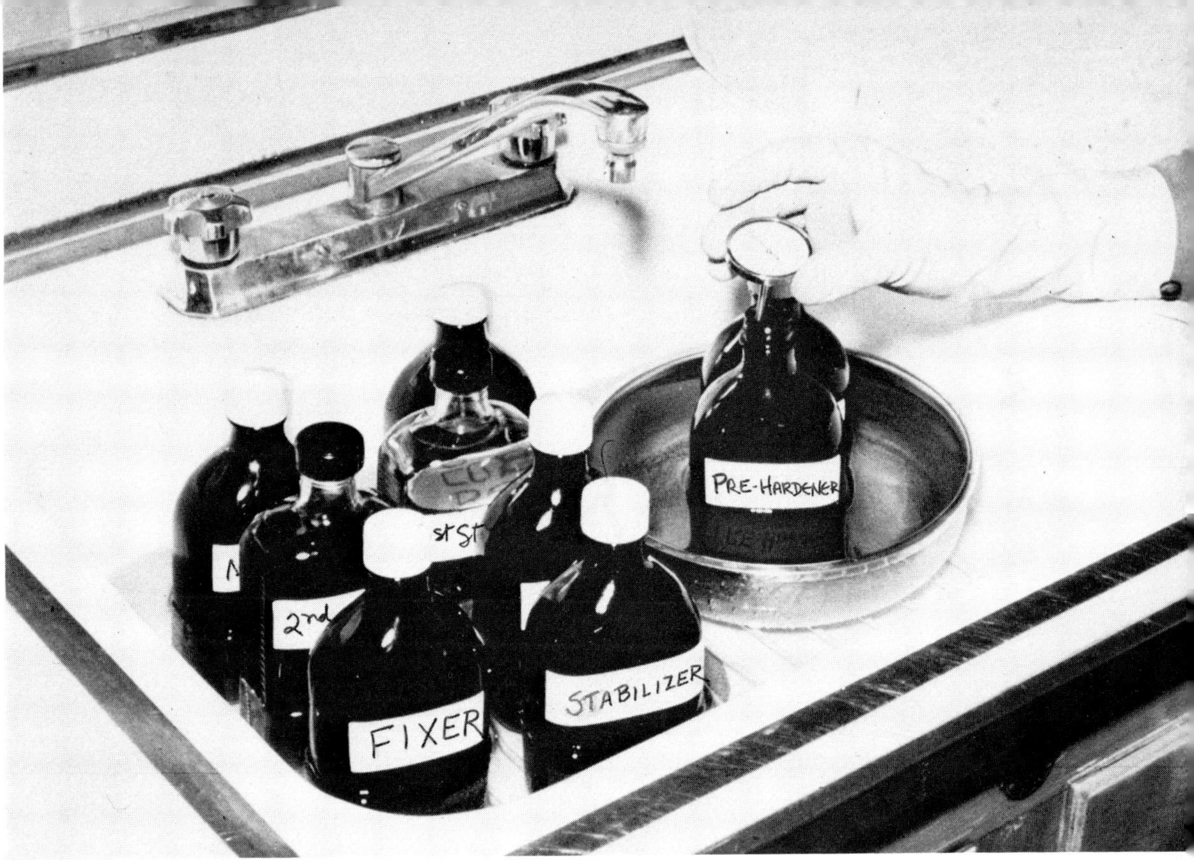

Fig. 5-3. Adjusting the temperature of the color baths is merely a matter of immersing the bottles in warm or cold water. Temperature control is an important part of the developing operation.

Fig. 5-4. Sandwich-type slide mounts are quickly heat-sealed with the tip of an ordinary iron, set for low temperature.

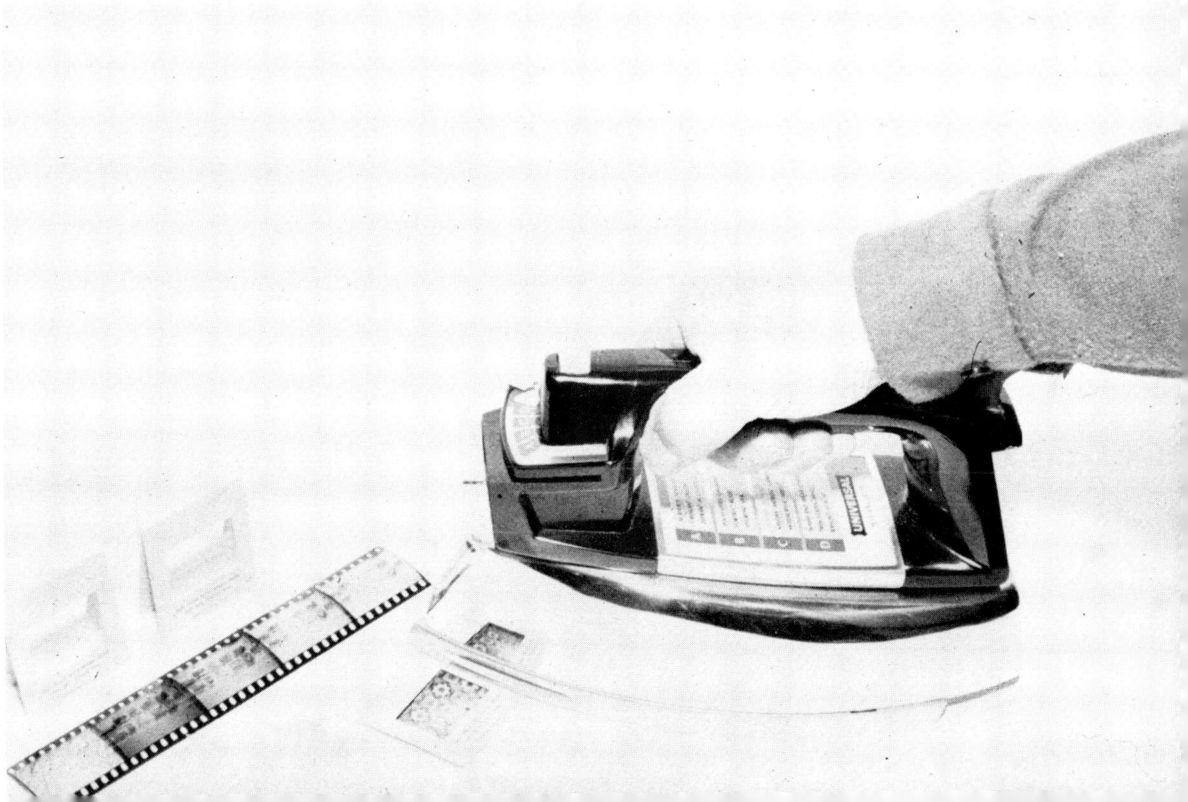

What really makes Ektachrome developing feasible in any kitchen or basement is the well-organized Kodak "Process E-4" kit. This contains 18 cute little bottles of concentrated liquid chemicals and 14 packets of dry powders, which require only mixing in warm water. You use half of these at a time, nine bottles and seven packets, to make nine 16-ounce (473ml) bottles of working solutions. Each of these pint combinations develops eight rolls of 20-exposure 126 film, or six rolls of 20-exposure 35mm film, or three rolls of 36-exposure 35mm film, or four rolls of 120 film. It is not advisable to mix nine full quarts, using all the chemicals in the kit at once, unless you have a lot of films to do and enough reels and a big enough tank in which to do them.

The best time to prepare the mixes is the same time you intend to process. Two different developers are provided, and after they have been used once they will keep for only about two weeks in full, tightly stoppered glass bottles. The other solutions will last about eight weeks, but they aren't of much use without the developers.

The full operation comprises 13 steps and takes 56 minutes. The sequence is as follows: 1. Prehardener; 2. neutralizer; 3. first developer; 4. first stop bath; 5. wash; 6. color developer; 7. second stop bath; 8. wash; 9. bleach; 10. fixer; 11. wash; 12. stabilizer; 13. dry.

An interesting feature of this Ektachrome processing is that the solutions all run much hotter than in black-and-white processing. The ones that need the closest temperature control are the prehardener, which is specified as 85° F. ± 1° (29.5° C.. ± ½°), and the first developer, 85° F. ± ½° (29.5° C.. ± ¼°). All the other chemicals can be between 83° F. and 87° F., and the wash water can range safely from 80° F. to 90° F.

Note that number 11, the third wash, is not the final step, as in black-and-white, but is followed by a stabilizer bath. You must **NOT** add another wash step after the latter, much as you might feel inclined to do so after your experience with black-and-white processing.

ADJUSTING THE WORKING TEMPERATURE

To start, adjust the hot and cold water faucets of your sink until the mix is about 100° F. Fill the sink to a depth of about four inches and put in all nine bottles. Uncap only the prehardener and put the thermometer into it. Stir gently and watch the meter. When the reading gets to 82° F. or 83° F. remove *all* the bottles, place them on the nearby work area, and drain the sink. As the glass is still warm, the temperature will probably climb a bit more. If the prehardener goes beyond 86° F., place the bottle in a bowl of cold water for about 15 seconds and check again. When the temperature is between 84° F. and 86° F. (ideally, 85° F.), set your timer for three minutes, pour the liquid into the tank, and agitate it as with black-and-white. Quickly rinse the thermometer and check and adjust the neutralizer and the first developer. The neutralizer goes in and out in one minute, but the first developer stays in for seven minutes. This gives you time to catch your breath and to work on the remaining bottles. They may have cooled off a few degrees, but another immersion, in a bowl of hot water, will bring them up.

It is necessary to empty the sink after the initial warm-up period so that the thermometer and the funnel can be rinsed thoroughly as they are shifted between bottles and the film tank, and to permit the tank to undergo washing steps number 5, 8, and 11.

When you hang up the film to dry you may be dismayed to find that it has a decidedly cloudy look, like a black-and-white strip of film that wasn't left in the fixer long enough. Don't be alarmed; this discoloration will disappear as the remains of the stabilizer solution evaporate.

MOUNTING THE SLIDES

This is an easy job with standard 2″ × 2″ cardboard or plastic mounts. When you cut the film handle it by its edges, and position the frames in the mounts with a pair of tweezers.

IS THE WORK WORTH IT?

This depends on whether you're considering mere money or personal satisfaction. There is a saving by doing the processing yourself, but it's not very much. What is more important is the pleasant glow . . . literally that, in full color . . . that you will feel when you flash your first slide on the screen.

An incidental advantage is that you can boost the effective exposure ratings of both Ektachrome-X and High Speed Ektachrome beyond their normal ASA values of 64 and 160, respectively, merely by increasing the time of the first developer. With popular Ektachrome-X, for example, ASA 64 almost doubles to ASA 125 when the time is 9½ minutes instead of 7, and it goes to ASA 160 at 10½ minutes. You can do some very interesting experiments along this line with short rolls of film.

WHAT ABOUT OTHER FILMS?

It is impossible to do Kodachrome at home. Several GAF color slide films can be processed with prepared GAF kits, but these are of marginal value because the prices of the films generally include commercial developing.

Kodacolor-X, a negative material, is altogether a different matter. You can process it with the Kodak "Process-22" kit, and then make prints on color paper with a specially-equipped enlarger. This is the most advanced form of do-it-yourself photography, and takes patience, materials, and know-how. It is also grand fun.

BLACK-AND-WHITE PRINTS
FROM COLOR PICTURES

It is sometimes desirable to have a quantity of prints from a color shot made at a fraternal or social gathering, for free distribution to friends or relatives who attended. However, the cost of even small color prints in quantity can discourage this generosity.

There is an easy solution to the problem if the scene was recorded on Kodacolor-X or Ektacolor. These are negative films, and while they are designed for color printing they also yield excellent *black-and-white* prints on a special Kodak paper called Panalure. You process this exactly as you would conventional papers; the only additional accessory you need is a dark amber safelight filter. You can turn out 5″ × 7″ and 8″ × 10″ prints at a fraction of the price of much smaller color prints, and while they aren't quite as flashy as the latter, their size alone makes them impressive. And since they're free, who will complain?

Black-and-whites from color slides are another matter, because these are positive films intended primarily for projection. It is difficult to make suitable black-and-white negatives from them with even sophisticated amateur equipment, and many commercial processors dislike the job enough to refuse it. An alternative is to print the slides on "direct positive paper," which requires special chemicals. The materials are expensive and not widely obtainable, and the cost per print can be so close to that of color prints made by Kodak plants that the whole operation becomes futile.

APPENDIX

Some random suggestions and "kinks" to make your darkroom work easier, quicker, and more pleasant.

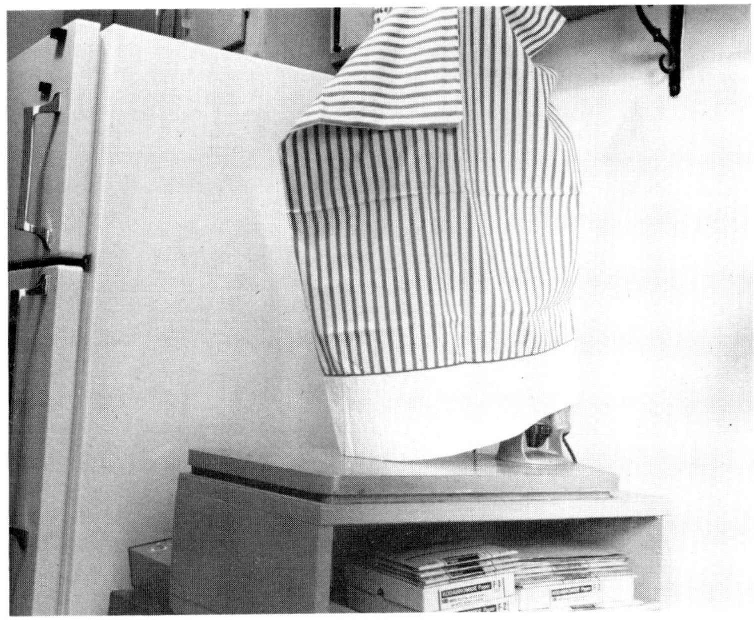

Whether you keep your enlarger in fixed position in a darkroom or store it in a closet, protect it from dust by putting an old pillow case over it.

CLEAN TANK — CLEAN NEGATIVES

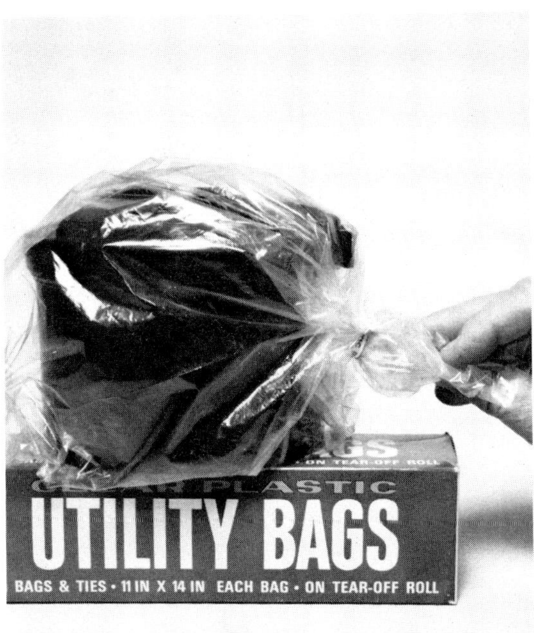

Keep a developing tank absolutely clean and free of dust between jobs by enclosing it in a plastic utility bag.

EASEL MAGNIFIER EASES FOCUSING

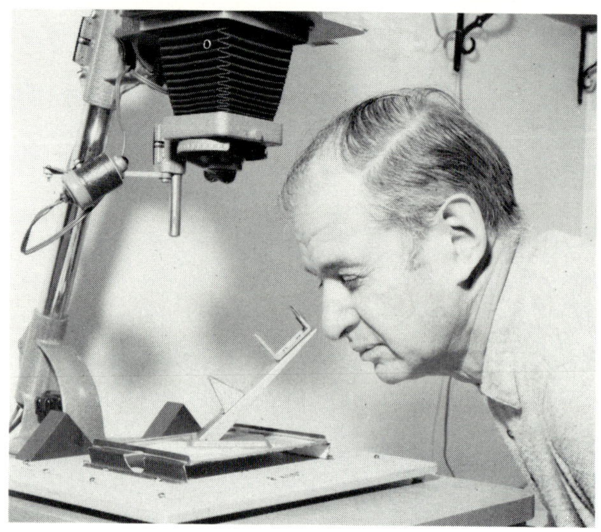

Do you have difficulty focusing dense negatives? Try an easel magnifier. It actually works on the grain of the projected image rather than on the image itself. It's a bit tricky to use at first, but it becomes quick and easy after you determine the best distance from your eye to the first lens.

EXTRA WALL SPACE IN THE KITCHEN DARKROOM

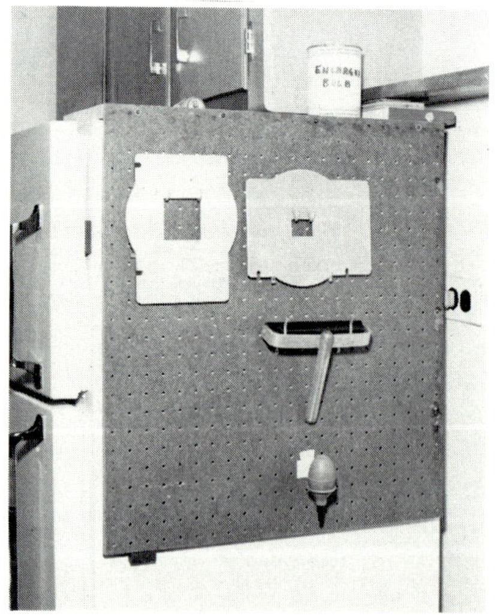

A convenient place for enlarger accessories is a piece of perforated hardboard on the side of the refrigerator in the kitchen. No holes are needed in the box. Instead, attach the top edge of the board to a piece of shelving and merely hang this from the top of the box. Its own weight keeps it in position.

After developing films with stainless steel equipment, you can dry the reels quickly, after shaking out as much water as possible, by placing them over the pilot light area of the kitchen range. The tank can be wiped clean with a paper towel.

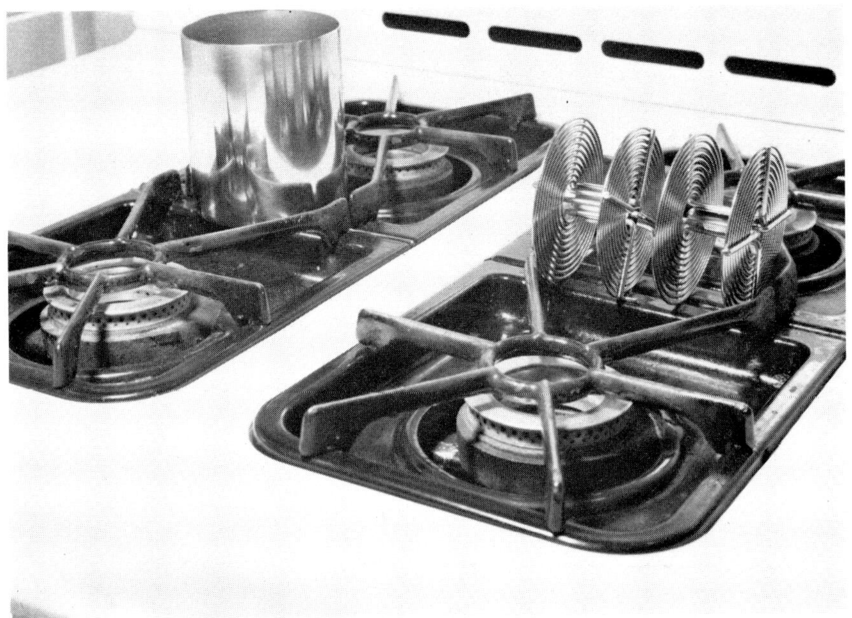

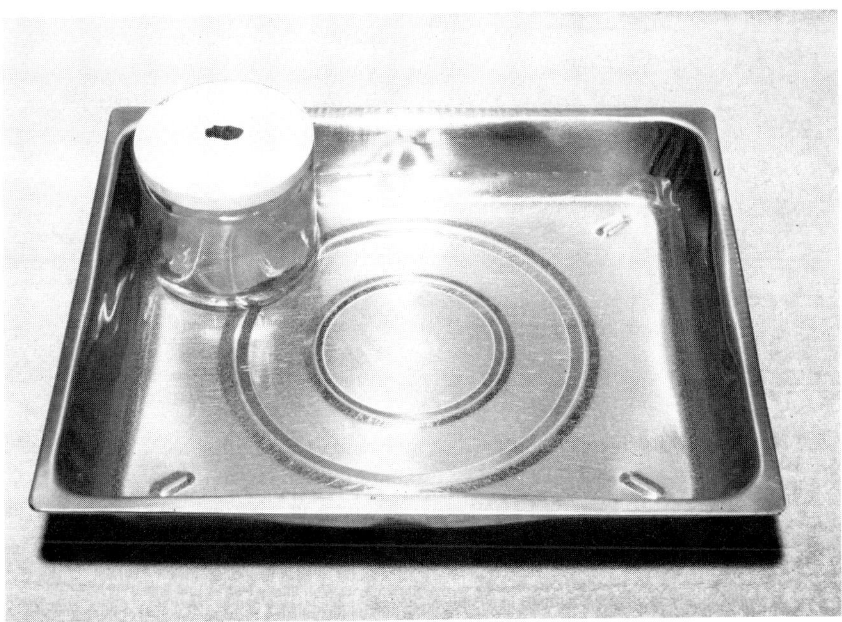

To keep print developer reasonably close to 68° F. or 70° F. during hot weather, put a glass jar filled with ice cubes in one corner of the tray.

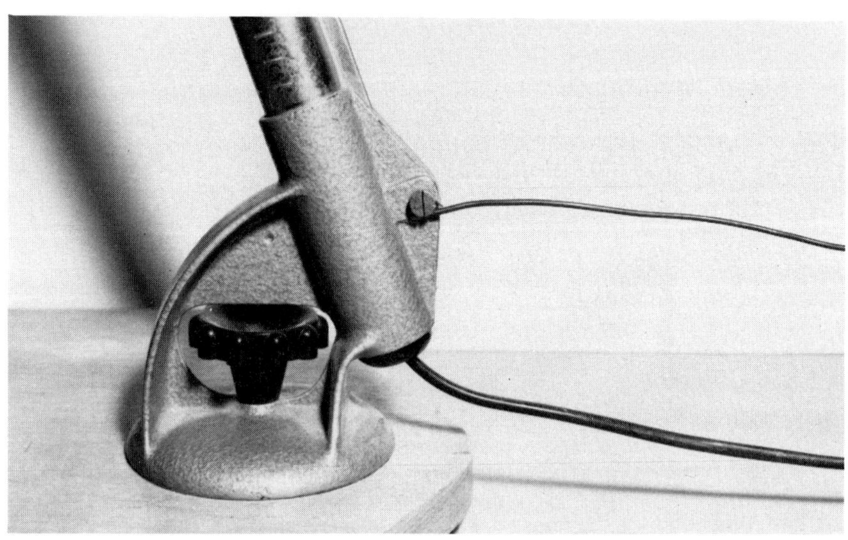

DE-DUSTING THE ENLARGER

In a dry room, an enlarger tends to build up electrostatic charges that attract dust out of the air. The effect can usually be eliminated by the addition of a grounding wire. Connect one end under any available screw on the machine and the other end under the screw that holds the cover of the wall outlet to its box in the wall.

CURING THE CURL

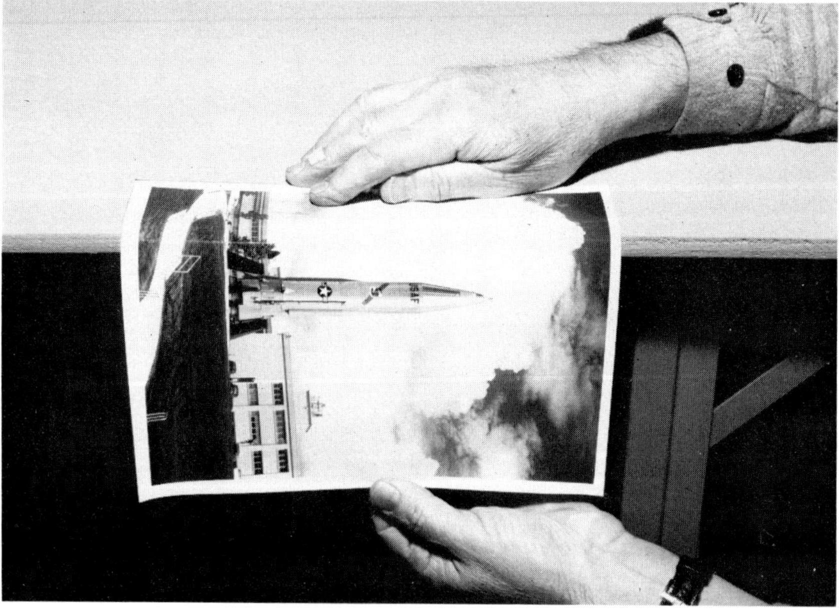

To take the stubborn curl out of prints that have not been treated in flattening solution, pull them gently but firmly over the edge of a desk or table. Two or three passes might be needed for large pictures.

COUNT THE PAPER

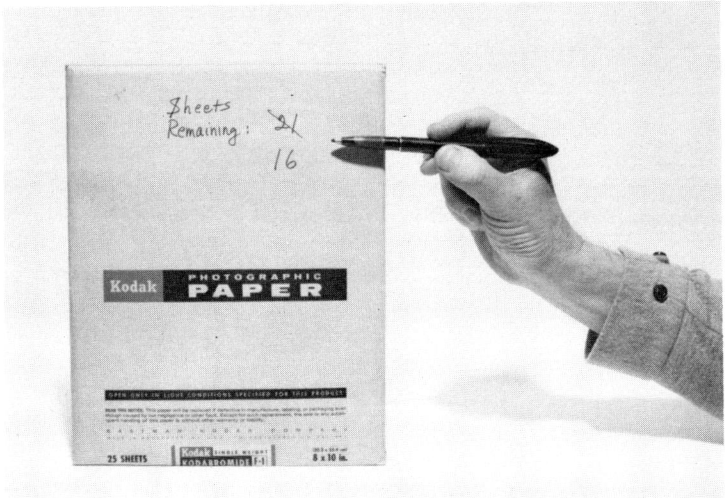

You won't be caught short during a printing session if you know in advance exactly how many sheets of paper are left in opened envelopes. At the end of each session count your paper, and mark the number of sheets remaining with a thick felt-tip pen so that you can read it quickly under a safelight.

CHECKING THE FIXER

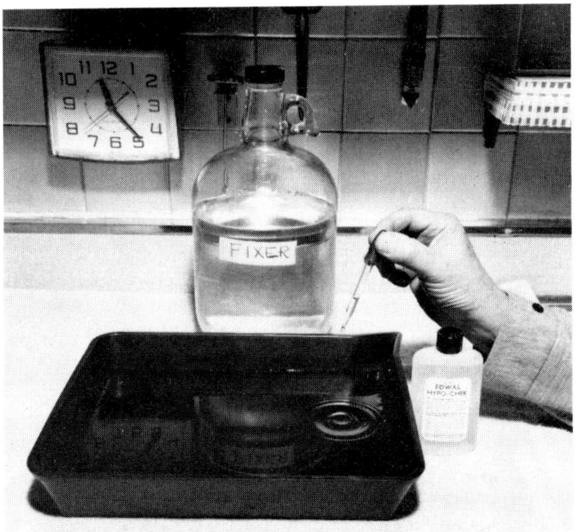

The only processing chemical you can check readily for working condition is the fixer. This is fortunate, since films and prints that are passed through an exhausted bath will fade more or less completely in a few months. To use any of the various "hypo-checks" on the market, simply add a drop or two to the fixer tray. If the bath shows no sign of discoloration it is okay; if a white spot comes into view immediately, it is no good. Fixer is cheap; it is poor economy to try to stretch it.

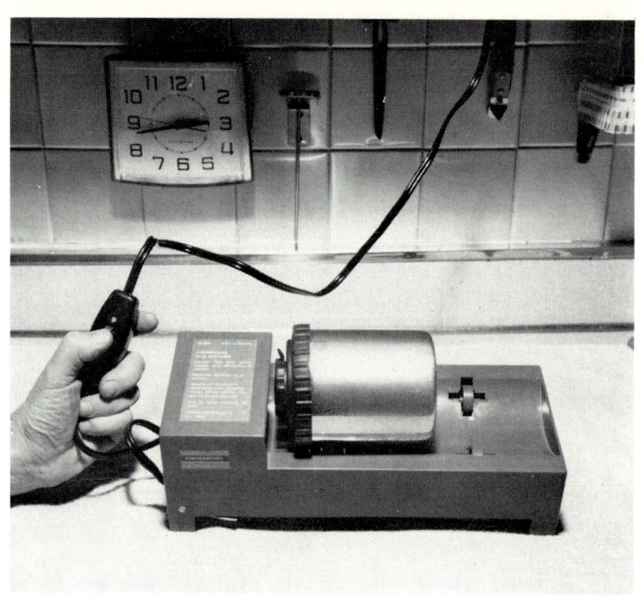

GREAT GADGETS

Two great time-savers that you will want to add eventually to your darkroom are the Kinderman film-tank agitator and the rapid-dryer, both motor-operated. The agitator takes a loaded stainless steel tank and rolls it around gently, at the same time moving it back and forth a little on its axis. This action makes for evenly developed, spot-free negatives. While it is churning away, you can be preparing the next solution.

The dryer pushes filtered air through a washed reel, which is bone-dry by the time you have cleaned up and put away the developing paraphernalia.

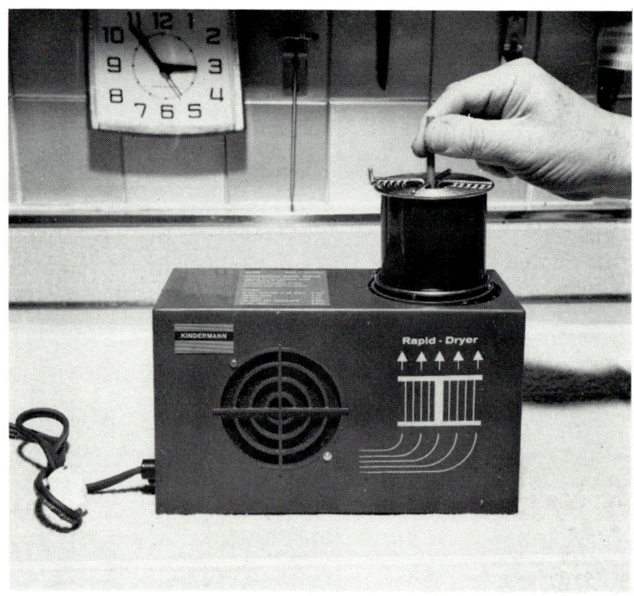

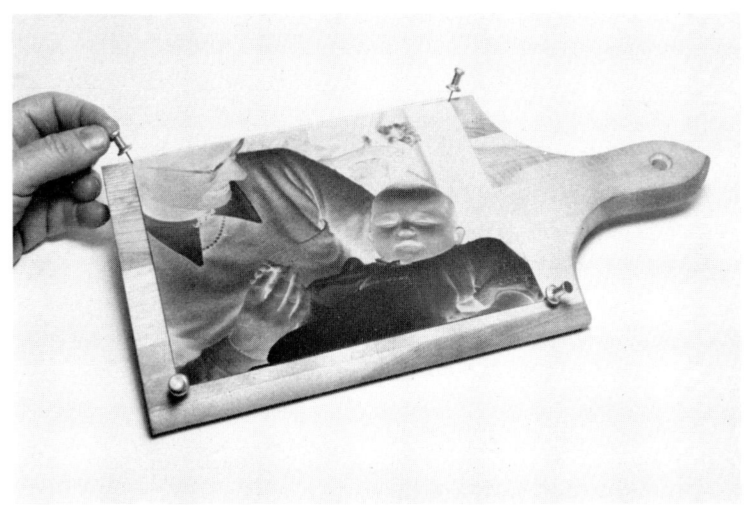

PRINTS WITHOUT BORDERS

Prints without the usual white borders are often more effective in appearance than with them. If you use a regular easel, you can trim the edges after the pictures are finished, but this is a waste of good paper. Another method is to secure the paper on a wood board with push-pins through the corners, and to "bleed" the image about a quarter of an inch over all the edges by adjusting the enlarger height.

For a quick trial of borderless printing, use a kitchen chopping block. Lay down a piece of plain white paper for focusing purposes and then replace it, under the enlarger's red safelight, with enlarging paper. If you like the effect, get a piece of half-inch plywood or a small drawing board, paint one surface white, and rule in rectangles for 5″ × 7″, 8″ × 10″, 11″ × 14″ print sizes.

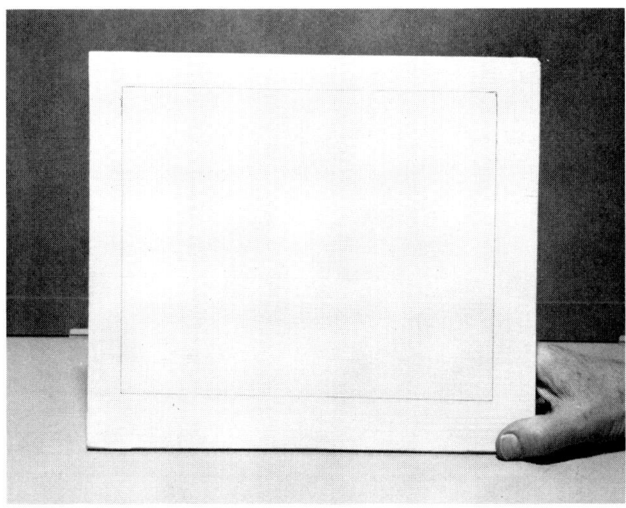

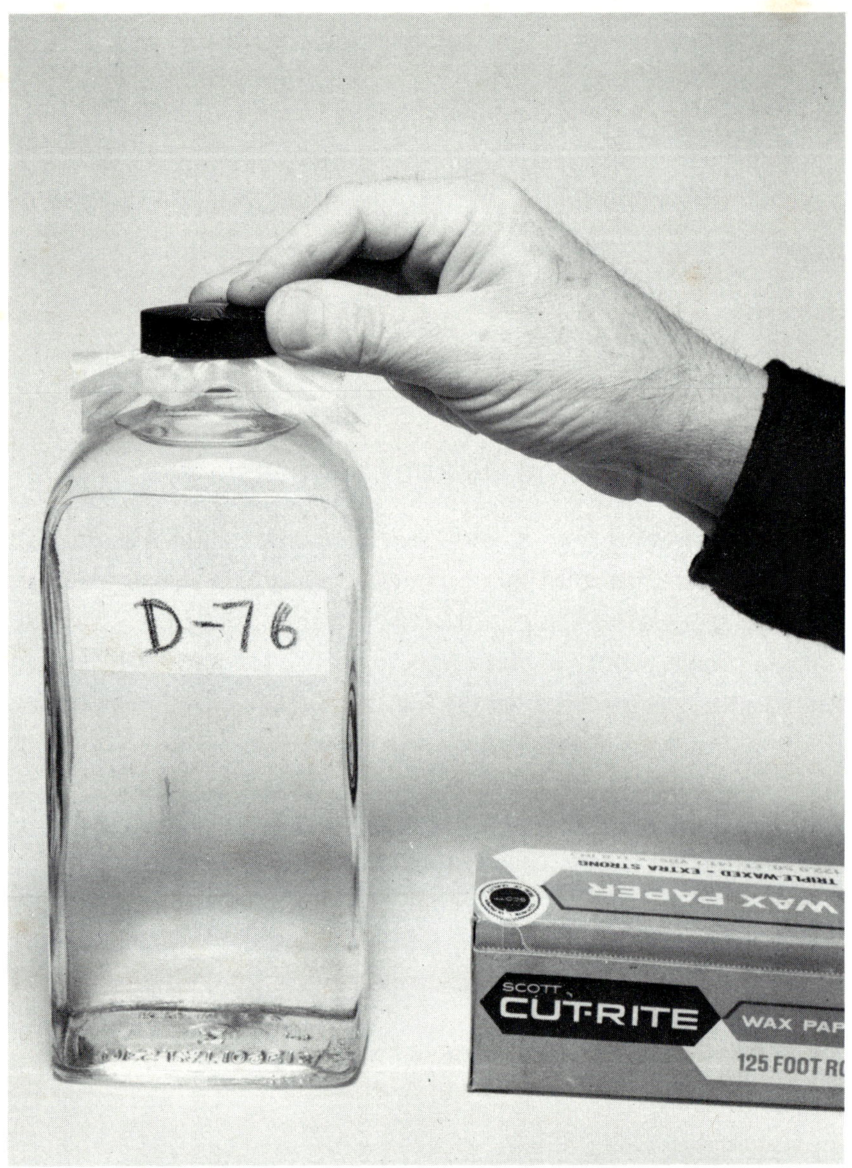

Photo solutions tend to deteriorate if left exposed to the air; developers are especially vulnerable. Therefore, check all bottle caps for leakage by inverting the containers. If there is the faintest sign of a leak, improve the seals by interposing a square of waxed paper between the cap and the neck. Tighten the cap slowly, and the paper will conform to the shape of the bottle.